Comparative History and Legal Theory

Recent Titles in
Global Perspectives in History and Politics

The Pure Concept of Diplomacy
José Calvet de Magalhães

Carl Schmitt: Politics and Theory
Paul Edward Gottfried

Reluctant Ally: United States Policy Toward the Jews from Wilson to Roosevelt
Frank W. Brecher

East Central Europe after the Warsaw Pact: Security Dilemmas in the 1990s
Andrew A. Michta

The French Revolution and the Meaning of Citizenship
Renée Waldinger, Philip Dawson, and Isser Woloch, editors

Social Justice in the Ancient World
K. D. Irani and Morris Silver, editors

The European Union, the United Nations, and the Revival of Confederal Governance
Frederick K. Lister

The Leviathan in the State Theory of Thomas Hobbes: Meaning and Failure of a Symbol
Carl Schmitt
Translated by George Schwab and Erna Hilfstein

Roman Catholicism and Political Form
Carl Schmitt
Translated and annotated by G. L. Ulmen

The Early Security Confederations: From the Ancient Greeks to the United Colonies of New England
Frederick K. Lister

Selected Works of Juan Donoso Cortés
Juan Donoso Cortés
Translated, edited, and introduced by Jeffrey P. Johnson

The Later Security Confederations: The American, "New" Swiss, and German Unions
Frederick K. Lister

Comparative History and Legal Theory

Carl Schmitt in the First German Democracy

JEFFREY SEITZER

CONTRIBUTIONS IN POLITICAL SCIENCE, NUMBER 392
Global Perspectives in History and Politics
George Schwab, Series Editor

Greenwood Press
Westport, Connecticut • London

Library of Congress Cataloging-in-Publication Data

Seitzer, Jeffrey.
Comparative history and legal theory : Carl Schmitt in the first German democracy / Jeffrey Seitzer.
p. cm.—(Contributions in political science, ISSN 0147–1066 ; no. 392)
Includes bibliographical references and index.
ISBN 0–313–30792–X (alk. paper)
1. Schmitt, Carl, 1888– 2. State, The. 3. Political science—Philosophy. 4. Law—Philosophy. I. Title. II. Series.
JC263.S34S45 2001
320.1'092—dc21 00–049496

British Library Cataloguing in Publication Data is available.

Library of Congress Catalog Card Number: 00–049496
ISBN: 0–313–30792–X
ISSN: 0147–1066

First published in 2001

Greenwood Press, 88 Post Road West, Westport, CT 06881
An imprint of Greenwood Publishing Group, Inc.
www.greenwood.com

Printed in the United States of America

The paper used in this book complies with the Permanent Paper Standard issued by the National Information Standards Organization (Z39.48–1984).

10 9 8 7 6 5 4 3 2 1

Copyright Acknowledgments

The author and publisher gratefully acknowledge permission for use of the following material:

Excerpts from "Carl Schmitt's Internal Critique of Liberal Constitutionalism: *Verfassungslehre* as a Response to the Weimar State Crisis" by Jeffrey Seitzer courtesy of *The Canadian Journal of Law and Jurisprudence*. Used with permission.

To Ethan McGinnis Seitzer,
a feisty lad

Contents

Acknowledgments ix

Abbreviations xi

Introduction xiii

Chapter 1
Retrofitting Liberal Constitutionalism: *Constitutional Theory* as a Response to the Weimar State Crisis 1

Chapter 2
Exorcising the Ghost of Composite States Past: Local Self-Government and Political Stability in the *Kaiserreich* 41

Chapter 3
Guarding the Constitution: The American Model in German Constitutional Politics 73

Chapter 4
Rethinking the Role of Courts: Constitutional Democracy as Institutional Dialogue 103

Works Cited 129

Index 155

Acknowledgments

I have incurred many debts during the completion of this work. I benefitted from the advice and encouragement of David Dyzenhaus, Rainer Forst, Eric Heinze, Gary Herrigel, Stephen Holmes, Oliver Lepsius, Bernard Manin, Ingeborg Maus, Peter Niesen, George Schwab, Michael Stolleis, Cass Sunstein, and Chris Thornhill. Valuable research assistance was provided by the library staffs of a number of institutions: the University of Chicago, the Warburg Institute and the Institute for Advanced Legal Studies, both of the University of London, the Max-Planck Institute for European Legal History in Frankfurt am Main, Germany, and the British Library. The Institute for Advanced Legal Studies proved a congenial environment for completion of the manuscript. Stimulating criticisms were offered by audiences at the Max Planck Institute for European Legal History, the Institute for Advanced Legal Studies, the Law Faculty of the University of Lancaster, and the Social Sciences Division of the University of Frankfurt. I am also indebted to Anna Maria Paczer for computer assistance, to the *Canadian Journal of Law and Jurisprudence* for permission to include previously published material in Chapter 1, and to the late Bob Seitzer for his herculean translation efforts. Finally, I am grateful to my wife, Janet Smith, for unstinting support and an abundance of good times over the years. I am still searching for someone besides myself to blame for the book's deficiencies.

Abbreviations

BP	*Der Begriff des Politischen*
CP	*The Concept of the Political*
CPD	*The Crisis of Parliamentary Democracy*
D	*Die Diktatur: Von den Anfängen des modernen Souveränitätsgedankens bis zum proletarischen Klassenkampf*
GU	*Gesetz und Urteil: Eine Untersuchung zum Problem der Rechtspraxis*
HP	*Hugo Preuß: Sein Staatsbegriff und seine Stellung in der deutschen Staatslehre*
HV	*Hüter der Verfassung*
LL	*Legalität und Legitimität*
PT	*Political Theology: Four Chapters on the Concept of Sovereignty*
RC	*Roman Catholicism and Political Form*
UR	*Unabhängigkeit der Richter, Gleichheit vor dem Gesetz und Gewährleistung des Privateigentums nach der Weimarer Verfassung*
V	*Verfassungslehre*
VRA	*Verfassungsrechtliche Aufsätze aus den Jahren 1924–1954: Materialien zu einer Verfassungslehre*

Introduction

The ever growing scholarship on the German legal and political theorist Carl Schmitt calls to mind the Big Bang theory of the origin of the universe. After an initial explosion, the universe of Schmitt studies continues to expand with no end in sight. The sheer volume of the scholarship on Schmitt begs the question: What remains to be written about him?[1] A systematic treatment of Schmitt's historical method in his major works on comparative constitutionalism, *Constitutional Theory* (*Verfassungslehre*) and *Guardian of the Constitution* (*Hüter der Verfassung*), makes possible a more effective criticism of Schmitt than commentaries which focus on his treatment of key normative concepts or texts in legal and political theory. This critical engagement with Schmitt also elaborates a comparative historical approach to democratic theory, which aims at enhancing the capacity of existing systems for democratic experimentation.

Schmitt continues to receive a wide readership partly for stylistic reasons. His works exhibit the rare combination of a brilliant polemical style with penetrating and stimulating analyses of law, politics, and society. Generations of critics have rightly criticized Schmitt's use of one-sided conceptual formulas (e.g. Kelsen 1930/31; Fijalkowski 1958; Fraenkel 1964; Scheuerman 1995). As such, however, Schmitt's concepts provide clear reference points for wide-ranging debates on a number of topics. Simply put, reading Schmitt may be at times enraging, but never boring. This is even true of his more staid writings in law and legal theory, which, combining insight with solid scholarship, have made lasting contributions to the fields of comparative law and legal theory.[2]

The fact that Schmitt is arguably the only German legal theorist to supply beach reading for late 20th century American academics cannot alone account for his extraordinary appeal. It is Schmitt's role in the politics of the troubled Weimar Republic and his early collaboration with the Nazis that makes his writings an enduring source of controversy. Throughout the Weimar period, Schmitt questioned the ability of liberal states to respond effectively to the challenges of mass democracy and insisted that the Weimar state act decisively against extremist opponents of both the right and left. In the Republic's eleventh hour, for example, Schmitt argued that the principle of "equal chance" for parliamentary representation posed a threat to the Republic, the preservation of which required putting the kibosh on political parties opposed to the Republic ([1932] 1988). On the other hand, certain features of Schmitt's writings and political activity prompt questioning of Schmitt's commitment to the Republic's core principles (e.g. Scheuerman 1993). Schmitt represented the *Reich* government in the trial before the State High Court (*Staatsgerichtshof*) concerning the former's consolidation of the Social Democratic Party (SPD)-led caretaker government in Prussia, an action many consider to be the final blow to the Republic. Schmitt's early thought on constitutional dictatorship ([1922] 1989) also provided theoretical depth to efforts of right-wing politicians to establish a quasi-authoritarian regime in the final crisis of the Republic through use of extensive presidential emergency powers. Schmitt was clearly not a democrat like his leading contemporaries, Richard Thoma and Hans Kelsen. Nonetheless, his intellectually astute criticisms of the radical right and left, as well as the liberal center, gave him an unusual degree of influence, even among Republican thinkers. Consequently, there was genuine surprise and consternation when he made a startlingly easy transition to the position of "crown jurist" in the early Nazi regime.[3]

Given this personal history, it is not surprising that a staple of Schmitt scholarship is the nature of his political commitment, particularly the question of an underlying continuity between his Weimar and Nazi era writings.[4] This study skirts this issue, but not because there are no grounds for criticizing Schmitt's politics. On the contrary, its central aim is to question Schmitt's understanding of the relation of theory and practice. The focus here is placed on Schmitt's analyses of the concrete institutional problems of the Republic in *Constitutional Theory* and *Guardian of the Constitution*, written while some chance remained for salvaging the Republic in its original parliamentary, welfare-state form. Only a critical engagement with

Schmitt's penetrating analyses of the institutional deficiencies of the Weimar state can produce an indictment against Schmitt which sticks. Otherwise, Schmitt can wriggle free by pointing out that the conditions necessary for more moderate forms of political and social action simply did not obtain during Weimar.

Responding to Schmitt in this way requires grappling with his use of comparative history to analyze the Republic's institutional problems.[5] It is a commonplace of Schmitt scholarship that Schmitt believed that the Weimar constitutional system rendered the German state incapable of responding effectively to a rapidly changing political and social environment. Schmitt's proposal for extensive presidential government was meant to respond to this circumstance by restoring to the state some of the potential for independent action that he believed it had in the pre-Weimar era. Current scholarship, however, does not take account of the fact that Schmitt thought comparative history itself could also revitalize the Weimar state.

Chapter 1 treats Schmitt's interpretation of the American and French Revolutions, in which he makes decisionism the defining feature of these seminal instances of constitution-making. This cleverly executed displacement gives his understanding of the independent state greater rhetorical appeal through association with liberal constitutionalism. Besides accounting for the initially surprising fact that Schmitt's *Constitutional Theory* takes the form of an internal critique of liberal constitutionalism, Chapter 1 applies more fully Schmitt's conceptual framework to show that the comparative history of constitution-making is inconsistent with his implicit claim regarding decisionism. A properly executed comparative history of constitution-making indicates that politically viable instances of constitution-making are not those resulting in a clear decision for a particular sort of political and social order. On the contrary, decentralized political structures and ambiguous constitutional compromises better advance the cause of democratic government than Schmitt's concern with the substantive results of the process of constitution-making.

Guardian of the Constitution can also be seen as a problem-oriented, comparative history, which aims to revive the independent state. But here, Schmitt expands the scope of his analysis beyond contrasting constitutional structures, narrowly defined, to include consideration of the political implications of long- and short-term developments in economy and society. Chapter 2 examines Schmitt's deft use of conceptually driven comparative history to identify the underlying structure of the Weimar state crisis, showing how short- and long-term trends in economics, law, politics, and society coalesce in patterned ways to limit the potential range of state action. Once again, Schmitt's argument is turned against itself by showing that his highly centralized institutional solution to the Weimar state crisis is premised on a problematical understanding of the nature of political stability in the *Kaiserreich*. Despite Schmitt's perceptiveness regarding the short- and long-term structural determinants of the Weimar state crisis, he did not fully understand how the composite German state worked. A more complete history of the relationship of politics and society in the *Kaiserreich* suggests that a more effective institutional response to the Republic's governability problems involves enlarging, rather than limiting, the role of local self-government in the system.

In both these works, Schmitt makes effective use of comparative history to highlight particular problems and to elaborate his understanding of the necessary institutional solutions to these difficulties. In each instance, however, he fails to carry his analysis far enough. Chapter 3 examines Schmitt's comparative-historical study of the structural and procedural limitations of the German judiciary. Central to this analysis is an examination of the appropriateness of the American model for German circumstances. Here, Schmitt's argument anticipates important aspects of current social science work in the fields of political development and comparative judicial politics. Through his use of conceptual frameworks, Schmitt is able to treat empirical issues economically without losing the thread of his primary normative concern. The problem lies in Schmitt's reliance on unexamined assumptions. Chapter 3 attempts to define the limits of Schmitt's critique by exploring conceptual and empirical issues implicit in his argument. Schmitt could have enhanced the persuasive power of his critique by addressing these issues. But attending to these questions would not have enabled him to make as strong a case for a unitary, centralized form of presidential government. The chapter concludes by suggesting that Schmitt's critique, when fully extended, highlights the importance of time to constitutional government in a way that strengthens the arguments for a decentralized solution to the Republic's governability problems presented in the first two chapters.

This historical reconstruction is an institutional form of deconstruction, which turns Schmitt's argument for highly centralized, almost unlimited, executive authority against itself by showing that Schmitt's conceptual frameworks, when applied properly, actually yield a directly contrary result. At the same time, the systematic criticism of Schmitt's comparative-historical methodology develops a substantive argument for decentralized forms of political order. Chapter 4 demonstrates that a proper application of Schmitt's conceptual framework of state types in *Guardian of the Constitution* indicates that a decentralized system with a fragmented judiciary, like that in Weimar, can actually better serve constitutional democracy, even in the midst of a constitutional crisis, than Schmitt's understanding of presidential government.

A fragmented court system contributes to an institutional dialogue over constitutional principle and practice.[6] Though Schmitt does not explore the possibility of, the conditions for, or the effects of such dialogue, my critical reading of his comparative history of the German judiciary indicates how courts can fulfill this important function without hindering decisive executive action in the short-term. By prompting officials to make an accounting of their actions, even of their own decisions, courts contribute to an institutional dialogue over constitutional principle that improves the overall system's capacity for experimentation in political and social forms. The various branches and levels of the state, or even subunits of these, can propose or implement innovations in law, politics, and society. Other components of the system can question such actions, either on substantive or procedural grounds, prompting changes in, or perhaps even abandonment of, a disputed action. On the other hand, such innovations might lead to questioning of the existing order and, perhaps eventually, to fundamental changes in the system.

In terms of the direction of change, this dialogic understanding of constitutional politics is open-ended. The important concern is the process of change, though, in the long-term, this procedural emphasis is understood in rather fluid terms as well. One can object to state action as exceeding the bounds of permissible discretion. Still, particular actions or developments may prompt changes in prevailing understandings of official discretion. Much in the same way, general views of the proper political and social order may change fundamentally as well.

Hence, the vision of democratic politics elaborated here understands procedural limitations in a way that ensures an ordered political process, while it facilitates wide-ranging experimentation in political and social forms.[7] This understanding of democracy as ongoing experimentation is in tension with Schmitt's insistence that state protection of a narrow understanding of the legitimate political and social order is necessary to maintain minimal political stability. Though this understanding of democracy agrees with Schmitt that minimal order is a necessary precondition for a viable democratic system, it takes issue with his understanding of the institutional basis of political stability. Enhancing the system's overall capacity for political and social experimentation better ensures political stability than the reification of a disputed political and social order.[8]

There is a methodological analogue to this vision of democracy as ongoing experimentation. Any proposed institutional changes are based upon assumptions about certain practices, structures, and procedures as well as about the expected impact of proposed changes in these. Rendering these assumptions explicit in formal models enables one to test them through carefully designed comparative-historical studies. As thought experiments postulating expected relationships among possible causal factors, such models enable one to develop and test hypotheses about conditions in specific contexts through controlled comparison with other systems, both past and present. Even if theorists themselves do not execute such a study, the very effort to construct a testable model provides a threshold requirement for normative arguments about institutions and facilitates critical review of their claims. No such inquiry can claim the potential certainty of laboratory experiments in the natural sciences. But it brings one as close as is perhaps possible to an experimental approach in human affairs.

Comparative history facilitates this more narrowly institutional form of democratic theory.[9] Focusing on the details of democratic government makes it possible to identify changes in outlook and institutions that enhance a system's capacity for democratic experimentation. This emphasis on institutional questions distinguishes my approach from a good deal of legal and political theory, in which analysis of concepts and/or of the tradition takes center stage.[10] Obviously, Schmitt's and my concerns are quite different. Nonetheless, Schmitt's willingness to apply comparative history to normative questions, despite the important methodological challenges involved in such an effort, make his work a useful vehicle for considering how one might better approach normative questions in this way. In this sense, my internal critique of Schmitt's comparative-historical state theory aims to use Schmitt's works as scaffolding for climbing beyond Schmitt.

NOTES

1. Schmitt has always been controversial in Germany, with major works appearing every decade or so over the last forty years (e.g. Fijalkowski 1958, Krockow 1958, Hofmann [1964] 1992, Maus [1976] 1980, Meier 1988a, and Mehring 1989). Schmitt studies in the United States are of a more recent vintage, beginning with Schwab ([1970] 1989). Bendersky (1983) sparked renewed interest. The Schmitt literature in the last decade defies citation. Recent works in English focusing on Schmitt's legal theory are Scheuerman (1994), Caldwell (1997), Dyzenhaus (1997), and McCormick (1997). On the Schmitt "renaissance" in Germany, see Schlink (1991) and Rudolf Walther, "Der verführerische Gestus: Zur fortwährenden Renaissance von Carl Schmitt," *Süddeutsche Zeitung*, January 3, 1994. For an analysis of the interest in Schmitt in the United States, see Habermas (1987).

2. Even a strident critic like Jürgen Habermas concedes that Schmitt is an "able constitutional theorist, as evidenced by his brilliant *Constitutional Theory*" (1987, 108). Schlink (1991, 160–176) notes four aspects of the current German con-

stitution, the Basic Law, giving Schmitt greater play among contemporary constitutional theorists than his leading contemporaries, Kelsen, Heller, Thoma, Smend, and Anschütz: Article 76; the constructive vote of no confidence; the Basic Rights; and the general concept of law. But the real reason for Schmitt's prominence, according to Schlink, is that his theoretic slogans, such as "political romanticism," "political theology," and "decisionism," resonate among normative theorists. On Schmitt's influence as a legal theorist in the Federal Republic, see Lietzmann (1988), Mehring (1995), and Mußgnug (1988). Regarding Schmitt's influence internationally, see the contributions of Quaritsch (1988, 17–20), Shiyaki (1988), and Kal (1988).

3. The standard biographies of Schmitt during the interwar period are Bendersky (1983) and Noack (1993). Rüthers (1994) supplies a more critical reading of Schmitt in the Nazi period.

4. For contrasting views on the question of continuity in Schmitt's work between the Weimar and Nazi periods, see Maus (1969) and Berthold (1999).

5. The important work *Legality and Legitimacy* ([1932] 1988) is not discussed in detail, partly because it appeared very late in the Republic when little chance remained for fundamental reforms, but also because Schmitt abandons the comparative-historical approach so prominent in *Constitutional Theory* and *Guardian of the Constitution* in favor of a highly abstract, conceptual one.

6. Legal and political theorists tend to assign a special role to courts in matters of principle. Because of their relative insulation from political bargaining, courts can engage in a form of discourse which transcends mere interest-group deals (e.g. Dworkin 1985 and Rawls 1993; cf. Sunstein 1993a). Even theorists who stress the importance of political practice in constitutional politics believe courts must guide developments (e.g. Michelman 1986) or sanction those already completed (e.g. Ackerman 1991).

The understanding of constitutional politics elaborated here stresses that court systems are democratic institutions to the extent that they contribute to an ongoing dialogue over constitutional principle. But it does not accord courts a privileged position in regard to principle. This view of the institutional basis of constitutional politics owes much to Louis Fisher's concept of coordinate construction (1988). Courts, the political branches, and even bureaucratic organizations, all engage in constitutional interpretation in an effort to respond to particular practical problems. Constitutional principle is defined through the give-and-take among governmental actors and organs over state action. The key consideration is not whether an understanding of a principle stems from a particular official or governmental organ. What matters is whether the proposed provisional solution persuades other actors of the appropriateness of the action as a solution to a specific problem and as an understanding of principle more generally.

7. This understanding of democracy as ongoing experimentation in political and social forms stems from the American pragmatist John Dewey, who evaluated specific institutional configurations on the basis of their consequences for human freedom ([1927] 1954, esp. 30–36 and 185–203).

8. Many consider Schmitt's call for greatly enhanced executive power and major limitations on the state's duties to provide social welfare a defense of the Weimar Republic, admittedly in a drastically modified form (e.g. Schwab [1970] 1989, Bendersky 1983, and Cristi 1998). Such a scaling back of the Republic's substantive commitments toward civil liberties and social rights, on the other hand, comes close to being the constitutional equivalent of George Washington's original hatchet, with two new heads and three new handles, according to others (Maus [1976] 1980, 121–159; also Scheuerman 1994). This study cuts a middle path between these alternative readings, in that it seeks to address Schmitt's concern for political stability without jettisoning the political and social experimentation promised by the Weimar Constitution in its original form.

9. A recent major work on democratic transitions in East and Central Europe makes extensive use of empirical data to address normative questions but does not address the question of the importance of comparative history to normative argument in a systematic manner (Elster, Offe, and Preuß 1998). Allison (1996) applies a Weberian ideal-typical methodology to the question of institutional borrowing. However, my concern with the potential uses of comparative history in normative argument extends beyond the issue of institutional borrowing.

10. As Cohen and Rogers point out, concrete institutional analysis has been mostly the province of neoliberals, not those committed to a more egalitarian political and social order (1995, 10).

Chapter 1

Retrofitting Liberal Constitutionalism: *Constitutional Theory* as a Response to the Weimar State Crisis

It is not entirely correct to speak of "the" German Revolution of 1918, for Germany experienced a number of revolutions simultaneously (Peukert [1987] 1991, 21–23). Besides the obvious change from a semi-authoritarian to a fully democratic political system, the Weimar Constitution established novel state institutions to mediate social conflict, an extensive set of constitutional rights, and a number of new courts for public law cases. The fledgling Republic also faced important challenges in the form of rival centers of political authority, such as the Workers and Social Councils (*Räte*) and various right-wing coup attempts. In the midst of this political tempest, major economic changes took place. The standard of living, for example, improved for a time, as workers gained greater leverage against management through new legal protections, and productivity rose when many industries fully mechanized. Finally, a number of trends in culture and society produced quite new living arrangements and social relations (Kolb 1972, esp. Part II, 103–275; Peukert [1987] 1991, 23–51, 81–117, and 129–190).

At the same time, there was considerable continuity with the prewar era. The federal system and the army survived the transition, though both in modified form, and the newly established Federal President (*Reichspräsident*) exercised relatively independent executive authority reminiscent of the recently retired *Kaiser*. Moreover, it was by no means certain that many innovations would actually displace their Imperial counterparts. The Catalogue of Rights suggested a fundamental change in the character of rights protection, but it was not clear whether any of the provisions would be enforceable as constitutional, as opposed to statutory, rights, as had pertained under the traditional system. And while on the defensive early in the Republic, capital gradually regained leverage against workers and forced changes in many postwar compromises (Peukert [1987] 1991, 52–77, 118–128, and 207–257; Maier [1975] 1988, 355–420).

Given the ambiguous nature of these developments in politics and society, it is not surprising that the relationship with the past was a central question in the Weimar era. Schmitt is no exception in this regard. His aim of revising or replacing outdated concepts and institutions necessarily entails attention to history in some form. But his approach to the use of history in normative argument varies considerably. In *The Crisis of Parliamentary Democracy* (CPD) (1985), Schmitt uses rather straightforward narrative intellectual history, what William Scheuerman aptly terms a "narrative of decline" (Scheuerman (1995, 138–142), whereas both *Constitutional Theory (Verfassungslehre* (V) ([1928] 1989) and *Guardian of the Constitution (Hüter der Verfassung*) (HV) ([1931] 1985) are forms of problem-oriented history. In other words, through use of conceptual frameworks, Schmitt analyzes a number of factors in various national contexts and time periods with a view to their relevance for a particular problem.[1] In *Constitutional Theory*, Schmitt develops a constitutional theory he considers suitable for the Weimar Republic through comparative histories of constitutional structure, while in *Guardian of the Constitution* he develops conceptual frameworks to consider the relevance for normative theory of developments in economics, law, politics, and society.

This chapter initiates a critique of Schmitt's comparative-historical state theory by examining his argumentative strategy in *Constitutional Theory*. The purpose of Schmitt's conceptual approach in *Constitutional Theory* is to create a form of constitutional theory capable of compensating for structural defects of the Weimar state (II).[2] The resulting understanding of constitution-making, decisionism, is in tension with liberal theory and practice. However, Schmitt elaborates the theory of decisionism through an historical reconstruction of the liberal constitutional tradition, which locates decisionism at its very core. Using his concept of identity as an organizing principle for a comparative history of constitution-making, Schmitt uses certain features of the English, American, and French Revolutions to define liberal democratic constitution-making in decisionistic terms (III). Unlike *Crisis* and other more directly polemical works, therefore, Schmitt's principal strategy in *Constitutional Theory* is not to discredit liberalism by showing that it is internally contradictory and incapable of responding to contemporary developments, though, clearly, he has not abandoned these beliefs. Rather, Schmitt recasts liberal constitutionalism so that the Weimar constitutional system, defined as liberal in *his* terms, can respond to the German state crisis as *he* understands it (I).

This shift in tactics indicates that an effective response to Schmitt requires treating *Constitutional Theory* as a work in comparative history. As in the Hollywood thriller *When a Stranger Calls*, it is necessary to warn friends of constitutional democracy that Schmitt is calling from inside the house, and this is only possible by carefully tracing the call. Just as Schmitt utilizes the raw material of the liberal tradition to found an illiberal form of constitutional theory, so it is necessary to work internally to Schmitt's argument to develop a more effective democratic response to Schmitt. Schmitt's conceptual framework, when applied appropriately, undermines his argument for a decisionistic understanding of the Weimar Constitution, because it suggests that decentralized political structures and ambiguous constitutional compromises account for successful efforts at constitution-making. This critical analysis of Schmitt's conceptual framework for examining the history of constitution-making points toward a more productive comparative-historical approach to the problems of constitutional politics in the modern era (III).

I.

It is often suggested that Schmitt's narrative of decline in *Crisis* is a myth in Sorel's sense, the purpose of which is to discredit parliamentary government (e.g. Scheuerman 1995). A comparison with Sorel also illuminates the argumentative strategy of *Constitutional Theory*. Of particular interest is Sorel's approach to history, "diremption," the central feature of which is the deliberate effort to isolate features of ideas, institutions, events, or developments from their respective contexts (Sorel 1950, 259 and 263–264). By abstracting away from contextual factors, which limit the usefulness of an idea or an institution for resolving a particular practical problem, diremption enhances the capacity of an object to serve as a rallying point for political action, because it heightens the perceived opposition between alternatives. With a zero-sum view of the world, one is far more likely to struggle to the bitter end, resisting the temptation to compromise for short-term gain.

The practical importance of diremption is illustrated by Sorel's analysis of the conflict between the Catholic Church and the French state. In the struggle with secular authority, the Church was forced to surrender control of ever more extensive portions of the social order. This was neither surprising nor disturbing, since secular authority is better suited to execute many essential tasks. Cooperation with secular authorities is especially important for the masses, for whom a degree of "economic-juridical uniformity" guaranteed by secular authority is beneficial. The problem is that the Church acquiesced on the truly important moral/religious issues, mistakenly seeking to preserve its position in secular society by compromising its stewardship of moral and religious truth, which is the true basis of its authority. Concessions on these larger questions eroded the Church's authority and, in the long-term, did much more to undermine the position of the Church within society than would have its steadfast refusal to compromise its principles (Sorel 1950, 253–273).

The issue of Hobbes' importance for liberal constitutionalism brings to light the structural similarities between Schmitt's and Sorel's approaches. Hobbes' insistence on the natural equality of individuals ([1651] 1968, 226–228) has important consequences for constitution-making. The stricture against alienating natural liberty without consent invalidates constitutions formed from contracts between rulers and the estates. In these agreements, monarchs concede or grant certain rights and privileges to the estates, retaining many for themselves, but the government remains independent of the people. Under Hobbes' new conception, the people form a covenant among themselves, establishing a state to protect their natural rights. The government is not independent of the people. In fact, the people "own" the actions of the sovereign (229), who acts as their "Representative" (220, 228). The act of constitution-making is legitimate to the extent that it ensures norms, the validity of which are independent of the act itself (223–228). The problem is, though Hobbes insists on the primacy of the natural rights of the individual, he rejects institutional limitations on the exercise of sovereign authority for purposes of ensuring those rights (230–231).

Schmitt defines constitutionalism in reference to this ambiguity. By stressing the "personalistic" core of the *Leviathan,* Schmitt attempts a startling reversal. There is an important ambiguity in the *Leviathan* regarding the ground of legitimacy of laws as commands. Is the legitimacy of law rooted in the purpose for which commands are issued, or is it the sheer act of issuing them that confers legitimacy?[3] Schmitt collapses this tension in favor of the latter. The fundamental question for Hobbes is not "what" is decided, but rather "who decides" (PT 33–35). This shifts the focus from the purpose for which order is established and maintained to the act itself of establishing and maintaining order, effectively stripping Hobbes' command theory of law, admittedly ambiguous, of any normative content.

There are theoretical reasons for Hobbes' failure to develop effective institutional restraints on the exercise of sovereign authority. The natural equality of the individual, based upon the universal possession of reason which can discern the natural law, limits sovereignty and locates it in the people, and the indivisible character of sovereignty ensures that the sovereign would not act against itself. The contextual and polemical reasons for this omission, however, are more important. Hobbes must be understood in reference to the struggle against traditional authority. In 17th-century England, the individual was caught in the cross fire between rival powers. In response, Hobbes sought to centralize authority and make its legitimacy contingent on the protection of the individual.

This also explains Hobbes' reliance on reason as a restraint on sovereign power. The religious wars of the 17th century were fueled by superstition and prejudice. Hobbes sought to counter this by insisting on the capacity of reason to provide a workable basis for a peaceful order. Hobbes, of course, never claimed that a thoroughly rational politics would ever obtain; in fact, he conceded that abuses would continue. But his emphasis on the clarifying, conciliatory power of reason was meant to dampen and modify the natural passions which fueled and, in turn, were aggravated by, superstition and prejudice.[4] Hobbes, ever attentive to the complexity of human motivation, knew that one does not bolster confidence in reason by stressing its deficiencies.

Leo Strauss agrees with Schmitt that any fundamental critique of liberalism must begin with Hobbes. But Schmitt does not engage Hobbes in a thoroughgoing manner, according to Strauss, for Schmitt ignores the essential civilizing core of the *Leviathan*.[5] Strauss argues that Schmitt's misreading of Hobbes is traceable to his concern with the moral, per se, in that it constitutes a "polemic" against "entertainment," which, rejects "civilization" for the sake of moral "seriousness" (CP 100–101).

This is very probably true. However, Schmitt's caginess regarding his underlying intentions makes it exceedingly difficult to prove that Schmitt deliberately misread Hobbes. Indeed, he may have simply been wrong. Nonetheless, the extraordinary one-sidedness of Schmitt's interpretation of Hobbes harmonizes so well with his argument concerning the centrality of "decision" in constitutionalism, considered in Section III, that it suggests strongly that this was a deliberate move on his part. Again, this begs the question: Why not simply reject liberal constitutionalism outright and assert the independent legitimacy of decisionism, much as Sorel insisted on the superiority of socialism over capitalism?

Sorel was initially drawn to the syndicalist movement because he thought its rich associational life could provide the basis for a complete break with the Third Republic. The vibrancy of syndicalist institutions is traceable to the great inspirational power of Marxist historiography, which reduces history to a final struggle between the proletariat and the bourgeoisie that the former is destined to win. The workers' movement has a distinct advantage over Christianity in that it still has a doctrine of eschatology which could inspire great acts of resistance. The problem is this eschatology is threatened by its very source. Because orthodox Marxism insists that the socialist revolution would result inevitably from the "iron law of necessity," it obscures the fact that a successful socialist revolution requires decisive human action. Sorel's myth of the general strike reinvigorates the Marxist view of history. Actively configuring historical materials to stress the desperate need for, and potential efficacy of, heroic action enhances the motivational power of Marx's idea of class struggle. Whether that which sparks heroic action is true or not is irrelevant if it is successful. For Sorel, in other words, history is strictly a tool that is useful in sparking radical social change.

Schmitt rejects Sorel's claim that Catholics no longer adhere to their doctrine of eschatology (1996, 25) (RC). They agree, however, on the purpose and mechanics of myth-making for political purposes. Much in the way the Marxist view of history draws enormous power as a motivational force from its reduction of history to an epic struggle between the proletariat and the bourgeoisie, Schmitt's theory of constitution-making as decision can take on added strength by being received as a defense of Western constitutionalism. This is not to say, of course, that Schmitt was actually a liberal, either in classic or contemporary terms. Schmitt clearly sympathized with the counterrevolutionary rejection of liberalism. But Schmitt accepted the need to work with existing materials, flawed though they might be, and, in his time, this meant, first, the democratic ideal. Because the counterrevolutionaries were uncompromisingly antidemocratic, their vision of social order found little resonance in a democratic era. This reactionary blindspot accounts for the peculiar book-report quality of Schmitt's treatment of the counterrevolutionaries in the final chapter of *Political Theology*. Schmitt opens the chapter by recounting in a sympathetic tone the counterrevolutionary "recognition that their times needed a decision" (PT 53). Since much of Schmitt's work in the Weimar period, but especially *Political Theology* itself, is devoted to showing the necessity of decision in his time, this leads one to expect Schmitt to conclude the work with an argument for the continued relevance of the counterrevolutionary vision of social order. Instead, he merely reviews their rejection of liberalism and advocacy of hierarchical authority without taking a stand on it. The closest Schmitt comes to a firm position, in fact, is his claim that Donoso Cortes' characterization of the bourgeoisie as the "discussing class" is "not the last word on Continental liberalism in its entirety, but it is certainly a most striking observation" (PT 62–63).

For Schmitt, the great challenge is to redefine the democratic ideal so that it enhances, rather than erodes, the social order (Thornhill 2000, 72–73). Pierre Bourdieu's concept of *habitus* ([1972] 1977) illuminates how Schmitt seeks to respond to this problem. According to Bourdieu, fluid configurations of shared ideas, assumptions, and attitudes, or "fields," provide not merely the raw material for theoretical innovations, the common stock of concepts and evidence from which theorists draw. The reigning *habitus* also constitutes a set of implicit rules regarding the construction of workable theories, how acceptable concepts and evidence are themselves formed. The efficacy of a particular theory, even the most seemingly original, depends on the way in which it uses these shared ideas and dispositions. If it ignores the rules of the *habitus*, a theory will fail to resonate within its field. On the other hand, a properly constituted theory may innovate with the shared ideas and dispositions of the *habitus* so that it causes a shift of the center of the interrelated components of the field. However, it may only succeed in doing so by working within the rules of engagement established by the *habitus* (Bourdieu [1988] 1991, 7–39).[6]

Schmitt's *Constitutional Theory* innovates within a field constituted by the democratic ideal and the concept of constitutionalism.[7] Simply rejecting democracy and constitutionalism in favor of a reconstituted form of the traditional German state would not have resonated with a broad segment of the Weimar public, which was often, at best, lukewarm about the Republic, and yet deeply divided about how best to respond to its difficulties. A far more efficacious response to the Weimar state crisis was to alter the "self-description" of reigning practices (to speak with Charles Taylor [1985, esp. 104–115]), in this case, liberal democratic constitutionalism, through a carefully crafted comparative history of liberal constitutional history. In this way, one can have one's cake and eat it, too: an independent state within the confines of the Weimar Republic's constitutional democracy.

It is important to keep this in mind when reading Schmitt's now classic exposition of the essential features of a liberal constitutional order (V 125–220). In formal terms, Schmitt's sympathetic and penetrating analyses of key elements of liberal constitutionalism permit one to speak of a limited rapprochement with liberalism in *Constitutional Theory* (Cristi 1998, 173 and 113–25). Nevertheless, even if one views Schmitt's acceptance of a strong state directed at protecting a free social sphere in classical liberal terms as a form of "authoritarian liberalism," as does Cristi (128–37), the fact that Schmitt's reading of the relationship of the political and the liberal elements of the Weimar Constitution, along with his deft interpretation of some of the institutional implications of key constitutional provisions, effectively circumvents the "limited" nature of the resulting constitutional system (Thornhill 2000, 73–78) and indicates he attaches greater importance to the concept of an independent state.

Take, for example, Schmitt's treatment of the relation between the president and parliament (V 343–359). At first blush, the square off between them seems to end in a draw. The directly elected president can exert considerable leverage over a parliament organized by political parties, but the parliament retains important checks on presidential authority, such as the power to rescind presidential emergency decrees. Also, the president's ability to escape the political polarization hindering parliament depends to a great extent on the personal characteristics of the particular occupant. In the context of *Constitutional Theory* as a whole, however, the president gains the upper hand. Because the president is directly elected, the office bears democratic legitimacy not accorded an unelected head of state or even the representative parliament. Moreover, while the president retains many of the *Kaiser*'s competencies, such as command of the armed forces (V 192), he also has recourse to expansive emergency powers. These emergency powers do not include setting aside the entire constitution, promulgating a new constitution, or even nullifying particular provisions. But the president can suspend seven important constitutional rights enumerated in Article 48(2).[8] And Schmitt's insistence in this context that the constitution as a whole is superior to any particular provision suggests that he believes the president can suspend any individual provision, not merely those mentioned in Article 48(2), if he deems this necessary to save the constitutional system as a whole (V 26–27 and 109– 112).[9] That the parliament can repeal emergency decrees is of little consequence in view of the chronic ineffectiveness of the Federal Parliament. Besides, Schmitt argues that the president can dissolve parliament, even if this exceeds narrow legal limits, if he deems a no confidence vote is merely an attempt at obstruction (V 357–358). This means that the president can effectively circumvent parliamentary control (Finn 1991, 145), as Schmitt urged late in the Republic ([1932] 1988). For, as Hobbes put it, "If there be a right in any else to dissolve them, there is a right also to controule them, and consequently to controule their controulings."[10]

Whatever concessions Schmitt makes to liberal theory and constitutional forms in *Constitutional Theory* are shallowed up by his understanding of presidential emergency powers. And Schmitt's narrow reading of the overall purpose and institutional core of the Weimar Constitution does violence to its compromise character. To the extent that liberal democracy rests on a belief in genuinely limited government and on a recognition that constitutional systems are comprised of irreconcilable visions of political and social order (e.g. Rawls 1993, xvi–xvii; Hardin 1993, esp. 168–170), Schmitt's reading of the Weimar Constitution in *Constitutional Theory* remains in tension with liberal constitutionalism.

Given these features of Schmitt's argument, in substantive terms it is difficult to attribute much tangible significance to Leo Strauss's claim that Schmitt's critique of liberalism occurs "in the horizon of liberalism" (1996, 107). On this point, I agree with many of Schmitt's more strident opponents who consider Schmitt an anti-liberal thinker (e.g. Holmes 1993, 37–60). Methodologically, however, one can see *Constitutional Theory* as an internal critique of liberal constitutionalism insofar as Schmitt elaborates the key components of his illiberal constitutional theory through a careful reconstruction of liberal constitutional history. Schmitt's interpretation does not put the Weimar Constitution in tension with its primary sources, the American and French Revolutions, as Ulrich Preuß claims (1993, 153). On the contrary, Schmitt's comparative history brings his interpretation of the Weimar Constitution into harmony with these sources by redefining their respective places in the Western constitutional tradition. Much like a constitutional theory version of *Invasion of the Body Snatchers*, Schmitt's comparative history of constitution-making leaves certain external features of the liberal constitutional tradition in place. Rendered recognizable in this way to those who know and trust it, Schmitt's reconstruction of liberal constitutionalism enhances the effectiveness of decisionism as a defense of the German state *qua* Weimar Republic.

A reexamination of Schmitt's approach to concept formation is clearly in order, if the nature of his challenge to liberal constitutionalism is to become evident. In this regard, Reinhard Mehring rightly stresses the connection between Schmitt's "sociology of concepts" in *Political Theology* and the conceptual framework of *Constitutional Theory*. Schmitt deems it necessary to resolve oppositions between conflicting principles and to produce harmony between reigning principles and the institutional structure of states. But Mehring mistakenly argues that in *Constitutional Theory*, Schmitt seeks to produce the necessary harmony by discrediting and replacing liberalism (1995, 214). Section III shows that Schmitt's approach is more subtle than this. For him, the radical contingency of norms means there is no principled reason that the liberal tradition cannot be simply transformed so that the necessary harmony is secured, if this seems the most effective means to this end. Schmitt's only concern is whether his reconstruction of liberal constitutionalism is able "to inspire confidence" and spark action in defense of the Republic as he interprets it.

Like Sorel, therefore, Schmitt uses history as a tool. Once recalibrated through his carefully crafted comparative history, the liberal constitutional tradition provides an effective response to the Weimar state crisis as he understands it. Before examining critically Schmitt's reconfiguration of the liberal constitutional tradition, it is necessary to elaborate the understanding of the Weimar state crisis that prompts Schmitt to ground state theory in a "new" discipline of constitutional theory.

II.

Stressing the need to read Schmitt in general, and *Constitutional Theory* in particular, in reference to Schmitt's understanding of the unique problems of Germany does not deny that Schmitt believed Germany was caught up in larger Western developments.[11] A full appreciation of Schmitt's project in *Constitutional Theory*, however, requires seeing how closely tailored Schmitt's approach is to his understanding of the German context, particularly the convergence of material and spiritual factors in 19th- and early 20th-century Germany, which, in his view, compel a fundamental change in the role of legal theory in politics.

Schmitt's analysis of German law and politics in *Constitutional Theory* follows a long scholarly tradition stressing the divergence of German political development from that of much of the rest of Europe and North America.[12] A leitmotif in this style of historiography is the emphasis on the fact that German legal and political reform in the 19th century proceeded at different paces. Prussia's devastating defeat by Napoleon in 1806 sparked the so-called "revolution from above." Liberal bureaucrats introduced important reforms which promoted legal unity and introduced a significant degree of civil freedom, and yet, on a political level, little had changed; the state retained an essentially absolutist character.[13]

The failure of the Revolution of 1848 brought with it important changes. After declining to accept the throne from the Frankfurt Parliament in 1849, the Prussian monarch finally promulgated a constitution which gave constitutional status to many of the progressive civil law changes achieved by the *Allgemeine(s) Landesrecht* (ALR), the General Law of Prussia. Though relatively progressive, the Prussian Constitution of 1850, modeled after the liberal Belgian Constitution of 1831, constituted a booby prize of sorts for those who favored a unified, liberal constitutional state under the aborted Paulskirche Constitution.[14]

The founding of the German *Reich* in 1871 did not constitute the complete victory of what we today consider modern constitutionalism. Nonetheless, it provided Germany with a concrete political framework for national aspirations. Of course, the *Reich* legal system was a composite of the legal systems of the various *Länder*, or the states forming the Reich. Still, there was a common framework, through which one could achieve genuine legal unity. Most legal professionals directed their attention to the task of achieving this legal unity through the promulgation of a civil code and the establishment of a unified federal court system (John 1989, 42–72).[15]

Of more immediate relevance is the fact that these conditions also made possible a shift in emphasis in legal scholarship from continuity to discontinuity, in Schmitt's view. For the previous half century, legal scholarship had compensated for the considerable confusion regarding sources of law due to the highly fragmented legal character of the German Confederation. Historical studies had discerned a national spirit behind the seemingly fragmented, often contradictory, sources of the law. This tendency is illustrated by Savigny's understanding of the role of the legal profession in German politics, especially where he praises Roman jurists for cultivating a system of customary law with the necessary scope and elasticity for a complex, rapidly changing society (Savigny 1975).[16]

With the establishment of the *Reich*, Schmitt argues, legal scholarship could afford to become decidedly ahistorical. Because Bismarck's complex constitutional compromise provided a minimum degree of legal and political unity, it was no longer necessary for legal theorists to compensate for a lack of unity through elaborate historical and philosophical constructs. The importance of legal unity was reflected in the fact that the dominant form of legal theory in the *Reich* period, legal positivism, bolstered the existing system by identifying legal legitimacy with strict adherence to formal procedural mechanisms for the establishment and execution of laws.

Schmitt opposes legal positivism because it ignores the fact that law is rooted in larger cultural, political, social, and economic contexts.[17] In the *Reich* period, according to Schmitt, legal positivists were safely able to efface the distinction between constitutional and ordinary law, because the conservative state Prussia had a hammerlock on the constitutional system. Prussia had enough votes in the Federal Chamber (*Bundesrat*), for instance, to veto any proposed constitutional changes. The structure of the system, in other words, provided an effective, though unacknowledged, substitute for a substantive distinction between constitutional and ordinary law.[18] In this sense, the "feeling of political and social security" of the *Reich* period allowed legal theorists to enjoy a comforting abstractness, according to Schmitt (V IX).

Schmitt insists that legal theory could not retain the same detachment from reality under the unique conditions of the Weimar Republic. Due to its highly democratic character as well as its difficult domestic and international position, the Weimar system was much less successful at containing social conflict than its predecessor. In Weimar, competing groups, *Weltanschauungsparteien*, sought to utilize the democratic system, first, to solidify their position relative to that of their opponents by lending constitutional status to their view of proper human association and, then, to eliminate their opponents altogether.

In view of the quasi-legal character of the early Nazi regime, the possibility of the use of democratic procedures to exclude potential opponents is an important concern. The Republic's chronic governability problems suggest that one's efforts would be better directed at facilitating the construction and maintenance of parliamentary majorities, than in hindering the establishment of supermajorities (Caldwell 1995, 297–298). Despite the unlikelihood of tyrannical majorities before the consolidation of the Nazi dictatorship, Schmitt insists on the need to develop normative and institutional hedges against bullying parliamentary factions, since several features of the Weimar Constitution facilitated the debilitating ideological conflict responsible for the Republic's governability problems. Most important was the Constitution's ambiguity in regard to overall purpose of the system (V 28–36). This was a hotly debated issue, which the Weimar Constitution never fully resolved. According to Schmitt, the resulting document was fundamentally flawed insofar as it sought to split the difference among rival views. The principal drafter of the Weimar Constitution, Hugo Preuß, advocated focusing on the basic organizational framework of government. Preuß' hestitation regarding rights provisions, however, was not rooted in a fundamental opposition to constitutional rights as such. Rather, he was concerned to avoid the mistake of the ill-fated *Paulskirche* Constitution, the promulgation of which was delayed by debate over rights provisions.[19] With the organizational framework of government securely established, Preuß believed, one could address the more divisive question of type of system, liberal-capitalist or democratic-socialist, for example. Another important component of Preuß' approach to constitutional reconstruction was his effort to build and maintain bridges between warring social factions. Preuß was favorably impressed by the fact that, at the "decisive moment," the Social Democrats opted for "political democracy" rather than "dictatorship." This boded well for the future, Preuß argued, because it indicated that the bourgeoisie and the socialists could work together. But it should not lead one to believe that the class struggle is over, nor that there are not real differences between the classes. Formal equality alone is not enough, in his view. The new Republic, rather, must infuse formal legal equality with the "social spirit" (Preuß 1964, 421–428, esp. 428).[20]

This desire for class harmony was shared by Friedrich Naumann, a prominent Christian social theorist and politician, who believed that the collapse of the Imperial system offered the opportunity to establish a new type of system combining features of the capitalist West and socialist East

(Theiner 1983, 283–304, esp. 292–294). The Second Principal Part of the Weimar Constitution reflected Naumann's vision in that it contained a wide array of rights provisions, including traditional political and civil rights as well as economic and social ones. The economic and social rights lent constitutional status to the extensive social legislation of the *Reich*. In practical terms, therefore, the inclusion of these rights represented, for the most part, only a symbolic change from the previous era, though not an altogether insignificant one.[21] Leaving aside the difficult question of the legal status of these rights provisions, their inclusion in the Weimar Constitution signaled that the system was not the sole preserve of one end of the political spectrum.

This indecisiveness regarding the overall purpose of the system, in Schmitt's view, had disastrous consequences for the Weimar Republic (V 157–182, esp. 181–182). By lending apparent constitutional status to a wide array of often contradictory claims for governmental action,[22] Schmitt believed the rights provisions encourage competing groups to seek special treatment, exacerbating rather than moderating the social tensions which caused political instability. Of course, class conflict was a major factor in the unstable politics of the era, but it is difficult to say that the Basic Rights provisions further exacerbated already tense social relations. For example, civil servants insisted their salaries not be curbed, and unions objected to increases in unemployment contributions for workers. Such disputes complicated greatly the task of governing the Republic (Abraham [1981] 1986; Kruedener 1985). But various groups, no doubt, would have agitated for their causes, even without constitutional provisions supporting their claims.[23]

Though it is not clear that the Catalogue of Rights itself produced what Schmitt considers the political equivalent of a hornets' nest, he insists that any effective response to the governability problems of the Republic requires that one discerns behind the confusing mass of seemingly contradictory provisions a solid core, which provides meaning to the document as a whole and is not subject to amendment. Focusing on the basic institutional framework of government, and this in only minimalist terms, means snipping away the Constitution's extensive commitments to the promotion of social and economic equality as well as restricting the status of political and civil liberties as subjective rights (Scheuermann 1997; Maus [1976] 1980, esp. 47–52). In this way, as Cristi emphasizes, Schmitt aims to establish a "'strong state, free economy,'" or a polity that would not be plagued by chronic governability problems due to an overburdened state (1998, 146–58). Moreover, by removing important principles from the divisive competition among political parties, this scaled-down substantive vision would provide a stable pole around which defense of the constitutional order could revolve (V 20–36, esp. 24–25).

The legal positivists are not able to achieve this aim, Schmitt claims, because they insist on following the letter of the law, even though the law offers little guidance. The text of the Weimar Constitution, for example, does not distinguish among different provisions, indicating which are primary or how conflicts about them are resolvable. The legal positivist response to such a problem, according to Schmitt, is merely to refuse to address it. Take, for example, the position of Gerhard Anschütz on the constitutional crisis over the military budget in Prussia during the 1860s

> (W)hen the highest state organs cannot agree on a budget, 'there is not only a gap in the law, that is, in the text of the constitution, but moreover in law as a whole, which can in no way be filled by juristic conceptual operations. Here is where public law stops;' the question of how to proceed in lieu of a budget law is not a legal question. (Quoted in V 332)

Legal positivism's insistence on strict adherence to the letter of the law is also problematical, Schmitt argues, because in some senses the law is too explicit. The Weimar Constitution is clear, for example, in regard to constitutional amendments, requiring only a two-thirds majority of parliament. This simplified amendment procedure creates the impression that all constitutional provisions are of equal status, since every provision is subject to the same simple amendment procedure. Such a view implies that the principles established in Article 1 of the Weimar Constitution, that the German *Reich* is a "Republic" and that "all state authority stems from the people" (Schuster 1983, 99), are subject to amendment in the same way as obviously less fundamental provisions, such as the protection of the "well-earned rights of civil servants" under Article 129 (121). Such mistaken views cause the Republic considerable difficulties in both an immediate and more long-term sense. In regard to the former, Schmitt argues that a subjective right of civil servants could contribute to the worsening financial condition of the Republic, because it might hinder necessary economy measures ([1958] 1985, 174–179). One must also oppose such views, because they lend credence to the view that the Weimar Constitution itself is merely provisional by bolstering the claim that the entire system could be transformed through simple amendment procedures. Schmitt believes this renders meaningless the distinction between constitutional and ordinary law, leaving everything open to divisive political competition (V 99–112).

If the constitutional order is to be preserved, Schmitt argues, it is necessary to determine which elements of the Weimar system are truly fundamental. We have seen that the text of the Weimar Constitution provides little guidance in this regard. Another alternative is to examine the materials pertaining to the drafting of the Weimar Constitution. Schmitt, however, rejects this alternative as well. For Americans, this neglect of the intent of the framers is quite striking, but it is not surprising in view of the German legal tradition.

In the interpretation and application of law, Germans stress "objective" over "subjective" factors.[24] For the most part, Germans are not concerned with what Americans term the "intent of the framers," since this involves subjective states of mind of particular persons. Instead, they attempt to place particular laws within larger wholes. During the *Reich* period, for example, the legal positivists positioned laws within an allegedly complete and coherent system of concepts.[25] Earlier in the 19th century, the theorists of the Historical Law School, associated with Friedrich Carl von Savigny, believed the diverse and apparently ever changing customs and practices of a people were more than contingent responses to the political and social environment. For Savigny and his followers, rather, these customs and practices were indications of a "*Volksgeist*," a composite greater than the sum of its parts. These apparently discrete instances, in other words, were merely different manifestations of an underlying continuity, and, as such, they had an "objective" status, because they were abstracted from the discrete actions and specific intentions of particular individuals and groups.[26]

When Schmitt occasionally turned to the drafting history of particular provisions to resolve interpretive questions, this analysis was clearly subordinate to determination of the larger purpose of the Constitution in general. In an appendix to *Dictatorship (Die Diktatur)*([1921] 1989) (D), for example, Schmitt draws on the intent of the framers to resolve a tension between the first and second clauses of the Weimar Constitution's controversial Article 48. Schmitt stresses that the intent of the framers has no independent normative validity; in other words, the drafting history is not examined for its own sake. Rather, it "demonstrates the dominant sentiment of the Weimar national convention that Germany is in an abnormal situation" (D 233). It is this "general awareness" which provides the "rationale" for the clauses in question. But this rank ordering of interpretive canons does not mean that Schmitt is committed to traditional modes of interpretation. On the contrary, Schmitt seeks to recast the way in which history is deemed relevant to law.

Theorists associated with the Historical Law School and the German Idealist tradition disagree about the ultimate ground of history. Those of the Historical Law School see the unique *Volksgeist* of a people as the ground of history (Savigny 1968, 1: 105–26; Emerson [1928] 1979, 28–29), whereas the German idealists follow Hegel in his emphasis on the "Idea," or "World Spirit" (Hegel [1821] 1967, 216–223 and [1837] 1953, esp. 68–95; Taylor 1975, 428–461). Savigny and his followers insist that national experiences are incommensurable (Savigny 1973, 95–192, esp. 128ff). Hegelian Idealism, by contrast, obscures the essential differences among cultures by examining their histories in reference to the development of "Mind or Spirit" (Hegel 1956). Nonetheless, both the Historical Law School and the German Idealists believe that history is characterized by an underlying continuity.[27]

Schmitt believes history is characterized by discontinuity, so it is problematical to assume continuity on any level. The greatest offenders in this regard are Enlightenment thinkers, who confuse the apparent repetitiveness of phenomena with permanence. That similar actions are taken over extended periods of time does not mean these actions are identical, nor that they will necessarily recur under similar circumstances. There is always an element of contingency in human affairs, but this is obscured in the drive to achieve universal principles through the exaggeration of similarity.

To the extent one can speak of continuity, according to Schmitt, it is only in reference to human action or decision, the conscious, deliberate effort to take up principles and apply them to particular circumstances. The principles themselves cannot claim validity outside such efforts. That they emerge in some form in different contexts and are then successfully applied does not indicate that they are generally applicable. The surface similarity between different contexts might suggest their potential usefulness at a particular point, but it is only after they are successfully applied that one can say that they were applicable (V 44–91, esp. 87–91).

The problem with legal positivism, in Schmitt's view, is not that it fails to recognize the contingency of norms. Kelsen's understanding of democracy is premised on this recognition (Kelsen 1981). The problem is that legal positivism does not come to terms with the institutional implications of this fact.[28] In the *Reich*, the structure of the system made the contingency of norms a nonissue, whereas the Weimar political system gave full vent to fundamental political differences, resulting in general state paralysis. Rather than automatically according legitimacy to the outcomes of a deeply flawed political process, as does legal positivism, legal theory should develop guiding principles which compensate for important defects in state structure. In other words, whereas, during the *Reich*, an independent state provided a safe haven for legal theory, in the interwar period, legal theory must create a "theoretical space" for a beleaguered state apparatus.

Schmitt's understanding of constitution-making as decision is carefully tailored to this purpose. By grounding legitimacy in founding moments with few, if any, concrete reference points,[29] Schmitt's decisionism renders inviolate the commitment to core principles, while, at the same time, giving the state extraordinary freedom of action in ensuring these principles. The peculiar abstractness of Schmitt's understanding of founding moments is illustrated by his claim that there is an underlying continuity between Bismarck's *Reich* and the Weimar Republic. In 1870, the Germans obviously attained a "national" identity. Less obviously, he argues, they recognized the democratic principle, even though they did not make full use of it. Germans established the Federal Parliament (*Reichstag*) as a limited means of expressing the democratic will of the people, but they still adhered to the monarchical principle in regard to constitution-making. With the discrediting of the monarchical principle in the aftermath of World War I, the Germans adopted the democratic principle to its fullest extent, including constitution-making. On the surface, this was a fundamental change, Schmitt argues, but it obscured the fact that the Germans merely sought to "renew" not eliminate the *Reich* (V 46–60).

Schmitt is referring here to the Republic's official title "the German *Reich*." Hugo Preuß emphasized that the retention of the designation German *Reich* aimed merely at placating potential rightist opponents and signified nothing in regard to the source of governmental authority or its particular form (1964, 421–428, esp. 428).[30] Schmitt's spin on this semantic continuity suggests that, for him, legal theory itself becomes a form of political action since theorists define the relevant points of continuity/discontinuity and similarity/difference in a way that the founding moment becomes an effective response to the Weimar state crisis. A critical engagement with Schmitt's understanding of normative theory as political action entails examination of how Schmitt develops a state-friendly form of constitutional theory through a systematic reconstruction of the liberal constitutional tradition.

III.

The Weimar Constitution, Schmitt argues, "conforms thoroughly" to the type of constitution, the *bürgerlicher Rechtsstaat* (V XI), which gained classic expression in the rounds of constitution-making surrounding the American and French Revolutions. The defining feature of this type of constitution is the guarantee of the separation of powers and certain basic rights (V, 38–40). But it is mistaken to identify this type of constitution with consti- tutionalism per se (V 36–38). In fact, its legitimacy and, consequently, that of the Weimar Constitution rests upon the sovereign power of the people to give itself a constitution, regardless of its particular form (V 49–51).[31]

This is Schmitt's famous distinction between the political and legal (*rechtsstaatlich*) elements of the Weimar Constitution (V 23–25 and 40–41). Critics are right to point out that this distinction enables Schmitt to preserve the form of limited government at the expense of its substance. What is underappreciated among commentators is the significance of the fact that Schmitt develops this distinction through a systematic reconstruction of the classic American, and especially French, efforts at constitution-making. That this reconstruction effectively redefines the liberal constitutional tradition becomes evident only when Schmitt's comparative history of constitution-making is examined in reference to the larger history of Western constitutionalism.

Most treatments of Schmitt, however, do this to only a very limited degree. For example, Scheuerman rightly stresses the importance of Schmitt's reinterpretation of Sieyès, but he wrongly argues that, according to Schmitt, "liberal democratic jurisprudence *implicitly* [emphasis Scheuerman's] recognizes the existence of an omnipotent, inalienable, and indivisible founding subject, the *pouvoir constituant*" [emphasis Scheuerman] (1996, 309). Reading Schmitt's reinterpretation of Sieyès in reference to Western constitutional history, rather than focusing narrowly on Schmitt's treatment of early modern liberal theory and the legal positivism of Hans Kelsen, as does Scheuerman, demonstrates that, for Schmitt, this recognition is not "implicit." In Schmitt's account, rather, a peculiar strand of Sièyes's thought comes to define liberal constitution-making.

According to Schmitt, early constitutional struggles, like that leading to the Magna Carta, involved groups which, to the extent they defined themselves at all, did so in contradistinction to other groups vying for control of the same territory. The nobility, "freemen," sought to wrest concessions from the monarch, for example. The results of these struggles were agreements or contracts which aimed to guarantee the relative positions of the contracting parties. In Schmitt's view, however, these agreements are not constitutions in the modern sense, because the actors involved do not act consciously as a unit in order to define themselves politically.

The Glorious Revolution marks the beginning of constitutional law in the modern sense. By that time, Schmitt argues, all relevant social groups, including the King, were represented in Parliament. This relatively inclusive representation reflected a common identity which enabled the English to act as a unity. The agreement with William of Orange, for example, did not constitute this common identity; rather, the agreement with William presupposed this unity (V 46–47).

This notion of preexisting unity has both spiritual and material components. It is the product of historical development understood in existential terms. There is no necessary development toward a common identity, the achievement of which constitutes an end phase of sorts, because this depends on circumstances which vary considerably between contexts as well as on decisive human action. Schmitt argues, for example, that the relatively high degree of centralization in France at the time of the Revolution distinguishes French constitution-making from that of the Americans less in an institutional than in a spiritual sense. Americans compensated for the splintered character of their political system by sending representatives to a constitutional convention. The crucial difference is that the French have a common identity, forged over many centuries, which came to full flowering in the absolutist era. The centralizing efforts of the French monarchs broke down the great multiplicity of local bonds, so that, increasingly, the French identified with the central state. The Americans, by contrast, had a long tradition of local self-government, a legacy of their unique development as English colonies, which solidified these local attachments. At the time of the Revolution, significantly, Americans saw themselves first as members of particular states, secondly as citizens of the United States.

Because of this common identity, the French were able to act in a way not possible for Americans. In fact, in Schmitt's view, the round of constitution-making inspired by the French Revolution was truly the first instance of a people reaching a "decision" regarding their "political existence" as a whole. During the Glorious Revolution, the English people, through Parliament, acted as a unity, but the Revolution involved a rearrangement, more or less, of an existing system, the sanctioning of a series of developments which occurred over an extended period of time. The French, by contrast, consciously made a radical break with their past, and, on the basis of their common identity, chose a new political form. The great French insight, Schmitt argues, was seeing the act of establishing a constitution as itself "constitutive." In other words, the authority of the people acting in its collective capacity is unrestrained by any norms prior to the act itself; it is the act of will itself which establishes norms (V 76–80, esp. 78).

The next closest instance was the American Revolution. But here again, Schmitt argues, only an institutional restructuring took place. The Americans anticipated this notion of a people consciously adopting a new political form, and yet they were unable to act upon it, because they were preoccupied with finding an institutional framework to accommodate their various political identities. The Americans had to "constitute" their identity through the act of constitution-making itself, whereas the French were able to "presuppose" this identity (V 76–80). Put differently, the Americans were stuck at some sort of preparatory stage, unable to grasp the great opportunity offered by their own Revolution.

Schmitt identifies an important aspect of the French tradition. The French are not defined by their constitutions in the way that Americans are by the U.S. Constitution. The French state was formed before the Revolution, and it is in an important, though ill-defined, or perhaps even undefinable, way, independent of particular forms of government. There are certain institutional loci of the French national identity—the centralized bureaucracy for example—and the French national identity has undergone some changes, most notably through the Revolution itself. Nonetheless, it was preexisting, independent.[32]

It is quite understandable that Schmitt oriented his attempt at a systematic comparative constitutional theory toward the "classic French constitutions" (V XI). The aborted Paulskirche Constitution of 1849 marked the apex of American influence on German law before the founding of the Federal Republic (Steinberger 1987). Otherwise, German legal institutions and legal theory were heavily influenced by the French model.

The problem is that Schmitt defines constitution-making not merely in reference to the French model, which he rightly argues occupies a central place in the Western constitutional tradition, and one of special relevance for civil-law countries, such as Germany.[33] Rather, Schmitt defines Western constitution-making exclusively in reference to the most radical strand within the French tradition.[34] This renders his reading of the Western constitutional tradition doubly one-sided. In this, Schmitt makes good on his claim that "(t)he rule proves nothing; the exception proves everything: (the exception) confirms not only the rule but also its existence, which derives only from the exception" (PT 15).

Schmitt correctly stresses the central role of Sieyès, who embodies, perhaps better than anyone, the ambiguities of the Revolution, as well as the importance to revolutionary thought of Sieyès' concept of a radical break with the past. But Schmitt ignores the great tensions in Sieyès' thought, as well as those between it and various other strands of revolutionary thought. Relatedly, he severs the concept of a radical break from its historical context, overlooking the pressing practical problems to which it was a response and which served as a potential limit on its scope. Sieyès links will with representation and identifies the national will with that of the National Assembly, first, in order to discredit the traditional system of representation, which tended to bolster traditional authority for the very reason it was more democratic: imperative mandates reinforced provincialism.

Sieyès links will with representation, also, in order to justify the activity of the National Assembly, which was already a going concern. As the National Assembly became tyrannical, however, Sieyès hedged and sought to limit its authority in a variety of ways.[35]

The blizzard of French constitutions in the first generation after the Revolution effaced the distinction between the form and substance of constitutions. Nevertheless, the French accepted, at least initially, something similar to the American understanding of a normative constitution, as evidenced by Articles 2 and, especially, 16 of the *Declaration of the Rights of Man and Citizen*.[36] Schmitt recognizes the importance of the concept of a normative constitution for the French and American efforts at constitution-making (V, 38–39), but he sees the concept of a normative constitution as merely another in a series of attempts to portray political aims as constitutionalism per se (V 36–38). The legal status of the *Declaration* is a matter of some dispute (e.g. Kühne 1990 and Philip 1989), and yet it is still not the case that the French rejected the notion of norms anterior to constitutions. Even in the late 19th century, when leading constitutional theorists turned from natural rights as conceived in the social contract tradition, they still believed that the lawgiver was bound in some essential way. And this was under a constitution, famous for its brevity, which established only the bare framework of government and provided amendment procedures only marginally more demanding than those for ordinary legislation.[37] Schmitt's great French contemporary Leon Duguit (1919, 1–66) provides an especially interesting contrast in this regard. Schmitt's reading of the French understanding of the nation and its importance for constitution-making echoes Duguit's position on these issues in important respects. Moreover, both Schmitt and Duguit stress the need to break from outdated concepts. And yet Duguit argues for an alternate understanding of the state centering on the notion of "public service, "in which the state is limited by its duty to provide public services. The principal problem in the French tradition, therefore, has been finding the proper institutional means through which such norms could gain expression.[38] Schmitt's focus on Sieyès' idea of a radical break with the past obscures this important connection between the French and American traditions.

One must always guard against interpretations which deny the plurality and ambiguity of rich, complex traditions (Tracy 1987). Bearing this in mind, it is still not too much of a stretch to claim that the American and French Revolutions form the epicenter of what we today consider liberal constitutionalism. More specifically, the seminal instances of constitution-making associated with these revolutions gave classic expression to the core liberal commitment to limited government in service of individual liberty. How one understands individual liberty changes over time. In fact, commentators are right to point out an important difference in this regard between the American and French Revolutions themselves (Arendt 1973 and Preuß 1995). But central to these revolutions and the traditions of constitutional theory and practice they inspired, including the Weimar Constitution itself, was the idea that the legitimacy of constitutions is intimately bound up with the protection of individual liberty, however one understands this concept. By systematically obscuring this important commonality between the American and French constitutional traditions, Schmitt does more than deny their rich diversity. Rather, he slips his theory of decisionism into the very core of the liberal constitutional tradition.[39] More specifically, in arguing that the central lesson of these classic instances of liberal constitution-making, particularly that stemming from the French Revolution, is the idea that the legitimacy of constitutions depends upon a sovereign decision of the people, and not whether the resulting constitution protects individual liberty, Schmitt effectively shifts the theoretical epicenter of the liberal constitution tradition. In this sense, Schmitt does not develop a theoretical antipode to the liberal constitutionalism so much as transform it from the inside out such that it serves as a theoretical foundation for his illiberal constitutional theory. Restoring the normative concept of constitutions to its rightful place historically has important implications for Schmitt's normative argument. Specifically, by qualifying the association of decisionism with these seminal instances of liberal constitution-making, it limits the capacity for Schmitt's theory to inspire the sort of decisive action he deems essential for responding effectively to the Weimar state crisis.

Schmitt's existential understanding of norms might still have enabled him to wiggle free of this difficulty. Perhaps it was historically inaccurate to locate decisionism at the core of the liberal tradition. Nonetheless, Schmitt might argue, his decisionistic reading of the Weimar Constitution, based as it was on his understanding of the essential difference between these seminal instances of constitution-making, better ensured political stability. Therefore, one should embrace his theory regardless of the fact that it is based on a one-sided reading of the normative and historical foundations of liberal constitutionalism.

Responding to such a defense of Schmitt's comparative history requires consideration of Max Weber's historical method, for, in a sense, Schmitt's *Constitutional Theory* is reminiscent of Weber's challenge to traditional German historiography. Weber was a major participant in a debate among historians known as the *Methodenstreit*. In 1896, Karl Lamprecht sparked the debate by calling for a reorientation of the traditional concerns and methods of German historians. He argued that recent advances in social psychology challenged the traditional insistence on the incomparability of national contexts. In fact, he argued, through the methods of social psychology, one could examine parallel developments in a variety of contexts in such a way as to enable one to discern "laws" of historical development, much as in the natural sciences.

With few exceptions, most notably Otto Hintze, who voiced only qualified support for certain of Lamprecht's claims, German historians were quite unified in their rejection of Lamprecht's proposals. Having successfully shouted down Lamprecht and his small group of followers, German historians stuck doggedly to the central tenets of 19th-century historiography until after the Second World War.[40] Though traditional historians won this battle, they lost the war. Whereas Lamprecht failed by conflating the central concerns of historians and social scientists, Weber established a bridge between them by mediating their respective focuses on generality and particularity.[41]

Historians, according to Weber, must become more self-reflective in the sense of recognizing their active role in the process of research. Historical materials do not merely present themselves ready-made to the historian. On the contrary, whether they acknowledge it or not, historians must quite literally constitute their object of study, using a variety of techniques to select out and organize their data. In the 19th century, for example, German historians focused on the historical individual, the minute particularity of human experience. Periodization and narrative were ideally suited for this purpose, it was thought, because they enabled the historian to forego using concepts to select out, organize, and examine data. One could understand the individual events within a period on their own terms, that is, without recourse to abstractions which would obscure the essential uniqueness of the events. In the words of Leopold von Ranke, who is credited with establishing the modern discipline of history in Germany, the task of the historian was to determine merely "how it really was" (*wie es eigentlich gewesen*).

In Germany, this inductive approach was seen as an alternative to French rationalism, which, through its abstract, universal categories, was said to have drained human life of meaning and to have legitimated horrendous tyranny. By determining, through careful inductive analysis, the precise positions of particular events and developments within ever larger constellations, it was deemed possible to identify the essence of leading institutions or even of an entire era. These essences, expressed in concepts, had a normative status, the basis of which was peculiarly circular. Though the product of contingent human action, they formed organic wholes, in which particular actions gained meaning. The normative legitimacy of these organic wholes was derived from their very distinctiveness. In other words, one believed it was possible to derive an "ought" from an "is" (Iggers 1983, 63–89 and 124–173).

In Weber's view, German historiography reverses the proper relation between concepts and historical research (Burger [1976] 1987, 77–93). Whether acknowledged or not, concepts are the principal means through which historical research is conducted. Following his contemporary, the philosopher Heinrich Rickert, Weber argued that the finite human mind could only comprehend a small segment of social reality, which is infinitely complex and ever-changing, and that certain presuppositions, such as cultural values, play an essential role in the human sciences by indicating which portion of the endless stream of events is worthy of study. Moreover, because even the smallest portion of reality is infinitely complex, the same process of selection is operative at every level of analysis. Even a single event is a composite not simply because it is constituted on the basis of which facts the investigator deems relevant but also because the facts themselves are constituted by the investigator. In other words, the investigator must act upon his or her object of study, quite literally creating it during the process of study, for otherwise it would remain a mass of undifferentiated material.

Presuppositions are also necessary in the attribution of causation, according to Weber. To claim that one thing caused another, even in the most mundane cases, presupposes an understanding of what one would expect in similar cases, which, of course, must also be defined, and so on. In other words, any argument regarding historical causation implies certain conceptual understandings of a wide range of phenomena. These conceptual understandings are brought in from the outside, that is, they do not stem strictly from the data which are themselves constituted in the process of study. There is no knowledge of mere facts, in other words.

Ideal types, for Weber, are a means of formalizing the logical dictates concerning the role of presuppositions in social research.[42] On the basis of certain perceptions of a problem, one identifies particular features of events or developments, which are then exaggerated in a deliberately one-sided manner. The resulting composites are fictional in that, though they have some basis in reality, they purposely distort it by highlighting certain relationships or sequences to the exclusion of others. In this way, they formalize one's expectations regarding particular phenomena under given conditions, providing a baseline for determining the extent to which the targeted events and developments deviate from the norm as postulated.

Ideal types are neither substantive claims nor even hypotheses. They are merely heuristic devices. They enable one to get at empirical data and are justifiable in a particular case only to the extent that they aid in determining the "cultural significance of concrete historical events and patterns" (Weber 1949, 111). Every concept creates associations by forging linkages among otherwise disparate phenomena. According to Reinhart Koselleck, for example, the concept of legitimacy had gone through myriad permutations which had proved useful in a variety of causes, legal, political, and scholarly. Weber "scientifically neutralized" this term by radically severing it from these rich associational linkages. Once isolated in this way, Weber rendered the concept of legitimacy "both formal and general enough to describe constitutional potentialities both long-term and short-term, shifting and overlapping, which then disclosed historical 'individualities' on the basis of their internal structures" (Koselleck 1985, 91).

Weber's emphasis on the potential experimental quality of the human sciences produced a working agreement between the discipline of history and the social sciences. The use of concepts enables the historian to proceed experimentally, eschewing periodization and narrative but without sacrificing attention to the historical individual. This is because, through use of concepts, one can isolate particular aspects of different periods and contexts and examine whether or to what extent they are relevant for the contemporary concern. Focusing attention in this way on specific features of otherwise widely disparate phenomena enables the historian to combine scope of coverage with attention to detail, mediating the particular concerns of historians and social scientists. Of course, one can take issue with the particular findings put forth in such works. Some of the findings in Weber's *The Protestant Ethic and the Spirit of Capitalism* ([1958] 1976) are now considered questionable.[43] Nonetheless, the approach serves a useful function. In calling attention to previously unexamined relationships among possible causal factors, such studies can open new areas of research, which may prove fruitful in understanding the issues in question (Furet 1984, 1–23 and esp. 54–67).

In terms of form, *Constitutional Theory* is innovative in an analogous way. Take, for example, Gerhard Anschütz's classic commentary on the Weimar Constitution. In the Introduction (1930, 1–28), Anschütz addresses a few general issues, such as whether revolutions are legitimate sources of new laws (3–11) and whether, if at all, there is legal continuity with the prewar system (11–15). The remainder of the work, however, is organized around the particular provisions of the Constitution, treated in chronological order. In regard to each article, Anschütz lists the relevant literature, analyzes its scope and substance, and discusses the political-legal practice relating to it. Throughout, Anschütz does not engage in a significant degree of comparative-historical analysis.

Schmitt's *Constitutional Theory* is divided into four major parts examining, in order, the concept of constitutions (V 2–121), the legal (V 125–220) and the political (V 223–359) components of constitutions, and the constitutional theory of federations (V 363–391). Each of these parts is organized into sections examining topics, such as the absolute (V 3–11) and relative (V 11–20) concepts of constitutions. Though within these topics Schmitt discusses major developments, there is no overarching narrative or chronology. His aim is to identify essential continuities and discontinuities in the development of key concepts and consider their relevance for major features of the Weimar Constitution. He does so by examining the principal features of the Weimar Constitution in reference to major developments in constitutional government in other countries, principally France, but, to a lesser degree, both the United Kingdom and the United States, and other countries as well. In this way, he intends to identify the peculiar challenges facing the Weimar Constitution and what might be done to make it more viable as a constitutional system. Along the way, Schmitt discusses 103 of the Constitution's 181 provisions (V 392–3), though only to illustrate larger issues. Article 153 concerning the right to property, for example, is considered under the headings of the "positive concept of a constitution" (V 27), constitutional amendments (V 101 and 111), the concept of statutes in the *Rechtsstaat* (V 152), and constitutional rights (V 160, 165, 166, 171, and 172). Schmitt's more general concern in addressing constitutional provisions in reference to a number of different issues is to provide a "systematic framework" for considering the problems of the "*bürgerlicher Rechtsstaat*" (V XL). In this way, Schmitt seeks to shift the center of gravity of legal theory debates away from the analysis of individual provisions of the Weimar Constitution by examining the constitution in a much broader comparative historical framework. By making use of conceptual frameworks to organize empirical materials that are relevant for normative questions, Schmitt's *Constitutional Theory* can be seen as an attempt to develop a more empirically grounded form of constitutional theory, one in which the issue of the practical relevance of the resulting normative concepts is addressed directly through the process of concept formation.

Weber also believed that comparative studies are quite relevant to normative debate. Near the end of World War I, other systems were proposed as models for the reformation of the German system, raising the question of to what extent these institutions were suitable for the German context with its unique characteristics. Comparative studies, Weber argued, indicate precise points of similarity and difference between the respective contexts, which aid in addressing this important question ([1918] 1978, esp. preface and 1449–1459). But in these political writings, Weber did not apply the ideal-typical method, relying instead on more impressionistic contrasts between systems (e.g. [1918] 1978, 1451–1459).[44] Weber's refusal to apply ideal types in his own normative arguments reflected his determination not to lend false scientific status to his claims. "The coming of age of science always implies the transcendence of the ideal type," in Weber's view (1949, 104). Take, for example, "Benjamin Constant's theory of the ancient state," which, according to Weber, "serves as a harbor until one has learned to navigate safely in the vast sea of empirical facts" (104). Weber argued that it "is still legitimate today to use the brilliant Constant hypothesis to demonstrate certain aspects and historically unique features of ancient political life, as long as one carefully bears in mind its ideal-typical character" (104).[45] For Weber, viewing ideal types as empirically valid was tantamount to assuming an affirmative, decidedly one-sided answer to the important question of the cultural significance of the object of study (98).

Schmitt's position in regard to the relation of theory and practice is the converse of Weber's. The unjustified conflation of empirical and normative components of social inquiry is clearly subordinate to Schmitt's concern to ensure the practical efficacy of normative theory in a period of political crisis. Nonetheless, Schmitt's *Constitutional Theory* reflects some aspects of Weber's ideal-typical method,[46] enabling one to examine it as a methodologically sophisticated application of comparative history to legal theory. Like Weber, for example, Schmitt develops guiding concepts through one-sided exaggerations of certain aspects of his object of study, in this case the Western constitutional tradition. As such, Schmitt's concepts may prove useful as heuristic devices, providing a means of comparison of actual instances of constitution-making. As with Weber's *The Protestant Ethic and the Spirit of Capitalism* ([1958] 1976) and other works utilizing ideal types (e.g. Bendix [1964] 1977), the appropriateness for this purpose of concepts, such as identity, does not depend on whether they accurately portray historical individuals narrowly defined, since such artificial constructs necessarily obscure important features of events and developments in order to achieve conceptual clarity. The question is, to what extent the categories enable one to determine the concrete significance for a particular problem of certain works, events, and developments. In *Dictatorship*, for example, Schmitt uses the concepts of sovereign and commissarial forms of dictatorship to identify and analyze changes in the theory and practice of constitutional dictatorship in the modern era (D). One can also say this of *Constitutional Theory* insofar as Schmitt uses the concept of identity to establish a spectrum of actual instances of constitution-making. Schmitt's concept of identity resembles an ideal type in that it does not represent what is common to the myriad instances of constitution-making before the founding of the Weimar Republic. In fact, according to Schmitt, the French Revolution was the first instance of a people reaching a decision regarding their political existence as a whole. Schmitt then argues that other instances of constitution-making, such as the English Revolution of 1688 and the American Revolution of 1776, deviate in different respects from the French model. Using certain aspects of the French Revolution as a baseline, in other words, Schmitt executes a "systematic" study of constitution-making.

The problem with Schmitt's comparative histories in *Constitutional Theory* is partly that he attempts to include an overly extensive set of disparate phenomena under one concept. Schmitt's tendency to characterize complex phenomena with a sharply drawn conceptual formula gives his works an extraordinary suggestiveness. At the same time, his use of highly abstract conceptual formulas reduces the utility of his categories as explanatory devices and renders his formulas open to misinterpretation, a danger Schmitt himself conceded (BP 13). In *Guardian of the Constitution*, we shall see, Schmitt partly responds to this difficulty by using conceptual frameworks which more effectively capture dynamic relationships among diverse phenomena relevant for particular policy questions. In *Constitutional Theory*, however, Schmitt has not fully taken to heart Weber's admonition that for concepts to be used effectively in historical research, they must be carefully calibrated to the range of phenomena under consideration. As the scope of the study increases, a point is reached beyond which one must break the concepts down into several, less general, categories covering narrower sets of phenomena. If one does not limit the scope of coverage of conceptual devices in this way, the concepts tend to obscure, rather than help identify, concrete points of similarity and difference which are potentially relevant to the question examined. "The more inclusive the relationships to be presented, and the more many-sided their cultural significance has been," according to Weber, "the *more* their comprehensive systematic exposition in a conceptual system approximates the character of an ideal type, and the less is it possible to operate with *one* concept" (Weber 1949, 97).

Schmitt fails to restrict properly the range of coverage of his conceptual formulas, limiting their usefulness in historical research. To criticize Schmitt in this way, however, is to miss the point in an important sense. Schmitt uses concepts, such as identity, not as a provisional means of identifying and explicating concrete points of similarity and difference among contexts, a tool to be discarded or revised depending on its usefulness for this purpose and applicable in normative discussions only as a means of explaining empirical findings. On the contrary, Schmitt uses concepts, like that of identity, to get *around* empirical data. Resorting to sound bites, one might characterize Schmitt's method in the following way: Schmitt draws on a Weber-like understanding of the importance of concepts in historical and social inquiry, a form of neo-Kantianism, in order to develop a politically efficacious alternative to what he considers a destructive version of neo-Kantianism, specifically, the legal positivism of Hans Kelsen. The end product, however, can no longer be considered neo-Kantian, because the empirical and normative dimensions of the inquiry are fused.

In this sense, Schmitt's *Constitutional Theory* can be seen as a return to the unified science of the state, which attained its fullest expression in Hegel. In fact, it is somewhat surprising that Schmitt did not title the work *State Theory*. Clearly, Schmitt's concerns extend beyond the confines of constitutional theory narrowly defined, for his analysis of the Weimar Constitution through a broad comparative historical framework is directed at identifying and reinforcing the grounds of the viability of the state in the modern era. *Constitutional Theory* also resembles a 19th-century work in state theory, to a lesser degree, in terms of the range of issues addressed: economics, law, politics, and society, all as they bear on the normative and empirical dimensions of the state. Nonetheless, Schmitt emphasizes that he is not offering a "general theory of the state forms" or a "state theory" (V XII), and quite rightly, for his concern is the German state, specifically the Weimar state. Still, it is somewhat surprising that Schmitt emphasizes so emphatically that he is developing a constitutional, not a state, theory.

The reason for Schmitt's caginess, I suggest, has to do with his peculiar relationship with Neo-Kantianism.[47] Specifically, though he draws upon some aspects of Weber's neo- Kantian understanding of history to develop a state-friendly form of constitutional theory, Schmitt seeks to sever any association between his conceptual approach in *Constitutional Theory* and that of the last great state theorist of the 19th century, Georg Jellinek, who exerted an important influence on Weber. Distinguishing himself from Jellinek is particularly important for Schmitt, because Jellinek's neo-Kantian approach to concept formation in the study of the state provided Weber with a springboard for completing the disintegration of the unified science of the state, which Schmitt seeks to rehabilitate in a suitably revised form.

In his monumental work, *General Theory of the State (Allgemeine Staatslehre)*, originally published in 1900, Jellinek examines the state from every conceivable angle. Among the many issues considered are the purpose of state theory (1922, 3–24), the history of state theory (53–70), and even "the name of the state" (129–135). Throughout this comprehensive treatment, Jellinek insists on distinguishing clearly between empirical and normative dimensions of his subject. The work is divided, for example, into sections treating either an empirical or a normative issue. And, in an extensive methodological discussion early in the work (25–52), Jellinek emphasizes the need to achieve methodological clarity about the nature of concepts in state theory (34–42). Weber followed Jellinek, insofar as both sought to distinguish between normative and empirical forms of inquiry. However, Weber recast Jellinek's understanding of ideal type concepts. Whereas Jellinek saw ideal types as normative concepts, Weber considered them artificial constructs useful in empirical inquiry. In addition, the purpose of Weber's ideal types was to highlight the differences between contexts, rather than express what is common to a range of phenomena, as in the case of Jellinek (Burger ([1976] 1987 and Kalberg 1994).

Schmitt effectively collapses what both Jellinek and Weber sought to keep distinct, the empirical and normative dimensions of social inquiry. Of course, given his different aims, Schmitt might respond that his failure to distinguish clearly between types of concepts is not a decisive objection, for his deft fusion of empirical and normative dimensions of politics and society might be the very means of bringing about a more efficacious form of normative theory. The next three chapters will consider this claim more fully in reference to *Guardian of the Constitution*. I conclude this chapter by reexamining Schmitt's concept of identity in *Constitutional Theory* as a potential heuristic device in the Weberian sense. Though Schmitt clearly did not intend his concept to be used in this way, he moved far enough in this direction to permit such a reconstruction. Moreover, turning Schmitt against himself in this way shows that Schmitt's approach fails in this sense as well. Nonetheless, it points toward how such a conceptual approach might serve constitutionalist aims, if applied appropriately and conscientiously.

Schmitt's theory of constitution-making hinges on a subsidiary claim regarding the role of the state in the American and French political traditions. Specifically, he posits that the relevant differences between the two seminal instances of constitution-making are attributable to the fact that the French state facilitated the development of a common identity among the French before the Revolution by centralizing political authority to a much greater degree than did the various states prior to the American Revolution. At first blush, there is a striking difference between the French and American constitutional traditions regarding degrees of administrative centralization, as emphasized by Tocqueville in his classic accounts of their respective political traditions (1955, 32–41, 57–60, and esp. 72–77; also 1969, 61–98, esp. 87–98). The United States was a confederation of relatively independent states at the time the Constitution was drafted and promulgated. Also at this time, and even into the 19th century, the political allegiance of Americans was directed first toward their state governments and only secondarily toward the federal union. Finally, there remained very important differences among the American states, both politically and socially, the institution of slavery being the most notable. It is not surprising that given these circumstances, the framers of the Constitution mostly sought to agree upon a basic institutional framework, within which substantive disagreements could be worked out over time, but without the states losing a considerable degree of their preexisting sovereignty.

Prior to the promulgation of the first French constitutions, by contrast, there was a much greater degree of centralization. But it is very important to qualify this contrast. The French kings under the Old Regime were absolutist, but not in the sense that they alone exercised governmental authority. Royal decrees, for example, were promulgated by the law courts, or parlements, which might refuse to enforce them in exchange for special privileges from the king (Doyle 1987, 157–67). This pattern of securing obedience to central legislative authority in exchange for special legal dispensations was a defining feature of the Old Regime. The king sent royal officers into the provinces to ensure execution of central dictates. But these central officials exercised authority alongside, and often in competition with, a multilayered, overlapping set of corporate bodies empowered by monarchs to carry out certain functions or activities. In fact, central state officials made extensive use of local institutions, in order to collect taxes efficiently, for example. Contrary to Tocqueville's famous claim, therefore, the spread of central authority did not necessarily occur at the expense of local institutions (Root 1987). The monarch's ongoing need for financing and administrative aid meant that the central government's undisputed legislative authority could not be easily used to further central control over the execution of law. The concessions granted in exchange for the funds necessary to bolster central state power limited the state's capacity to interfere in the social order and, thereby, initiated a "dialectic of subversion" against central authority (Furet 1981, 107–111, esp. 110). At the same time, the parlements and other corporate bodies with special privileges were, in a roundabout way, a bulwark of the Old Regime. Settling disputes over the incredibly complicated system of special privileges and concessions greatly complicated the task of governing. By serving as intermediaries for the state, corporate bodies provided the monarch access to short-term credit. This was especially important, for lacking a central parliament and national bank, as in England, monarchs were not considered especially creditworthy. Often governed by representative bodies, the corporations were better able to spread burdens among their members, making them much better credit risks (Bien 1994).

This complex mosaic of agreements between the central state and myriad corporate bodies produced complex loyalties among citizens. By reaffirming the authority of Paris throughout France, this process of government by ongoing negotiation produced some of the conditions that Schmitt considered essential for the development of the concept of the nation. Despite the growing authority of Paris, corporate bodies regulated much of everyday life. In terms of their internal organization and mode of exercising their privileges, these corporate bodies were often miniature states, with assemblies responsible for establishing policy and procedures for resolving internal disputes. Whatever the French knew of self-government, according to David Bien, they learned in these corporate bodies (1994). Over the course of the Old Regime, the authority of the central state expanded greatly, and yet, on an institutional level, the gaze of citizens was typically directed at the defense of specific corporate privileges against encroachments by rival organizations and by central authority.[48]

In general terms, therefore, Schmitt is right that the French and the American Revolutions differed more in a spiritual than in an institutional sense. In both systems, there was self-government at the local level, even though the nature of this self-government and the larger state framework in which these organizations functioned differed considerably. In this sense, Tocqueville was closer to the mark in regard to the early American forms of government than he was to that in Old Regime France.[49] The French, however, came to understand themselves as a political community far earlier than the Americans, for whom a national consciousness emerged briefly during the Revolutionary War, only to be subordinated to the long-standing state loyalties until after the Civil War (Geiter and Speck 1997).

The problem is that it is not clear that the French national identity forged by the Old Regime carries the explanatory power Schmitt ascribes to it. The national political consciousness, which Schmitt sees as a prerequisite for a genuine act of constitution-making, was produced to a great extent by the Revolution itself (Bossenga 1987 115–140, esp. 131–134; also Jones 1995, 176–214), as illustrated by the so-called Municipal Revolution. During the Old Regime, town governments were tightly integrated into the hierarchical royal system. With the breakdown of the Old Regime in 1789, local committees were established throughout France, some alongside existing town councils and others in place of traditional institutions, depending on local circumstances. Initially quite autonomous from central authorities, the perceived need for greater central control for the war effort sparked efforts to integrate committees more tightly into the national system (Tilly 1993, 169–170). Though enjoying only short-lived autonomy, the local committees played a very important political role in the French Revolution. For the most part they excluded the poor and uneducated, and yet, as representative bodies, they constituted a substantial widening of participation in comparison with the Old Regime. Moreover, while the initial impetus behind their establishment was often to protect property, they provided for the emergency needs of the poor as well, greatly expanding the powers and responsibilities of government. Thus, while committees tended to exclude common people, they attended to some of their concerns. And, because the committees conducted their business publically, they gave common people an outlet for political participation, creating a "political space, " in the words of Lynn Hunt, and, with it, a new political culture (Hunt 1976, 321–346 and 1978; also Jones 1995, 215–236).

The fact that the communes tended to support revolutionary changes in Paris lends credence to Schmitt's claim about the importance of preexisting unity to French efforts at constitution-making. But one must analyze further the basis of this unity. Municipal committees were established to respond to local problems. Early on, committee actions often anticipated developments at the center. However, the more important point in terms of Schmitt's argument is the fact that the committees did not tend to support the National Assembly and then the Convention because of a preexisting national identity. Rather, their support of central authorities stemmed from the perceived national dimension of local problems. When one attends to events on the ground, one gets an entirely different image than that of the French nation acting in its collective capacity to provide itself a new political form. Instead, one sees a series of ad hoc responses to pressing circumstances, with the only common thread being the perceived need for some fundamental change in the existing system.[50] That particular groups were able to seize the opportunity to give direction to change and, for a brief time, control it to a limited degree should not mislead one into thinking this was a unified process. Particular constellations of forces at the local level accounted for the complex motivations of leading agents and the character of changes there. Commercial interests in some cities were fearful of greater central control, for example, because it might mean central interference in commercial affairs, while other groups advocated decentralization in order to preserve local privileges, such as tax indemnities. Thrown into the mix were also some deeply rooted regional identities, which had proven quite resistant to efforts at national integration throughout the Old Regime.[51] Moreover, in those localities where city officials were open to reform and permitted more inclusive forms of participation, the push for a complete housecleaning was not as strong.

The messy character of the lead-up to the radical break with the Old Regime does not mean that the concept of the French nation did not predate the Revolution, nor that it did not play an important role in the early French efforts at constitution-making. It indicates that it is necessary to understand how the need to develop practical solutions to local problems facilitated the identification with national level institutions, which, according to Schmitt, was so important in the process of constitution-making. In both the American and French systems, non-national institutions played an important role in bringing about more centralized, democratic governments. Only the American system, however, provided for political stability and remained intact beyond its infancy. This suggests that, if a relative degree of national consciousness is the prerequisite of constitution-making in the modern sense, stressing national identity did not serve Schmitt's purposes. He needs to better account for the role of national identity, or provide an additional argument about why a comparative history of constitution-making demonstrates the superiority of *his* understanding of the French model.

I will not attempt to answer the question of what accounts for the relative longevity of the early American efforts at constitution-making, nor do I propose the American model as the appropriate one generally. My concern is to illustrate a basic point about Schmitt's use of comparative history. The connection Schmitt makes between degrees of centralization/decentralization, on the one hand, and national/subnational identities, on the other, is too crude if one's aim is to develop a politically efficacious constitutional theory. This is because, as presented, it cannot account for the relative political stability of the American political system. At best, one might use these pairings as heuristic devices to address the relative importance of various factors accounting for the different character and results of the two classic instances of constitution-making. One might ask, for example, what accounts for the fact that non-national institutions played an important political role in each system prior to both Revolutions, and, yet, were mostly excluded from the process of constitution-making and the resulting constitutions only in the French context?[52] One should ask further whether the character of centralization in the process of constitution-making and subsequent constitutions accounts for the relative stability of the American system, and, if so, how? The difference might be not attributable to institutional factors, narrowly defined. Perhaps France's relatively more exposed external position (e.g. Skocpol 1979, 60–64 and 1994, 282–284) or the use of local institutions by reactionary opponents of the Revolutionary Regime (e.g. Soboul 1988, 174–178) produced a tendency toward political instability in France. The general point is that one must move beyond general contrasts between systems if one is to make effective use of comparative history in normative theory. Instead, one must examine how systems actually operate, especially whether, and/or how, they respond to pressing practical problems over time. It is precisely such issues that are central to the proper design and maintenance of constitutional systems. In *Guardian of the Consti-*

tution, Schmitt took important steps in this direction. But despite his sophisticated use of conceptually driven comparative history, he failed to adequately understand the underlying character of the German state in a way that prevented him from developing more effective theoretical and practical solutions to the Weimar state crisis.

NOTES

1. On the differences between narrative and problem-oriented approaches to history, see Furet (1984, 54–67).

2. Adam (1992) also focuses on Schmitt's concern with the Weimar state crisis, but he stresses the importance of Catholic thought for understanding *Constitutional Theory*.

3. On the ambiguity in Hobbes' understanding of political obligation, compare Warrender (1957, esp. 299–329) with Johnston (1986, esp. 116–133).

4. For an excellent treatment of Hobbes' effort to counter the destructive power of irrational beliefs, see Holmes (1995, 69–99).

5. On the relationship between Schmitt and Strauss, as well as important changes in their respective interpretations of Hobbes in the interwar period, see McCormick (1994) and Cristi (1998, 169–178).

6. For a helpful analysis of Bourdieu's concept of *habitus* stressing the idea of thought as action, see Brubaker (1993, 212–34).

7. Richard Wolin (1992) utilizes the concept of *habitus* to account for Schmitt's transformation from a respected Weimar academic to the "crown jurist" of the Third Reich. The concept is useful in understanding Schmitt's relationship with the counterrevolutionary tradition. Here, however, it accounts for the peculiar fact that Schmitt's *Constitutional Theory* takes the form of an internal critique of liberal constitutionalism.

8. These are Article 114 (personal liberty), Article 115 (inviolability of the home), Article 117 (confidentiality of communications), Article 118 (freedom of expression), Article 123 (freedom of assembly), Article 124 (freedom of association), and Article 153 (right to property). Translations of these and selected other provisions of the Weimar Constitution are included in Tribe (1987, 194–201).

9. On the exercise of emergency powers during Weimar, see Rossiter (1948, 31–73), Finn (1991, 139–78, esp. 175–177), and Watkins (1939).

10. From the *Leviathan*. Quoted in Wehler (1985, 54).

11. For a overview of Schmitt's understanding of world history, see McCormick (1993, 119). The issue is handled more extensively in Ulmen (1991).

12. Generations of scholars have devoted themselves to explaining Germany's belated transition to a full-fledged liberal democracy. See, for example, Veblen ([1915] 1966), Plessner (1974), Meinecke (1950), Krieger (1957), Dahrendorf (1968), and Blackbourn and Eley (1984).

Schmitt's emphasis on the peculiarities of German federalism and Bismarck's brilliant political leadership echoes Weber's famous argument to this effect (Weber [1918] 1978, 1381–1469).

Unless otherwise indicated, my analysis in this section draws from Schmitt's treatment of parliament (V, 303–359), particularly his discussion of constitutionalism in the *Reich* (V 330–338).

13. The best work on the Prussian reform movement, particularly the relation of political and legal reform, remains Koselleck (1989).

14. For a thorough analysis of the tumultuous events surrounding the Prussian Constitution of 1850 and the legal and political changes it effected, see Huber (1960, 2: 35–128). An overview is offered in Grimm (1988, 175–217).

15. Blackbourn and Eley (1984) provide an excellent treatment of the failed "bourgeois revolution" during the *Reich* period. Though they underestimate the significance for German political development of the failure to institute full political reform in the 19th century, they are right that legal reform at the federal level provided liberals with many of their demands. Also, many of the individual *Länder* constitutions protected an extensive array of civil liberties, compensating somewhat for the absence of constitutional rights under the *Reich* Constitution (Luebbe-Wolff 1990).

16. For an excellent discussion of the importance for 19th century German politics of the reception of Roman Law by Savigny and his followers, see Whitman (1990).

17. Ott (1992, 32–116) offers a good overview of the diverse strains of legal positivism in Germany. On the basic issues and positions in the debate over legal positivism in the Weimar Republic, see Wendenburg (1984), and Heun (1989). For an extended critique and a defense of Kelsen, see Dyzenhaus (1997, 102–160) and Dreier (1990), respectively. Maus (1986, 205–226) offers a nuanced understanding of legal positivism, while Caldwell (1995) disputes the oft-repeated charge that legal positivism is politically naive.

18. For an overview of the complex constitutional structure of the *Reich*, see Craig (1978, 38–60).

19. On the difficulties presented by the issue of rights provisions, see Eyck (1968, 211–214).

20. Despite his stature as a legal theorist in the *Reich* period and his important role in the early part of the Weimar Republic, Preuß has not received much scholarly attention. On Preuß' political theory, see Lehnert (1992). For an analysis of the basic features of and debate about Preuß' drafts of the Weimar Constitution, see Jellinek (1930, 127–138).

21. For a good overview of the Basic Rights in the politics of the era, see Peukert ([1987] 1991, 129–146). On the politics of the welfare state more generally, see Hong (1998) and Crew (1996).

22. Nipperdey (1930) is the authoritative commentary on the legal status of the various provisions of the Catalogue of Rights. See also Thoma (1932, 607–623).

23. On social conflict in the Weimar Republic with a view to the Basic Rights, see Peukert ([1987] 1991, 132–147).

24. The classic statement of this tendency is Mohl (1860, 1:96–143). An excellent contemporary treatment in reference to constitutional law is Hesse (1991, 19–32).

25. For an excellent overview of legal theory in the *Reich* period, see Emerson ([1928] 1979, 47–91).

26. A useful introduction in English to Savigny's view of history and of the state is the famous lecture *Vocation of our Age* (Savigny 1975). On Savigny's method, see Savigny (1951). Böckenförde (1976, 9–41) offers an interesting discussion of theoretical problems with the Historical School approach. Consult Rückert (1984) on Savigny's "idealism."

Schmitt does not elaborate his understanding of history explicitly in *Constitutional Theory*, so it is not surprising that Savigny and the Historical School do not emerge there. My reconstruction of Schmitt's position on this issue is based upon Schmitt's works prior to *Constitutional Theory*, such as *Political Theology*, which address the subject directly, as well as on the methodological implications of Schmitt's interpretation of Western constitutional history in *Constitutional Theory* considered below. Schmitt's first extended treatment of Savigny is *Die Lage der Europäischen Rechtswissenschaften* (1943/44). Ulmen (1991, 74– 86), provides a thorough discussion of Schmitt's treatment of Savigny in this work.

27. Carl Friedrich provides a useful comparison of Hegel and the Historical Law School on this point (1963, 131–142).

28. Though Schmitt expressed disdain for Kelsen, there are important parallels between his theory of decisionism and Kelsen's value relativism, as many commentators have pointed out. For a recent reworking of this claim in reference to Schmitt's critique of liberal constitutionalism, see Scheuerman, (1996).

29. Bruce Ackerman's understanding of dualist democracy is structurally quite similar to Schmitt's decisionism, both in terms of their respective views of a sovereign people asserting its will in founding moments as well as in their insistence on a qualitative distinction between the founding moment and ordinary politics (Ackerman 1991, 3–33). An important difference between them is that Schmitt, but not Ackerman, accepts the concept of an unconstitutional constitutional amendment.

30. Mattern (1928) provides a critical analysis of prevailing views on the continuity between the *Kaiserreich* and the Weimar Republic.

31. Schmitt's distinction between the legal and political components of the Weimar Constitution has kept theorists busy for generations. A good recent treatment is Thornhill (2000, 72–74).

32. For an excellent brief comparison of the American and Continental understandings of the state and an analysis of the implications of these understandings for constitutionalism in the United States and Europe, see Casper (1989).

33. Merryman (1985) provides a concise introduction to the civil law tradition and how it differs from its common law counterpart.

34. For an overview of the complex strands in the French constitutional tradition, see Stone (1992, 23–45).

35. Baker (1989, 313–323) provides an excellent discussion of Sieyès' role in the French Revolution.

Stefan Breuer (1984) also examines Schmitt's appropriation of Sieyès. We agree that Schmitt radicalizes Sieyès' understanding of constituent power by failing to properly contextualize Sieyès' writings and political activity. But, whereas Breuer's treatment focuses on social relations, my analysis stresses the immediate political context and Sieyès' place in the French constitutional tradition.

36. "The aim of every political association," according to Article 2, "is the preservation of the natural and imprescriptible rights of man. These rights are liberty, property, security, and resistance to oppression." Article 16 reads: "A society in which the guarantee of rights is not secured, or the separation of powers not clearly established, has no constitution" (Baker 1987, 237–239).

37. On this crucial period in French constitutional history, see Geny (1927, esp. sections 130–132).

38. This concern was reflected in the debate in France over the appropriateness of American style judicial review early in this century. Cf., especially, Malberg (1984) and Lambert (1921). On the importance of this controversy for French constitutionalism generally, see Stone (1992, 33–40).

39. In this regard, Bruce Ackerman and Schmitt arrive at a common destination via different routes. By refusing to read the American constitutional tradition through the distorting lens of dangerous foreign theorists, such as Locke, Hume, and Kant, Ackerman gives pride of place to what he considers the most distinctive American contribution to political theory, specifically, his own rather Schmittian notion of "Dualist Democracy" (Ackerman 1991, 3–33).

40. For a sense of the bitterness of this debate, particularly of the unfair treatment of Lamprecht by traditional historians, see Whimster (1987).

41. Weber's contribution was a series of essays published in the first decade of the last century (Weber 1949; [1906] 1977). For an overview of Weber's role in the debate, see Burger (1987, 140–153). On the importance of Weber for the discipline of history, see McLemore (1984), Kocka (1986), and Kocka and Peukert (1986).

42. There is considerable disagreement about Weber's theory of ideal types. An important question is whether Weber aimed to provide the means for determining causality in a narrow historical sense or categories suitable for generating general theories of social action. The focal point of this dispute is the apparent tension between Weber's use of ideal types in early and later works. Kocka (1986), for example, distinguishes between the more concrete/historical ideal types of the early methodological essays and works like *The Protestant Ethic*, on the one hand, and the more abstract/theoretical ideal types of *Economy and Society*, on the other, whereas Mommsen argues that Weber "remained faithful throughout his life to the methodological position which he had taken up between 1903 and 1907" (1974, 11), even though his "epistemological goals . . . undergo a certain displacement" over time (1989, 123). Finally, Kalberg argues that, in *Economy and Society*, the often

lengthy digressions into comparative history aim at developing ideal types that might be used to organize further empirical studies; Weber does not really ever get to the next stage of the testing and revising the models (1994, 82–91, esp. 90).

For my purposes, it is not necessary to attempt to resolve such scholarly donnybrooks about ideal types. I focus on those aspects of Weber's theory on which there is general agreement: specifically, that ideal types are formed through one-sided generalizations and that they serve as heuristic devices in empirical research. Both of these features are particularly helpful in understanding and responding to Schmitt's use of concepts in *Constitutional Theory*. On ideal types generally, see Hekman (1983), Bendix (1987), Lindbekk (1992), and Kalberg (1994, 50–78 and 92–142).

43. On the scholarly controversy surrounding the *Protestant Ethic*, see Fischoff (1944), Nelson (1973), Giddens (1976, 8–12), Winckelmann (1978), Bergler (1987), and Lehmann and Roth (1993).

44. Roth and Schluchter (1979, 195–206) offer a good discussion of Weber's approach to history in his political writings. For a major recent attempt to apply Weber's theory of ideal types to the issue of institutional borrowing between systems, see Allison (1996).

45. Weber is referring to Constant's famous essay, "The Liberty of the Ancients Compared with that of the Moderns" (1988, 307–328).

46. Schmitt was rather tight-lipped about his relation to Weber. Nonetheless, their relationship constitutes an important product line in the Schmitt studies growth industry. There are numerous attempts to compare their respective political theories (e.g. Mommsen [1959] 1984, 381–893; Slagstad 1988; and Mehring 1990).

Regarding their respective methodologies, Mehring (1991, 214) makes note of the fact that Schmitt puts ideal types to use in normative discussions in a way that Weber would not condone. However, he does not demonstrate precisely how their respective approaches differ, nor does he take account of the fact that Schmitt's use of ideal types enables him to decenter and recast the liberal constitutional tradition for his own purposes. Other leading criticisms of Schmitt's misuse of ideal types also fail to take account of this feature of *Constitutional Theory* (e.g. Kelsen 1931, Fijalkowski 1958, and Hofmann [1964] 1992). Finally, other notable treatments of Schmitt's approach to concept formation do not focus on *Constitutional Theory*. See, for example, Meier's (1988) treatment of *Political Theology* and *Concept of the Political*.

Two studies by G.L. Ulmen address issues of greater relevance to my treatment of Schmitt's methodology. Ulmen (1985) examines Schmitt's relationship to Weber on the question of the "sociology of the state," arguing, rightly, that Schmitt seeks to "link the historical and sociological methods (1985, 27). Ulmen focuses, however, on Schmitt's political existentialism, not on his legal theory, particularly the constitutional/state theory elaborated in *Constitutional Theory*. In a subsequent work, Ulmen (1991) offers the most comprehensive comparison to date of Weber and Schmitt. Here Ulmen focuses on the controversy over value-free social science and on their respective views of world history. These issues are rightly central to any full-fledged comparison of Schmitt and Weber. My concern, however, is with methodology in the micro, not macro, sense: specifically, Schmitt's use of ideal types to reconstruct core principles of the Western constitutional tradition. Moreover, I show that Schmitt's approach to concept formation does not aim so much to "obtain a concrete understanding of the political" (Ulmen 1985) as it does to redefine the central concerns of liberal constitutionalism by obscuring points of similarity and difference among important components of the tradition.

On concept formation among legal theorists, generally, in the Weimar period, see Lepsius (1994).

47. Regarding the origins of neo-Kantianism in law and its fate in the Weimar Republic, see Lepsius (1994, esp. 156–164 and 304–341).

48. Sewell (1980, 25–32) examines the corporations' control over members and their antagonistic relations with one another.

49. On the changing political culture in the Old Regime, particularly the complex, though important, role of corporate bodies in collective will formation, see Bien (1987), Bossenga (1987), Root (1987), Doyle (1987), Van Kley (1987), and Revel (1987).

50. In terms of the fluid nature of the developments leading up to these seminal rounds of constitution-making, the American and French Revolutions resemble one another a good deal more than Schmitt's decisionistic account allows. On the complex and ever changing relationships among theory and practice in the American Revolution, see Wood [1969] (1972).

51. Soboul (1988, 168–193) discusses the political and social roots and significance of regional variations and loyalties.

52. A principal theme of *The Federalist Papers*, for example, was not that state institutions and loyalties were no longer vibrant, nor that they were per se inimical to the common good. The unifying theme of the collected papers was the need to provide a more expansive institutional framework, which could attend to limited problems outside the scope of effective individual state action. Even Hamilton, who advocated strong central government, emphasized the continued importance of the states in the new system. See, for example, *Federalist* 9 (Madison et al. 1961).

Chapter 2

Exorcising the Ghost of Composite States Past: Local Self-Government and Political Stability in the *Kaiserreich*

In his study of the American Civil War, James McPherson points out that the narrative form of historical writing is especially well-suited for treating the role of contingency in history. By placing events in a sequence leading to a particular outcome, the narrative form highlights the possible impact of individual actions on subsequent events and developments. This sequencing also suggests that if actors had chosen otherwise at key points, things might have turned out differently.[1]

As one of this century's great theorists of the political, one would expect Schmitt to rely primarily on narrative political history when attending to contextual issues. At times, this is true. Note, for example, the so-called narrative of decline presented in *The Crisis of Parliamentary Democracy* (CPD) (1985). However, Schmitt can be rather surprising in this regard. In *Constitutional Theory* (*Verfassungslehre*) (V)([1928] 1989), for example, his decisionistic understanding of law and politics comes of age, so to speak, and yet, methodologically, Schmitt relies primarily on problem-oriented, comparative history to elaborate his argument. *Guardian of the Constitution* (*Hüter der Verfassung*) (HV) ([1931] 1985) continues Schmitt's turn toward the use of comparative history to address the concrete institutional problems of the Republic. At the center of *Guardian of the Constitution* is a relatively brief discussion of the Weimar state crisis (HV 71–108), the central premise of which is that one cannot adequately address the Republic's governability problems absent a clear understanding of the concrete conditions under which its constitutional system operates. An emphasis on the importance of context is a familiar mantra among legal and political theorists. What distinguishes Schmitt's analysis of the Weimar state crisis in *Guardian of the Constitution* (*Hüter der Verfassung* [HV] [1931] 1985) is his use of conceptual frameworks to consider the relevance of a wider range of contextual factors. Often, for example, legal and political theorists make reference to key political developments (e.g. Dyzenhaus 1997, 17–37), or they note certain general conditions, such as chronic economic problems (e.g. Schwab [1970] 1989, 29). Through his use of concepts, Schmitt is able to address contextual issues in a more systematic fashion, outlining in relatively short compass how certain features of the Weimar economic, legal, political, and social systems tend to coalesce in patterned ways to affect the state's ability to respond to pressing problems. The intersection of these factors might not prove debilitating in another context, he concedes. But under the relatively unique conditions of the Weimar Republic, they greatly restrict the range of alternatives available to the Republic.

This chapter examines Schmitt's use of concepts to examine the structural limits of state action in *Guardian of the Constitution*. After introducing Schmitt's conceptual framework through a critical examination of changes in his position on the problems of parliamentary government (I), a more general criticism of Schmitt's approach to the problems of the German state is provided through an analysis of his claim that local self-government is the primary institutional vehicle for the erosion of the distinction between state and society. More specifically, though Schmitt displays a clear sense of the political implications of important structural defects of the Weimar state, his incomplete understanding of the structural basis of political stability in the *Reich* period causes him to overlook the importance of decentralization to the effective functioning of the German state (II).

I.

Of the three elements of Schmitt's conceptual framework, federalism (*Federalismus*) is the most familiar and straightforward. It refers to the presence of a number of formally equal states within a larger organization of states, the latter maintaining a degree of separateness from the member states either individually or collectively. In a federal system, the individual member states have some influence over the process of will formation at the federal level, while they each retain limited autonomy from the federation as a whole (HV 94–96).

Pluralism (*Pluralismus*) is also a familiar concept. In the postwar American context, it refers to a form of political competition, in which a wide range of groups organize in order to influence the process of government at various levels of the system. Schmitt's concept resembles the American version in his emphasis on the presence of formally organized groups at all levels of the political system seeking to influence the process of will formation to their own advantage. But Schmitt's understanding differs in terms of the postulated relationship of state and society. For American pluralists, the state does not have an identity apart from the amalgam of private groups participating in government at all levels. The state merely serves a mediating function among the myriad groups seeking to define policy on a wide range of issues. Pluralism in Schmitt's usage calls to mind the English pluralists, who criticized unlimited state power and the relatively independent hierarchy of government authority associated with it. Harkening back to 19th century German state theory, Schmitt places a positive value on the independence of the state from society. But in its emphasis on social groups seeking to influence the state, all the while remaining distinct from the state (HV 73–91), Schmitt's model of pluralism traces its roots to the older English understanding.[2]

The final concept, polycracy (*Polykratie*), is least familiar. Borrowed from his friend Johannes Popitz (HV 91–92), the influential State Secretary for Finance in the Weimar period (Dieckmann 1960, 130–142),[3] polycracy refers to a large number of organizations that are relatively autonomous from the state in a formal legal sense and, yet, bear responsibility for important public functions. The most obvious examples are the large number of firms implementing social policy for the state, such as health insurance organizations. But polycracy also includes firms granted autonomy from the state, in varying degrees, because they play a role in fulfilling state responsibilities, such as reparations payments. Finally, it includes firms that are taken over and/or organized by governments, but which function otherwise like private companies. The common element among these diverse forms of economic organization and public/private partnership is the fact that these organizations retain a degree of independence from the will of the state (HV 91–94).[4]

As concepts, these terms do not accurately portray the complex reality of politics and society. In fact, taken alone, they misrepresent actual conditions, for they typically appear in combination with one or the other factor (HV 72). One cannot fully understand the practical implications of pluralism apart from the political, economic, and social changes summarized under the terms federalism or polycracy, and vice versa. But the three concepts provide points of departure for examining the complex reality of state action in the Weimar Republic (HV 71–72).

Schmitt's aim in utilizing this conceptual framework is to identify and analyze the underlying structure of the Weimar state crisis. In other words, Schmitt seeks to determine how the economic, legal, political, and social trends summarized under these three concepts intersect to limit the range of options available to the Weimar state, not just in responding to particular problems but also in seeking to reform the basic structural defects of the state. Though Schmitt's analysis retains some of the familiar conceptual character of his earlier, more polemical works, his use of concepts in this section of *Guardian of the Constitution* aims at defining the peculiar limitations of the Weimar context, not the general deficiencies of liberal theory or practice. And, while there are a number of particular problems with Schmitt's use of these interrelated concepts, he is generally able to make clear in relatively short compass the deep structural nature of the governability problems of the Weimar Republic.

An appropriate starting point for understanding Schmitt's conceptual framework is his analysis of the central political problem of the Republic, the inability of the Federal Parliament (*Reichstag*), to provide effective political leadership. Over the preceding decade, Schmitt's approach to the question of the legitimacy and viability of parliamentary democracy changed markedly. A triangulation point for treatments of Schmitt is the short polemical tract, *The Crisis of Parliamentary Democracy*. This controversial work appeared originally in 1923, the high point of the first extended crisis of the Republic, and was reissued with a new preface in 1926, at approximately the middle point of a period of relative stability. Schmitt's principal criticisms of parliamentary government are drawn from more extended, early treatments of the issue, such as Moisei Ostrogorski's *Democracy and the Organization of Political Parties* ([1903] 1922). Schmitt's application of many of these ideas, however, particularly the connections he draws between long-standing problems of parliamentary government and important contemporary developments, both intellectual and political, has proven quite influential.

Crisis clearly displays Schmitt's gift for synthesizing works from diverse disciplines for the purpose of addressing important theoretical and practical problems. This makes the work noteworthy, but it does not explain its widespread influence. The book continues to fascinate due to an underlying ambiguity. Schmitt crystalizes profound doubts about the viability of parliamentary government in the form of a plea for more concerted action in its defense. For "reform proposals (to) gain perspective," Schmitt argues, it is necessary to identify the "moral" underpinnings of parliamentary government (CPD 18–21). Identifying the moral foundation of parliament as "government by discussion," the effort to attain "relative truth" through open debate, Schmitt insists that one must then examine whether these principles continue to inspire. For adherence to outdated principles is not merely "embarrassing, as though someone had painted the radiator of a modern central heating system with red flames in order to give the appearance of a blazing fire" (6), it is also pernicious, because it prevents taking necessary steps for fruitful change by obscuring the true source of the problem.

Schmitt's enduring hold on the imagination of those across the political spectrum is due to the fact that he can be seen as speaking simultaneously for both liberals and their opponents. Presenting a lofty vision of parliamentary government, many of Schmitt's critical remarks are comparable to a shot across the bow, or an attempt to alert the proponents of parliamentary government to the true nature of their opponents. At the same time, Schmitt's treatment of the extraordinary obstacles to effective parliamentary government posed by fundamental political and technological changes is perhaps even more devastating to the cause of its reform than an all-out frontal assault (Sontheimer [1964] 1978, 78–80; also McCormick 1997, 170–175). By presenting himself as a proponent of reform, Schmitt seems to be saying that government by discussion is a noble idea, but one whose time is clearly past. Schmitt's treatment of the Weimar political crisis, in other words, has more the feel of a *post mortem* of parliamentary government, or a *coup de grace* at any rate, than a call for reform. By dispensing with quaint notions, such as government by discussion, it is possible to move on to more promising alternatives, he seems to be arguing. Nonetheless, his portrayal of the ideal of government by discussion holds considerable appeal for those seeking an alternative to interest group politics.

Schmitt's primary claim in *Crisis* is that parliamentary democracy is facing a challenge to its very foundations, because important social changes, summarized under the heading "modern mass democracy," render problematical the open discussion essential to this form of government. Universal suffrage has given rise to "mass parties," which demand total loyalty from their members and are expert at the manipulation of the rapidly changing communications media. Parliamentary representatives are no longer independent of particular interests and constituencies, willing to concede the force of the better argument. They are the instruments of various political-social groups which determine their position in closed session outside parliament or in its back chambers and which are unwilling to compromise their positions once they are determined. Parliament has become a "showplace," controlled by groups, many of which are irresponsible in that they have no genuine commitment to the system other than to use it for their own purposes (Scheuerman 1995, 136–142).

Schmitt is right to stress that rapid social change contributed to the Republic's difficulties. As Detlev Peukert emphasizes, the problem in Weimar was not that the Revolution failed, so much as the fact that there were several revolutions going on at once. In addition to the introduction of full democratic government, there were rapid and fundamental changes in industrial production, living conditions, and social relations, which outstripped the ability of new and existing institutions to produce lasting political and social compromises. In fact, many of the innovative institutions established during the war and carried over into Weimar did not lessen social tensions, as they were intended to do. On the contrary, they may have actually heightened friction among opposing groups, in that bargaining was then passed on to the state, with each side encouraged to press their most extreme demands (Peukert [1987] 1991, 3–51 and 87–190). The state's ability to meet such demands, perhaps never fully up to the task, declined over time. Changing conditions caused the social compromise that produced the Weimar Republic to unravel. Each side had its reasons for initially accepting the compromise. Fearing a socialist revolution and needing the cooperation of labor to ensure production, some leading industrialists saw these corporate mediating devices as a means of reestablishing their hegemony over the economy, which was uncertain in revolutionary times. Trade union officials and the Social Democrats in the Weimar Coalition thought that along with the expansion of social welfare programs, these mediating devices were the best means of achieving socialist goals within the established framework. Even leaders of the Workers and Soldiers Councils (*Räte*), who were instrumental in bringing down the Imperial system and controlled considerable territory after the war, accepted these compromises initially (Maier [1975] 1988, 136–153).

The tragic irony of these innovative institutions was that their establishment and continued effectiveness was dependent on the unstable, uncertain circumstances of the war and the early postwar period. Postwar inflation was one of the conditions for the successful establishment of these cooperative frameworks. This is because business could easily pass along higher costs to consumers, while the declining value of the *Mark* made German goods more competitive internationally. With the stabilization of the currency in late 1923,[5] the international competitive advantage of industry diminished. Also, the success of government initiatives against threats to the established system from both the right and left, but especially the right, meant that the threat of more radical socialist experiments seemed to have passed. For both reasons, industry became less cooperative with earlier radical plans for economic reform, though not with all redistribution programs which continued through the 1920s (Maier [1975] 1988, 249–272, 356–387, esp. 364–387). Many leftists were also disappointed with the results produced by these institutions. While work conditions improved with the introduction of the eight-hour day, and though there was some rise in the standard of living, these gains were not as substantial as expected initially. Moreover, in order to ensure the establishment of the original experiments, the Social Democrats in the Weimar Coalition used traditional elites in the army and bureaucracy to put down leftist rebellions throughout Germany. Not surprisingly, many leftists felt betrayed by more moderate trade union officials and the Social Democratic Party leadership. After cooperating with the government in a general strike to put down the Kapp putsch, the time for revolutionary action seemed to have passed, and yet labor had little to show for its efforts. This rift between moderate and radical leftists was to complicate the task of governing throughout the Republic (Peukert [1987] 1991, 33–35).

Beside the fracturing of the political spectrum, another challenge to governability was the lack of money to fund compromise settlements fully. Though the German economy had enormous productive potential after the war (Petzina and Abelshauser 1974), it remained weak throughout the Weimar period. Only by 1927 did it return to 1913 production levels (Peukert [1987] 1991, 118–124). Even if the Parliament could have agreed on a program of action, it is not clear what it could have done, as the chronically weak economy provided it with very little room to maneuver (Abraham [1981] 1986, 1–41 and 229–318).

The extent of these objective difficulties suggests strongly that parliamentary calculus, no matter how ingenuous, could not have ensured effective parliamentary government (e.g. Stürmer 1967 and Conze 1968). In view of these practical obstacles to effective government, one must ask why Schmitt would measure so beleaguered an institution by such high standards. This seeming anomaly prompted a leading contemporary of Schmitt, Richard Thoma, to question why Schmitt sought out the "moral underpinnings" of parliamentary government in works written long ago in response to significantly different problems. Thoma suggested that Schmitt would do better to examine the works of those actually involved in the establishment of the current system, such as Hugo Preuß, Friedrich Naumann, and Max Weber, to discern the "purpose" of parliamentary government, because they were responding directly to current conditions (Thoma 1985, 79–80).

Thoma's criticisms obviously struck a nerve. For not only does Schmitt formally respond to Thoma in the preface to the second edition of *Crisis*, but, in both *Constitutional Theory* and *Guardian of the Constitution*, Schmitt also bitterly recounts Thoma's charge that he wrongly focuses on the "moldy greats" of political theory in addressing the problems of parliament (e.g. V 313 and HV 89). In these later works, moreover, changes in

Schmitt's method suggest he is responding to Thoma's insistence on the need for a more pragmatic, context-sensitive approach. In the preface to the second edition of *Crisis*, for example, Schmitt mostly only reiterates his claim that the present challenge to parliamentary democracy was a "spiritual" one rooted in fundamental social changes since the 19th century. Any approach to reform not focusing on the moral/intellectual foundations of parliamentary government will not get at the root of the problem. Parliaments might continue to function, in Schmitt's view, but only as hollow shells teetering on dangerously unstable axes. In *Constitutional Theory*, by contrast, Schmitt examines the actual history of parliamentary government in Europe in order to address the distinctive problems of the Weimar Republic. Reinhard Mehring and William Scheuerman are both right that there is a sense in which Schmitt's elaborate comparative history in *Constitutional Theory* constitutes a more empirical reworking of his argument in *Crisis* (Mehring 1991, 206 and Scheuerman 1995, 142). Schmitt reviews the "ideal foundations" of parliamentary government, though with much greater attention to the actual legal, political, and social developments that render parliamentary democracy obsolete in his view (V 307–319). Nonetheless, Schmitt's treatment of parliament in *Constitutional Theory* constitutes an important shift in emphasis from the interrelationships among normative theory, social change, and politics, on the one hand, to the structural determinants of the Weimar state crisis, on the other.

Note, for example, the treatment of the importance of social change for the ideal of the government by discussion, which was so prominent in *Crisis*. While an examination of the ideal of government by discussion (V 307–319) is the first substantive section of Schmitt's treatment of parliament in *Constitutional Theory*, it is arguable whether it forms the pivot point of his approach. In fact, this section is oddly out of place in the context of the entire discussion (V 303–359). It is preceded by a brief section (V 303–307) which effectively serves as an introduction to the subsequent problem-oriented history of the various structural means of organizing political leadership. In this introductory section, Schmitt sketches the four "parliamentary subsystems," which together form an "elastic total system." Schmitt argues it is "necessary to distinguish among these subsystems "in order to understand parliamentary government in general, but *above all* (emphasis mine) to understand the exceptionally difficult and rather opaque system established by the Weimar Constitution" (V 306–307). With the aid of this conceptual framework, Schmitt examines how constitutional structures in Belgium, France, and Germany reflect and shape political practice in these countries (V 320–359).

This shift in emphasis toward a comparative-historical analysis of the structural determinants of political practice is also indicated by the fact that besides the section examining the ideal of government by discussion, the only other point at which analysis of social change figures prominently is the brief review of English parliamentary practice (V 320–326). These sections aim primarily at revealing the hollowness of German liberal visions of parliamentary government, which are based on the English model. Schmitt argues, for example, that the cabinet, not the allegedly sovereign parliament, provided political leadership in the 19th century. The parliament was, at best, the point of connection between the electorate that reached political decisions, and the government, which provided political leadership. This partial deconstruction of Schmitt's own ideal standard is, indeed, peculiar, if his purpose is to lend more muscle to the rather sketchy narrative of *Crisis*.

These features of the treatment of parliament in *Constitutional Theory* suggest that Schmitt seeks to engage critics like Thoma on the concrete institutional level as well. Through his comparative history of parliamentary government, Schmitt seeks to show the ways in which the peculiar constitutional structure of the Weimar Republic reflects more or less unique German developments and concerns (V 334–338 and 340–341) and why European-wide trends have been telescoped in a particularly disastrous way in Weimar. More importantly, Schmitt attempts to identify how the Republic's constitutional structure simultaneously limits and enhances the ability of particular institutions and that of the state generally to pursue coherent long-term policies (V 343–359).

Given this shift in emphasis toward an analysis of constitutional structure, it is clear that Scheuerman's examination of Schmitt's critique of parliamentary government works much better as a contemporary response to Schmitt than as a critique of Schmitt's treatment of parliament in *Constitutional Theory*. Scheuerman is right to point out the limited generalizability of many of Schmitt's claims. But when Scheuerman argues that many of the social trends Schmitt cites were factors in parliamentary paralysis only "in a few central European countries (such as Weimar Germany), yet hardly can be taken as a universal explanation of parliamentary failure" (Scheuerman 1995, 145), he is more or less reiterating the very point Schmitt makes in his historical overview of parliamentary government and his analysis of the political practice of the Weimar Republic. Also, Scheuerman's argument that many of the social trends noted by Schmitt "leveled out and even decreased after the 1930s and 1940s" applies to *Crisis* more than *Constitutional Theory*, since social change did not figure nearly as prominently in the latter treatment of parliament.

To respond effectively to Schmitt, therefore, it is necessary to recognize the extent to which the intellectual history approach of *Crisis* has given way to comparative historical analysis of the structural determinants of the Weimar state crisis. Similarly with *Guardian of the Constitution*, one must take account of the fact that Schmitt's analysis of the practical obstacles to effective parliamentary government displays more sophistication in both methodological and empirical terms than the previous two treatments of the topic. In *Guardian of the Constitution*, Schmitt emphasizes that any treatment of the issue of parliamentary democracy must consider two important changes in the position of Weimar Republic in comparison with that of the *Reich*. In constitutional terms, Parliament is now the lead institution responsible for setting policy and supervising administration. In the *Reich* period, these roles were mostly filled by bureaucrats under the direction of traditional monarchical authorities, both at the *Land* and *Reich* levels. The bureaucracy could continue to provide expert advice and would be relatively impervious to capture by pluralist forces given its tradition and constitutional position (HV 101–102). But the bureaucracy was an instrument incapable of political leadership itself. Moreover, state responsibilities and the need for direct control had greatly expanded since then, and yet the means needed to carry out central state responsibilities often enhanced the autonomy of society from the state.

This trend is illustrated especially well by the politics surrounding the coal crisis. Leaving aside Schmitt's polemical references to Germany as a "reparations" state, he is right about some of the political consequences of Germany's reparations obligations. To meet its payment schedule, the *Reich* government promoted industrial production for export, which, in turn, provided export industries with enormous political leverage. In exchange for their cooperation in this, as well as in the campaign of passive resistance in the Ruhr valley, some leading industrialists sought the establishment of regional conglomerates, or "industrial duchies," which would be mostly free from public control. Ultimately, the crisis dissipated as the scarcity problem was resolved. But German industry retained a degree of autonomy from governmental control unrivaled in Europe (Maier [1975] 1988, 194–225).

The capacity for long-term state intervention into the economy, in Schmitt's view, is also limited by the infusion of pluralism into the entire political system. Groups from across the political spectrum, both in and outside the government, can threaten to derail the policymaking process at different levels of the system, compelling other parties to make significant concessions. Of course, given the prevailing conditions of scarcity, the necessary concessions might not be possible to fulfill. And when it is possible to cobble together a workable majority on a particular issue, the coalition might not last long enough to ensure long-term commitment to the policy. It may also be the case that the resulting policy might be either so diluted or internally conflicted that it would not address the problem that initially prompted unified national action (HV 92–93).

Parliament's time arrived in Germany just as its ability to fulfill the role envisioned by liberal theorists was declining (HV 82). It was increasingly difficult for Parliament to carry out even a negative checking function, let alone provide the sort of coherent, unified, long-term political leadership deemed essential by Schmitt (HV 82–83). Political parties are the chief culprits in the enervation of Parliament, in Schmitt's view, for they accentuate the tendency toward pluralization of the political system, with all its attendant negative consequences. Through tight control of their members, parties sharpen long-standing social divisions and give expression to these tensions in Parliament, in effect preserving the autonomy of society mostly as a beachhead for assaults on the primary institutions of the state. Internally, moreover, they display the tendency toward a quantitative total state evident elsewhere in the society in that they provide a full range of services to members. In this sense, they do not stop the process of totalitarianization so much as advance it by "parceling" it out (HV 84). And, by doing so, they render the political system, particularly Parliament, incapable of coherent, unified, long-term leadership.

For Schmitt, the electoral system is a primary institutional defect of the system, because it reinforces the position of political parties. The shift from single member districts in the *Reich* period to strict proportional representation in the Weimar Republic encourages fragmentation of the party system. Based on a winner-take-all conception of democratic competition, the previous system was not to the advantage of small parties. Weimar's system of proportional representation aims at ensuring an accurate portrayal of the electorate, generally, by providing representation even to parties unable to achieve a plurality in any individual district (HV 85–86). The great advantage of the *Reich* electoral system, Schmitt argues, is that it establishes a direct connection between voters and the Parliament, rather than one mediated by parties. According to the Weimar Constitution, members of Parliament are to represent the entire people, not a particular constituency or political parties, the latter of which have no basis in the Constitution. When candidates are selected and supported by centrally managed political parties, they lose any claim to independence from the party leadership. Tightly integrated in this way into party organizations, representatives merely express the views of the party leadership and are not open to persuasion through debate. The resulting hollowness of parliamentary deliberations puts the lie to the liberal concept of Parliament as an institutional mechanism for the shaping of diverse interests into a national will (HV 86–90).

Apart from problems with Schmitt's take on the liberal concept of representation (e.g. McCormick 1997, 157–205), it is questionable that a single-member district, winner-take-all form of election would have had the effects Schmitt desired. It is not clear that it would have produced a two-party system or even a substantial winnowing of parties. There were single-member district elections in the *Reich* period, and yet there was considerable continuity between the party structure in the *Reich* period and early Weimar period (Lepsius 1993, 31–38), suggesting that the system of proportional representation alone was not responsible for this fragmentation (Peukert [1987] 1991, 38). In the *Reich* period, for example, the two-stage election process tended to discourage party mergers in the initial stages. The basic institutional weakness of Parliament in the overall system, moreover, discouraged consolidation at both phases, because there was little potential reward to gaining leadership in Parliament, as Weber made clear ([1918] 1978), 1381–1469, esp. 1410–1416). Correction of these deficiencies, along with the elimination of proportional representation, and, perhaps the addition of a threshold requirement like that of the Federal Republic, might have induced some consolidation of the party system.[6] However, the fact that many Weimar-era parties had strong regional and local bases suggests that these changes would not have had as dramatic an impact as one would expect (Braunthal 1996, 54–55 and 156–58). While lacking strong national support, such parties could still have gained some representation by achieving a plurality in a few districts and/or at the *Land* level.

Even if such a change would have resulted in a two-party system, which the case of early 20th century Britain suggests is not at all certain (Butler 1963). A single-member district system may not encourage the sort of independence of mind among representatives Schmitt seeks.[7] In the United States, for example, the central party organizations do not pick individual candidates at the local or regional level, and yet it is not the case that representatives remain open to rival views, particularly when they conflict with strong regional or local interests. Policy in the U.S. tends to represent ad hoc compromises among diverse groups, which are typically aggregated in regional or even local terms (Sharkansky, 1970). The need to produce national candidates for presidential elections prompted the development of the two-party system in the United States. But this national cooperation was only possible through tolerance of considerable regional and local variation in party platforms at the expense of strong central political leadership and because of a huge spoils system to pay off local supporters, with all the attendant consequences in terms of effective administration (Skowronek

1982, 24–26). So even if a nationally elected German presidency were enough to encourage party mergers for electoral purposes, which is unlikely given differences in civil service selection and type of party identification, the resulting system would probably be less fragmented in name only. It would still be necessary to cobble together on an ongoing basis the sort of fragile coalitions decried by Schmitt. The only difference would be that much of this work would take place internally in the two major parties, which would themselves resemble separate party systems.

While Schmitt was unrealistic about the potential impact of electoral law changes, he was right to criticize the political effects of the splintered party system. Leaving aside ideological hot button issues, such as the nature of the economy, there was some consensus throughout the Weimar period on the need for central state action on certain issues, as illustrated by the perceived problems with the tax system. During the *Reich* period, taxing power was primarily exercised by the *Länder* and local governments, compelling the *Reich* to borrow considerably, particularly with the onset of World War I. The Weimar Constitution reversed this relationship among levels of the government (Schuster 1983, 99–131). Article 8 gave the *Reich* jurisdiction over all taxes and income (100–101). Under Article 11, the *Reich* could prohibit the *Länder* and local governments from levying taxes on the same basis as the *Reich*. It also prohibited the *Länder* and local governments from raising revenue in ways that hindered the *Reich* financially. According to Article 11, moreover, the *Reich* could administer its own taxing system (101), but Article 84 gave the *Reich* supervisory authority over the revenue generation of the other levels of government (113–114). The financial position of the lower levels of government had some protection, with Article 8 stipulating that the *Reich* must compensate these levels of government for sources of income deprived them by the *Reich*. Article 54 also forbade the *Reich* from placing new burdens on the lower levels of government without supplying them with new sources of revenue (109; generally, Newcomer 1937, 42–97 and Huber 1981, 486–504). There was a big glitch in the new system, however. Compensation for lost revenue did not take into account changes in obligations other than those imposed by the *Reich*. In other words, the *Reich* would reimburse governments at previous levels of taxation, not with a view to current revenue needs, nor with regard to equalization of revenue sources. The resulting revenue shortfalls at different points in the system became themselves a major political problem. Localities, for example, shouldered a good portion of the burden of relieving the economic hardship caused by the Great Inflation. Supplying funds according to previous revenue levels did not meet these new demands for social services. Moreover, certain areas of the country were especially hard hit by the economic instability, and yet the *Reich* was not required to provide them funds commensurate with their needs. Finance Minister Matthias Erzberger described the position of these governments well, when he pointed out that they have "(t)he almost unlimited right to find new taxes" (Gerloff 1928). At times, this was possible, since the financial position of the different levels of government was not always bad. The Great Inflation wiped out much government indebtedness while it created greater demands for governmental services. So, despite increases in social expenditures, many governments were able to balance their books, or even achieve a surplus (Newcomer 1937, 135–158; Lieberman 1998, 83–91 and 114–115).

With the onset of the Great Depression, long-neglected problems in this complicated financial system reached crisis proportions. Under the tradition of local self-government stemming from the Prussian reform era, cities saw themselves as responsible for the promotion of culture (Lieberman 1998, 27–56). Cities also competed actively with one another for prestige. Mayors of large cities, such as the future chancellor of the Federal Republic, Konrad Adenauer, in Cologne and Ludwig Landmann in Frankfurt am Main, often pushed projects with a view to short-term political success and their large visions of cities (Hofmann 1974, 99–106). Increasingly, however, they were hindered by the *Reich*. Besides the important constitutional limits on the powers of local government taxation, there were also efforts to limit borrowing by cities combined with a shifting of burdens downward to municipalities. Not surprisingly, this led to a major squeeze on city finances, leaving them relatively few options other than a massive reliance on short-term credit (McNeil 1986, 6–9; Lieberman 1998, 91–105).

The wide-spread perception of inadequacies with the federal system prompted the calling of *Länder* conferences in 1924 and 1928 devoted to reforming the federalist system (Frotscher 1983, 130; Huber 1984, 7:668–679). Neither conference produced significant changes in the federal structure, despite the perceived need for reform (Huber 1984, 7: 669–670). Besides the fact that the *Reich* government did not present a reform plan,[8] many *Länder* resisted change. The south German states, like Bavaria, resisted any reforms that might impinge upon their privileges under the current system, particularly their tax advantages (Karsten 1995, 89–90; Huber 1984, 7: 679). Prussia also dragged its feet, though in the interest of democratic government. Prussia rejected a diminution of its prominence in the current system as lessening its ability to serve as a line of defense for parliamentary democracy in Germany. Another obstacle to reform was the fact that many of the divisive disagreements among political parties at the national level emerged at this one as well (Schulz 1963, 486–515 and 564–612; Frotscher 1983, 136; Huber 1984, 670–679).

The inability to respond to such problems was a defining feature of the Weimar Republic. Even when there was agreement on the need for action, it was often impossible to develop a proposal acceptable to all parties. Social Democrat participation in, and toleration of, diversely constituted coalition governments indicate that some parties were more willing to compromise than others. Generally, though, the structural inducements to compromise were relatively weak. Parties sought to retain core constituencies in tightly contested elections, as the ever more splintered party system encouraged supporters to jump ship in favor of parties more attuned to their narrowly defined interests.[9] Not surprisingly, throughout Weimar, coalitions were chronically unstable and political improvisation was the norm (Stürmer 1967, 265–273; Conze 1968; Jones [1988] 1998).

Nonetheless, there were some bright spots in the relation of state and society at the time, Schmitt emphasized. Encouraging certain countertendencies to debilitating political fragmentation would enhance the state's capacity to govern. Take, for example, the role of the state in the management of the economy. The Weimar Republic extended the trend toward greater state involvement in economic affairs initiated during World War I. Economic reconstruction and mediation, along with expanding social welfare programs and substantial foreign obligations in the form of reparations and governmental loans, particularly at the local level, all compelled the state to become actively involved in economic affairs (Huber 1978, 5: 73–115; Petzina 1984, 55–66). Parliament was responsible for providing much of this central direction. At the same time, though, a number of other state organizations took on greater responsibilities for economic and financial management. Organizations like the Imperial Central Bank (*Reichsbank*) reflected a belief in the importance of politically neutral, expert advice in economic affairs. By providing long-term central direction in important areas of economic activity, it was thought that such experts could serve as a counterbalance to the debilitating tendencies of the party state (HV 96–111). The National Economic Council (*Reichswirtschaftsrat*), for example, was charged with suggesting policies it deemed best for the economy overall, rather than what advanced the aims of a particular party, region, or sector of the economy (Glum 1929, esp. 13–20 and 25–51; Thornhill 2000, 106–107).[10]

According to Schmitt, the very features of such organizations that enable them to serve as a limited counterbalance to the pluralization of the political system renders them incapable of providing the sort of unified political leadership he seeks. This is because these "nonpolitical" organs are effective only insofar as they address technical questions within their area of expertise. Their very independence from politics prevents such bodies from providing what the Weimar Republic needs: political leadership beyond limited solutions in narrowly defined areas.

Schmitt is right that government by experts is not a sorcerer's stone, capable of delivering the Weimar Republic from its chronic governability crisis, though not merely for the reasons he emphasizes. Clearly these institutions are not mere instruments, following central dictates or pursuing rational policy aims. Such organizations often pursue policies promoting their own advancement in relation to other bureaucratic organizations or advance policies that are in tension with larger political goals. The machinations of the Central Bank President Hjalmar Schacht (Schulz 1987, 2: 99–107) illustrate the important consequences these supposedly nonpolitical state institutions have for the governability of the entire system. In the late 1920s, local governments faced financial crisis because of the difficulty of receiving short-term credit after the onset of the Great Depression. The dire position of the local governments was exacerbated by the position of other governmental organs. There was a widespread concern with the extent of foreign borrowing, because this was believed to foster foreign domination. But there was somewhat less concern with borrowing by private organizations, which was thought to produce immediate returns. Much of this private borrowing actually went to unproductive organizations. Nonetheless, as credit tightened late in the Republic, governments at both the *Reich* and *Länder* levels, along with the German Central Bank, considered it necessary to limit borrowing by localities. Through a presidential emergency decree later approved by Parliament, the *Länder* were empowered to supervise borrowing by towns and cities. While localities often found ingenious ways of circumventing these controls, it was ever more difficult to find financing for extensive governmental services, including burdens placed upon them by the *Reich* and *Länder* governments. This situation was exacerbated by Schacht, who actively campaigned abroad to convince foreign banks and governments to restrict lending to local governments, mainly in order to increase his control of credit in Germany (McNeil 1986, 112–133; Lieberman 1998, 106–121).

The issue of short-term credit cuts both ways for Schmitt's argument. On the one hand, it illustrated the problem of pluralization in that it was increasingly difficult to pursue a unified policy when groups at different levels of the government were working at cross purposes with one another. Even the *Reich* government was divided against itself in financial questions, since the finance and economic ministries were often run by opposing parties. Representing different constituencies, various ministries might advocate policies in tension with one another (McNeil 1986, 35–68). On the other hand, it illustrated the problem of personal power. Individuals like

Schacht often sought to promote themselves rather than the platform of a particular party or social group (McNeil 1986, 255–274; Schulz 1987, 2: 461–467). Placed in powerful positions with little or no direct political responsibility, they could do considerable mischief as well as serve to counterbalance the larger system-wide tendency toward pluralization.

In an argument stressing the tradeoffs facing any state action due to structural features of the Weimar state, it is surprising that Schmitt would not consider more fully the doubled-edged character of politically independent institutions. The problem with Schmitt's analysis of the Weimar state crisis, however, is more subtle than his obvious myopia about the character of personal authority. Despite his, at times, astute sense of the political consequences of the structural features of states, Schmitt failed to grasp the political implications of the composite nature of the German state in the *Reich* period, which, in turn, caused him to discount potentially more effective institutional responses to the Weimar state crisis.

II.

Like many in his generation, Schmitt looked to the state to ensure the primacy of the public interest over the particular interests of individuals and groups. Though he bemoaned the fact that the Weimar state seemed unable to fulfill this role,[11] Schmitt stressed the limits of state action even in the heyday of the independent state, the so-called absolutist period. The important consideration, in his view, was that the state in the pre-Weimar era was strong enough to ensure that social relations did not have overly deleterious political spillover effects. Because the state was strong enough to prevent different groups from capturing the system for their own advantage or engaging in street battles with one another, it was possible to have a vibrant social sphere with considerable diversity (HV 73–74).

The peculiarly weak position of the Weimar state in regard to society, according to Schmitt, was rooted in the changing nature of the composite German state. In short, the different levels and branches of government were working at cross-purposes with one another in the Weimar period. To a degree, this was also the case in the *Reich* era. But, since then, there had been fundamental changes in the nature of political competition, in Schmitt's opinion. Specifically, the permeation of the entire system by pluralist wrangling undermined many of the structural tensions that enabled the state in the *Reich* period to function effectively, despite its extraordinary internal complexity.

The Weimar Republic was, indeed, governability-challenged. The combination of a federal structure with a more democratic political system certainly contributed to its problems. One peculiar difficulty was the fact that political parties from one level could utilize the national forum to advance their particularistic agenda, while, in the end, only disrupting the process at the national level. The Bavarian People's Party, for example, refused to support a governmental austerity measure, forcing an early election, because, *inter alia*, the proposed measure contained a tax affecting Bavarian breweries (Eyck 1963, 264–265; Huber 1981, 6: 498–499; and Patch 1998, 94–95). Score one for the home side.

The unanswered question remains: Was the *Kaiserreich* really so different? Such an inquiry is especially important for evaluating Schmitt's position, because his argument for presidential authority that is almost unlimited in practical terms is premised on his understanding of political stability in the *Kaiserreich* period. Examining the political function of local self-government in this period indicates that Schmitt's stated aim of preserving the basic structural integrity of the system would have been better served by a more decentralized and democratic response to the Republic's problems.

Determining the appropriate purpose and means of local self-government was essential, in Schmitt's view, because the long- and short-term developments represented in the concepts of pluralism, federalism, and polycracy had coalesced with disastrous consequences for the Weimar state. The sense of urgency in Schmitt's analysis of the institution of local self-government is not accounted for merely by the Republic's governability problems. It is due to the fact that Schmitt saw local self-government as representing both the beginning and end of the modern state. What this means will become clear once we better understand Schmitt's polemical references to the return of the medieval *Ständestaat* (e.g. HV 84).

From a modern perspective, a striking feature of the early *Ständestaat* during the 14th and early 15th centuries was the fact that political authority was based mostly on contractual agreements among individuals. Though the parties to these contracts exercised what we today consider public functions, such as adjudicating disputes and waging war, their claims to political authority were considered personal property (Barraclough [1946] 1949, 332–339). There were representative bodies, provincial estates, which facilitated revenue generation for specific purposes (Strayer 1970, 64–69; Tilly 1975, 21–25; Ertman 1997, 28–34). However, these parliaments were merely more convenient, cost-effective means of exercising political powers that were rooted in individual agreements. Merely because these contracts and statutes applied beyond the individual parties does not mean they constituted "public law" in the contemporary sense (Strayer 1970, 7–56; Tay and Kamenka 1983, esp. 69–77).

While the fragmentation of political authority calls to mind the modern concept of limited government through a separation of powers and federalism, the dispersal of political power did not work to the advantage of individual liberty in the modern sense.[12] The essential political problem in the early *Ständestaat* was not merely that authority was fragmented but that it overlapped as well. Different noblemen, often not within the same region, could lay claim to the same territory or to the exercise of particular functions. Therefore, there was limited commitment to the general good. However, the rise of territorial states in the 16th century brought major changes, such as the establishment of more broad-based representative bodies. In contrast to the provincial assemblies of the early *Ständestaat*, these territorial legislatures, known as States-General or *Landtage*, addressed issues of more general import, thereby encouraging more of a sense of the priority of the common good over particular interests (Barraclough [1946] 1949, 339–352). Also, the Imperial Cameral Court (*Reichskammergericht*), established in 1495, offered a limited, centralized, peaceful means of dispute resolution (Hartung 1972, 122–138; Stolleis 1988, 134–138). Despite these changes in the later *Ständestaat*, conflicts over rights to political authority were still often resolved through warfare. In this sense, the Thirty Years War was merely an extreme instance of a more or less chronic condition. The traditional belief that the emperor cared for the general interest had a moderating effect (Berman 1983, 482–519, esp. 493–505; Heimpel 1972, 43–72; Bloch 1961, 408–437, esp. 408–420). But it was not sufficient to counter this underlying structural defect of the system (Ertman 1997, 226–245).

It is this history Schmitt seeks to conjure up by warning against a "feudalization" of the Weimar Republic. Like the bundle of particular rights and privileges under the early *Ständestaat*, according to Schmitt, the extensive Catalogue of Rights of the Weimar Constitution, especially the right to local self-government, produces disunity and encourages conflict, while it precludes effective central state action. These rights and privileges suggest the primacy of particular interests over the general good, in his view, and the institution of local self-government provides individuals and groups an especially useful means of achieving their narrow political aims. Much as in the early modern period, he believed it necessary in the Weimar Republic to enhance the abstract coercive power of the central state by limiting particular rights and privileges, both those of individuals and of subnational governments.

Interestingly, while Schmitt believed the institution of local self-government was bound up especially tightly with the intersecting trends producing a refeudalization of German politics, local self-government initially compensated somewhat for some of the negative consequences of the establishment of the modern state in Germany. Even the establishment of absolutist monarchies in the modern era did not change the dualistic nature of the state, for much of the collective action associated with the state today was undertaken with the approval of the estates (Barraclough [1946] 1949, 349–352). Imperial armies, for example, were organized and financed at the local level, providing the estates considerable control over the nominal overlord, the German emperor (Spangenberg 1912, 44–66 and Haan 1968, 297–345). The struggle between monarchs and the estates continued into the middle of the 19th century (Grimm 1988, 138–141). Nonetheless, over time, absolutist monarchs gained independent sources of income and administration, so that by the end of the 18th century state action was no longer always contingent on the approval of the estates. By this time, however, the demands of effective state action worked in the opposite direction, as it became necessary to "bring society back in," so to speak, in order to ensure a vibrant state.[13]

In Prussia, most famously, bureaucratic reformers of the absolutist monarchy introduced sweeping legal changes that recognized and furthered the development of the emerging middle class. Besides myriad civil law reforms, Prussia introduced local self-government, which empowered localities to manage their own affairs through locally elected town councils, with some legislative authority and an executive branch accountable, in part, to the local councils. The institution of local self-government advanced the interests of both the bourgeoisie and the state. Leading liberal proponents like Rudolf von Gneist saw local self-government as a means of cultivating individuality without encouraging the political instability widely associated with the French Revolution (Hahn 1995). For traditional authorities, carefully limited local self-government enhanced state power by relieving the state of a number of functions while it integrated the ascendant bourgeoisie, who might otherwise have been prompted to push for more sweeping reforms. The principal architect of the liberal Prussian reforms, Karl vom Stein (1757–1831), sought to give localities almost exclusive control over their affairs. The original decree in 1808, however, excluded judicial matters from the jurisdiction of the communes and provided for continued central control of traditional police powers. Subsequent reforms further limited communal autonomy from central control. Along with the power of central authorities to dissolve local councils, for example, was added ever increasing central control over the local executives (*Aufsicht*) (Gunlicks 1986, 5–26).

Political and social changes in the final third of the 19th century worked to the advantage of proponents of local self-government. Though 19th century Germany never attained what we today consider full constitutional democracy, democratic reformers gained substantial victories. In several constitutional reforms culminating in Bismarck's *Reich* Constitution, there was an ever larger voice for society in state affairs in the form of parliamentary representation at the *Land* and *Reich* levels. The *Reich* Constitution was particularly noteworthy in this regard, because it established universal manhood suffrage for elections to the Federal Parliament. By the end of the 19th century and early 20th century, popular political movements achieved significant parliamentary representation, with the Social Democrats in 1912 becoming the largest party in Parliament, which, however, still did not have the power of initiative. Because it could, at most, block an action proposed by the government responsible to the Federal Chamber (*Bundesrat*) composed of *Länder* governments, the Parliament did not provide an effective outlet for demands for political and social change. Because of this political roadblock built into the structure of the system, Social Democrats increasingly looked to local governments as a vehicle for change. Early in the *Reich* period, Social Democrats dismissed local governments as tools of the bourgeoisie. At the time, there were substantial grounds for their suspicions. The *Reich* government would use its power of removal to prevent Social Democrats from occupying positions of authority at the local level. The *Reich* government also would not hesitate to dissolve local councils dominated by Social Democrats. With the end of the Anti- Socialist Laws, and after substantial electoral victories near the end of the century, it was more difficult to stymie Social Democrats at the local level. Leading Social Democrats became enamored with English local government, particularly with what was known as "municipal socialism," and began to agitate for a reformist posture at the local level. In the prewar era, the Social Democrats and their allies were using political representation at the local level to expand government services, gain control of and regulate utilities, and even pursue business enterprises. In this way, it was thought that socialists could gain a considerable degree of their national goals at the municipal level through incremental reform (Briggs 1996, 13–34).

The ground was shifting under liberals' feet, though not merely in the sense that the working class was gaining greater political representation at the national level. The changing nature of capitalist enterprise and the growing complexity of administration in the industrial age increasingly induced large industrialists to forgo active participation in local government. In their stead, more well-educated, socially conscious bourgeoisie began to exert ever greater influence over local affairs. While they, too, mostly opposed Social Democratic participation in government, they were not as uncompromising in this regard as the large industrialists. Moreover, they were open to economic and social reforms that appealed to Social Democrats. New political constellations, involving both bourgeois and working class groups, made local governments the most dynamic point of government in the *Reich* (Heffter 1950, 759–766 and Steinmetz 1993, 188–214, esp. 193–197).

Despite this limited *rapprochement* between liberal social reformers and labor at the local level, there was still considerable apprehension among the bourgeoisie about growing local government involvement in the economy and society. Critics of local government enterprise and social programs dubbed these local initiatives "cold socialization" (Lieberman 1998, 111–113). Nonetheless, while critics considered these actions an illegitimate use of local government, the law governing local government did not preclude them, for the extent of communal authority was not defined clearly by statute. This legal ambiguity meant that German localities could undertake any action deemed in its interest, so long as it was not specifically forbidden by statute (Dawson 1916, 28–34 and 38–39).

This is the so-called "universality principle" resoundingly criticized by Schmitt (HV92). In a strict sense, he argued, it was not comparable to the *Reich*'s power to define the extent of its own authority (*Kompetenz-Kompetenz*), because cities had to work within the boundaries established by the *Länder*. The *Länder*, especially, and even the *Reich*, could reign in local governments by passing statutes prohibiting certain actions. But in the composite state of the *Reich*, it was difficult to pass such measures, particularly given the growing strength of Social Democrats and their allies at all levels of government. In view of the peculiar conditions of the *Reich* period, therefore, local governments had considerable freedom to pursue an active program of expansion of local services and involvement in the private economy (HV 92–93).

This trend toward expanding local government services continued into the Weimar period. Here, too, legal uncertainty prevailed. The Weimar Constitution did not clarify the legal position of the local governments in the larger system. Article 127 established a right to local self-government (Schuster 1983, 121). Like many other rights established in the Second Part of the Weimar Constitution, this provision did not specify the extent of local government authority. It merely stated that "local councils (*Gemeinden*) and associations of local councils have the right of self-government within the limits of law." Even this closing phrase, "within the limits of law," was ambiguous. Traditionally, local governments were subject to the authority of *Länder* governments. Under the Weimar Constitution, however, substantial authority was shifted upward to the *Reich* government. Moreover, many officials in the *Reich* government actively sought a streamlining of authority in favor of the *Reich*. A major law in 1922, for example, shifted considerable taxing authority to the *Reich*, with the partly negative consequences already discussed. For much of the period, the relationship among the three levels of government remained fluid and a point of significant controversy (Wirching 1996, 37–64).

In Schmitt's view, local self-government was at the heart of the Republic's difficulties, because it was the primary institutional vehicle for the erosion of the state/society distinction (HV 72 and 92–93). Local self-government in the 19th century, Schmitt argued, was grounded in the state/society distinction, both substantively and institutionally. Local governments could manage their own affairs without too much state interference, as long as they restricted themselves to local, "nonpolitical," matters. The "state" was the appropriate forum for political issues, such as proposed changes in the basic organization of society and the character of the private economy. Municipalities were to concern themselves with "technical" questions like waste removal and transportation matters (HV 75).[14]

Schmitt's criticisms of local self-government reflected widely held concerns at the time. Many critics of city politics during the Weimar Republic were not per se opposed to local self-government. These critics were adherents of the 19th century understanding of the state as devoted to ensuring that the general/public interest would be given priority over particular/private interests.[15] Under this view, it was quite appropriate that the state remain independent of society to some degree. Otherwise, it could not avoid becoming the tool of rival social interests seeking to use state institutions for their own purposes. With an independent state, rival visions of social order could be expressed, and one might safely consider to what extent these particular visions reflected and/or served the public interest.[16] This distance from particularism was the essential advantage of the moderately authoritarian *Reich* system over more fully democratic Western ones. Insofar as local self-government was no longer a "technical" instrument of societal self-regulation, Schmitt argued, it was another tool in a potentially all-encompassing political competition,[17] which, in piecemeal fashion, might lead to a "quantitative total state," the key feature of which was that all of society would be open to governmental interference (HV 92–93).[18]

Social Democrats in the *Reich* period did not share this bourgeois belief in the positive role of the independent state in protecting the social order. The Anti-Socialist Laws established in 1879 caused considerable hardship for Social Democrats and produced among them deep-seated suspicion toward the state, which was considered the tool of the ruling class. The lapsing of official legal sanctions against Social Democrats in 1890 did not mean the end of state hostility toward them. It was not until the SPD supported the national side in World War I, at the cost of considerable internal dissension and eventual splintering of the party, that a more positive attitude among state officials developed. During the period of legal discrimination, a distinct subculture developed among Social Democrats, which reinforced separation from the state. This feeling of separateness continued into the period after the end of the Anti-Socialist Laws. The continued hostility of state officials, along with the subculture of separation, were effective obstacles to full integration of Social Democrats into society.[19]

A number of factors facilitated the development of a more reformist posture. Among these were the opportunities for reform offered by changes in composition of the bourgeoisie noted above and a growing political presence in both the National Parliament and at the local level. More interesting for our purposes is the fact that though Social Democrats did not embrace the bourgeois understanding of the special role of the state, they continued to distinguish between state and society in a way that facilitated reform efforts. Because many Social Democrats continued to adhere to the bourgeois belief that local government was social, not state, action, significant numbers of working class politicians could set aside their hostility toward the state and participate actively in local affairs (Steinmetz 1993, 194–197).

This reformist posture bolstered the state in a roundabout way. Local level reforms, facilitated in part by political success at the national level, helped convince some Social Democrats that the state could serve working class interests and that the working class could achieve some of its aims in the bourgeois social order. The resulting moderation of working class demands helped relieve pressure for more fundamental changes. In fact, Guenther Roth claims that the commitment to reform within the system left the SPD leadership unprepared to seize the opportunity to attempt more sweeping changes at the end of the war. Accustomed to tinkering with existing institutions, the leadership lacked a full-fledged blueprint for an alternative society, leaving it little option but to preserve major portions of the traditional order in the early postwar era (Roth 1963, 316).[20]

Presented a similar alternative much earlier, things might have turned out differently. But no such opportunity occurred. The stranglehold of traditional authorities on the state, particularly the Prussian dominance of the complicated federal structure, effectively blocked full-fledged expression of the growing popular support for the Social Democrats. During Weimar, there were no such institutional obstacles to sweeping legislative change, even though the implementation of any such changes might have been uneven, given differences in the political orientation of the various *Länder* governments. The obstacle to fundamental change in Weimar was the lack of consensus on the precise shape of any proposed changes.[21]

The preceding sidelong glance at local government politics calls into question an important premise of Schmitt's argument. It is important to qualify Schmitt's claim regarding the independent state in the *Reich* period in two ways. One can question the association of the state with the national-level institutions. Though contemporaries continued to distinguish between the national and local levels in this way, it is clear that in terms of actual governmental activity, this distinction was misleading at best. A number of factors besides those mentioned above produced increased reliance on local governments in the *Reich* period. Both the Junkers and the bourgeoisie saw local governments as a useful means of circumventing the constitutional limitations on governmental finance at the national level (Steinmetz 1993, 151–152).[22] In this sense, the tendency in the Weimar Republic to shift responsibilities for social welfare policies downward to localities had very deep roots. The larger point is that much of what one associates with state action was occurring at the local level. When one expands the definition of the state to include local governmental action, it is no longer possible to see the *Reich*-era state as relatively impermeable to social pressure (Steinmetz 1993, 41–54, esp. 46–50).

Expanding the understanding of the state in this way leads to a second point. While the peculiar structure of national-level institutions served as an obstacle to fundamental changes in the political system, it also facilitated the channeling of dissatisfaction to different levels of the system, where it could be more effectively managed. The fragmented *Reich* system shared this attribute with the federal system in the United States. During the preceding half century, the structure of the American system limited the scope of political competition and channelled it into fora where challenges to the overall system could be more easily managed,[23] as illustrated by the so-called Great Compromise of 1877. Bolstered by problematical Supreme Court decisions later in the century, the Compromise left contentious racial equality issues to the states. By ending federal supervision of civil liberties in Southern states, the 1877 settlement produced enduring sectional peace at the expense of freedom for African Americans (Woodward ([1951] 1956).[24] Since the states had significantly different laws and customs regarding race relations, it did not matter whether the same parties were in power at both the state and national levels of the system in the same way it might have in Weimar. Attenuating the political connection among local, state, and national levels in the United States meant that such political constellations were not a threat to the overall system.

Perhaps a decentralized system serves the cause of political stability better than a highly centralized one because a centralized system concentrates the expression of political and social dissent at the center. In the

Kaiserreich, this might have produced more effective pressure for systemic change, first, because traditional authorities might not have had a stranglehold on the system through their control of state governments. And, if traditional authorities could have blocked change at the national level in a more centralized system, proponents of fundamental changes might have had no alternative to radical, suprasystemic forms of opposition.

While Schmitt had a clear sense of some of the basic structural deficiencies of the Weimar state, he did not have a full understanding of how the German state worked. Reconsidering Schmitt's history of the German state shows the practical importance of a decentralized state structure, even in the *Reich* period. With this in mind, one can reexamine the problem of local self-government to reach a quite different result.

Clearly, local self-government presented problems for the Weimar Republic. The most important problem involved the need for short-term credit to fund a wide range of cultural and social programs at the local level. With the onset of the Great Depression, we have seen, the financial position of cities reached crisis proportions, as the credit market tightened substantially. Facing bankruptcy, many cities were unable to meet local social welfare needs, let alone continue to fund the sort of cultural programs long associated with municipalities. Since local governments were in many respects the most direct contact point with the democratically constituted state, the failure of municipalities to meet the growing need for social welfare assistance had a negative impact on perceptions of the Republic's legitimacy.

Assuming, for the sake of argument, the validity of this claim, the preceding analysis shows that a fuller understanding of the institutional basis of political stability in the *Reich* period suggests that an extreme unitary solution to these difficulties was not appropriate. Instead, one should focus on how one might enable localities to better fulfill their long-standing role as providers of state services. Seeing the localities as a potential support beam of the state, rather than as a fifth column, as does Schmitt, directs one's attention to the structural features of the state that undermine the position of localities in the larger system. In the *Reich* period, as noted, ruling parties looked to localities as a means of getting around financial restrictions on state action at the national level. After World War I, local governments lost their independent tax base, and any attempts at financial balancing occurred between the *Reich* and the *Länder*, with the local governments receiving whatever scraps fell from the table. Moreover, local governments were subject to the supervision, not just of the *Länder* but also of the *Reich* in regard to government financing through loans. Prior to the final crisis of the Republic, leading reformers like Popitz sought to streamline the tax system, eliminating much double taxation as well as reducing any redundant bureaucracy needed to assess and collect taxes. He also sought to consolidate small, economically nonviable *Länder*, provide municipalities with additional, independent sources of revenue, and establish a more direct relation between the *Reich* and local governments in regard to financial balancing. In this way, local governments could generate revenue needed to pay for expanding governmental services, thereby reducing reliance on short-term loans, and revenue transfers from the *Reich* to local governments would not be headed off at the pass by the *Länder* governments (Dieckmann 1960, 113–129).

Many city officials supported a similar proposal by the president of the Association of Cities, Oskar Mulert (Lieberman 1998, 115). Not surprisingly, fearing a loss in political leverage stemming from their middleman position between the *Reich* and cities, *Länder* governments consistently opposed changes in the postwar constitutional compromise over federalism.[25] By the time the book-length version of *Guardian of the Constitution* appeared in 1931, there was effectively no chance to bring about fundamental changes in the system. Consequently, it is unfair to criticize Schmitt for his failure to consider possible reforms that were clearly not obtainable. My point is that Schmitt's understanding of political stability in the *Reich* period obscured the important role of local self-government in the German state. So, even if Schmitt had made his turn to the analysis of the concrete institutional problems of the Republic much earlier, when there was still some hope of productive reforms, his incomplete understanding of the nature of political stability in the *Reich* period would have blinded him to the potential effectiveness of a more decentralized response to the Republic's governability problems.

Taking at face value Schmitt's claim that his primary concern was to preserve the basic organizational framework of the Weimar Republic, his failure to fully appreciate the underlying structural grounds of political stability and governability in the *Reich* period was an especially significant deficiency in his overall argument. For it caused him to look too much to national-level institutions to provide the stable political core for politics in the Weimar period. In the final crisis of the Republic, perhaps a national orientation was the only viable one, since only the federal president was capable of responding effectively to pressing problems. But, during the relatively stable middle period, when major reforms of the federal structure were considered and rejected, providing more support to local governments might have bolstered the tottering state apparatus. In this period, when national level institutions were incapable of the sort of coherent, long-term policy leadership deemed necessary by Schmitt, local governments were able to develop and implement extensive initiatives for economic recovery and for social welfare. Local governments were also able to achieve a level of governability not possible for national level institutions, even though they operated in an hostile political environment and faced opposition, both internally and externally, from other levels of government and from private organizations, such as banks and trade associations (Lieberman 1998, esp. 7–12). Despite his keen sense for the legal and political implications of the structural features of states, therefore, Schmitt did not fully understand how the German state worked. His problematical understanding of the operation of the German state, in turn, blinded him to alternative understandings of how the state might have been made to work better in *his* terms.

NOTES

1. McPherson (1988, ix and 857–858), as reported in Callinicos (1995, 46). On the political and social implications of narrative, see White (1987).

2. On the difference between the English and American understandings of pluralism, see Hirst ([1989] 1993, 2–4). Runciman (1997) offers a more extended analysis of English pluralists. Because of its focus on Hobbes and the state, this work is particularly illuminating for understanding Schmitt's understanding of pluralism. The classic elaborations and criticisms of American pluralism are provided by Dahl (1961) and Lowi ([1969] 1979), respectively.

3. On the cross-fertilization between the Popitz and Schmitt understandings of the relation of politics and society in the Weimar state crisis, see Bentin (1972, 13–18, esp. 13–14 and 123–141, esp. 129–131).

4. The blurring of the state/society distinction through the development of quasi-governmental organizations was not just occurring in Germany. In turn-of-the-century France, leading thinkers, such as Durkheim and Duguit, advocated an understanding of the state stressing public service as opposed to sovereignty. An important component of this vision was "hybrid" organizations, which fulfilled public functions while remaining relatively autonomous from the state. For an overview of this development, see Allison (1996, 59–66). On the importance of such developments for American law and the state, see Jaffe (1937, 201–253) and Brand (1988, 1–22 and 49–52).

5. The hyperinflation that continues to shape German attitudes cannot be attributed to the Weimar Coalition. While there is no certainty on its precise cause, it is clear that the postwar inflation found its roots in 1914. This is because the imperial government, in order to pay for the war effort, opted to borrow rather than raise taxes. While prices rose steadily after the war, financing the passive resistance to French occupation of the Ruhr in 1923 set off the unprecedented inflation. The principal problem was that government printing presses ran day and night in an attempt to pay salaries to striking workers and to continue to fund generous so-

cial welfare provisions. The best work on the German inflation remains Feldman (1997).

6. On the role of the 5 percent hurdle in consolidating the German party system in the early postwar era, see Padgett and Burkett (1986, 28–29). Braunthal (1996, 182–184) and Roberts (1997, 128–157) consider the stability of the postwar party system and the consolidation of the system in the post-reunification period, respectively.

7. Sartori ([1994] 1997, 3–79) exhaustively analyzes the basic tendencies attributed to various electoral systems and concludes, more or less, that precise effects of different types of systems depend on the circumstances.

8. Among the proposals considered was one championed by Arnold Brecht. Inspired by Hugo Preuß' original unitary vision, Brecht advocated making the Prussian provinces into separate *Länder*, with the position of the *Reich* strengthened vis a vis all *Länder* (Brecht 1945, 73–89, esp. 77–80; see also, Brecht and Kutzer 1928, esp. 1–16). Another proposal by the former chancellor Hans Luther envisioned the consolidation into Prussia of most of the smaller northern *Länder*. This enlarged Prussia would then be administered from the center as a federal district (Brecht 1945, 73–89; Orlow 1991, 126–129; and Frotscher 1983, 130–135).

9. There is a long-standing controversy about how much political room for maneuver was enjoyed by the parties supporting the Republic. Borchardt (1982, 162–182 and 183–205) sparked a debate over the limited range of options available to the German government in responding to the economic crisis in the final years of the Republic, which, in turn, rendered effective parliamentary government increasingly difficult, if not impossible. For reactions to the so-called Borchardt thesis, see Holtfrerich (1984), Kruedener (1985 and 1990), Maier (1985), and Voth (1993). In a recent reassessment of Brüning's role in the Weimar Republic, Patch argues that the collapse of the coalition government in 1930, leading to the first big electoral breakthrough for the Nazis, was "probably inevitable," because bourgeois parties risked further loss of votes through cooperation with the SPD (1998, 94–95). Berman (1998), by contrast, argues that the SPD might have broadened its base, if it had been willing to give up certain firmly held beliefs.

10. On the importance of corporatism in German political theory prior to the Weimar Republic, see Bowen ([1947] 1971).

11. For Schmitt's understanding of the long-term intellectual, political, and social changes causing the decline of the German independent state, see especially *Hugo Preuß* (HP) (1930).

12. One of the legacies of the *Ständestaat* in 19th century Germany, according to Leonard Krieger, was the German concept of freedom, which differed significantly from that in other Western countries. Rather than associating freedom with individual liberty from government interference, Germans conceived of it in terms of the autonomy from central control of corporate bodies, such as principalities and municipalities (Krieger 1957, 3–85).

13. See Skocpol (1985, 3–37) for a review of the extensive literature on the role of the state in effecting major social reforms in the modern era with important political implications.

14. Take, for example, an 1886 opinion of the Prussian Supreme Administrative Court, which reaffirmed the commonly held view that local governments could not legitimately meddle in "politics." The legitimate authority of municipalities only extended to "local affairs." (Dawson 1916, 37).

15. On the importance for understandings of the state of changes in politics and society during the 19th century, see Stolleis (1992, 229–265).

16. Thornhill provides a good overview of the importance for German political thought of the idea of an autonomous political sphere in contrast to the private order of interests (2000, 2–16) as well as a discussion of the importance of this idea for Schmitt in both the Weimar and early Nazi periods (55–91, esp. 84–91).

17. On this point, Schmitt echoed a widely held view. On the perceived threat to the independent state posed by local self-government in the Weimar period, see Herzfeld (1957, 32–37).

18. On Schmitt's distinction between a "quantitative" and "qualitative" total state, see Cristi (1998, 188–199).

19. On the "negative integration" of the Social Democrats in the *Reich* period, see Roth (1963). Bismarck's Anti-Socialist Laws had a negative impact on labor generally. For their importance for trade unions not legally part of the SPD, see Moses (1982, 66–87).

20. For a short history of the drafting and promulgation of the Weimar Constitution, see Rürup (1972, 218–243). On the practical obstacles to sweeping reform measures generally in the immediate postwar period, see Peukert (1991, 21–51). Schieck (1972, 138–164) examines the question of socialization of the economy in particular.

21. While dividing on the question of what accounts for the collapse of the Weimar Republic, historians agree that the lack of consensus on basic values greatly complicated the task of achieving political compromises. Compare, for example, Karl Dietrich Bracher's ([1969] 1970, 3–49 and 142–227) account stressing political factors with one emphasizing political economy, such as Abraham ([1981]1986, 35–41 and 59–74). Then, compare both of these works with Peukert's multicausal account (1991, 66–77).

22. On the restrictions on revenue generation by the *Reich*, see von Kruedener (1987, 111–135). Under the universality principle, municipalities were relatively unrestricted in regard to revenues, spending, and direct economic activity (Dawson 1916, 32).

23. Nedelsky (1990) argues, for example, that the original Madisonian vision for the Republic utilized constitutional structure to reinforce the political position of the propertied elite, while Tomlins (1985) shows how the common law system kept the early labor movement in a hammerlock in the late 19th century.

24. William H. Riker and Jonathan Limco argue that there is some empirical evidence that a federal system, comprised of a large number of units of approxi-

mately equal size, as in the United States, is conducive to political stability (1987, 113–129). On the liberal insight of removing contentious issues from politics, in order to enhance the overall effectiveness of democratic government, see Holmes (1988, 19–58).

25. On reform efforts generally, and South German particularlism as an obstacle to reform specifically, see Apelt (1946, 386–403 and 408).

Chapter 3

Guarding the Constitution: The American Model in German Constitutional Politics

The Weimar Constitution presented an impressive vision of democracy in the industrial age. Long-standing demands for parliamentary government were realized when Parliament received substantial new powers and a broader democratic base. The Constitution also established a directly elected president with considerable executive authority and provided for referenda and initiatives, making it arguably the most democratic constitution of its time. Among its novel features was the National Economic Council (*Reichswirtschaftsrat*) and a set of constitutional rights that included economic and social rights in addition to traditional civil and political liberties.

While innovative and ambitious, the Weimar Constitution also raised many unanswered questions. The Catalogue of Rights suggested a fundamentally new system of rights protection, without, however, specifying the legal status of particular provisions or of the Catalogue generally. Were they directly enforceable by the ordinary courts of law, as in the United States, or would the anticipated State High Court (*Staatsgerichtshof*) have jurisdiction over them? The inclusion of legislative-reservation clauses (*Gesetzesvor- behalte*) in many of the provisions suggest that the scope and substance of these rights would be subject to definition by ordinary law, as were rights in the prewar era. In fact, some of the rights provisions seemed to be merely programmatic, setting out general goals for future legislation. Did such provisions render the government legally accountable to undertake the necessary action? The text of the Constitution provided little guidance on these important questions.

In time, it might have been possible for the complex mixture of old and new institutions and legal forms to gel effectively; yet, time was a luxury the Republic did not enjoy. The collapse of the Weimar Republic, with its momentous consequences, suggests that the true test of an effective constitutional system is not whether it can authoritatively resolve contentious political and social questions, as Schmitt claims. It is to what extent the existing system can keep such questions open long enough to find provisional compromises. Seen from this angle, the challenge of constitutional engineering includes not merely the designing or reforming of entire institutions or whole systems, but also extends to the patching or tweaking of existing institutions and practices. In short, there is a pressing need for constitutional theory as building engineer.

The next two chapters evaluate Schmitt's record as building superintendent. The extensive Catalogue of Rights, along with the new and proposed courts, raised the question of the proper role of the judiciary in resolving political and social conflict. Though the Constitution was ambiguous regarding the legal status of the new rights provisions, and while it was silent on the general question of judicial review, there was substantial support for an enhanced judicial role. By expanding the competence of the Federal High Court (*Reichsgericht*) so that it could occupy a position in the German system comparable to that of the U.S. Supreme Court, or by establishing new courts along the lines of the Austrian Constitutional Court, the world's first constitutional court, some argued that judges could serve effectively as "guardians of the Constitution."[1]

Schmitt considered these proposals escapist fantasies. In *Guardian of the Constitution* (*Hüter der Verfassung*) (HV) ([1931] 1985), Schmitt argued that the German judiciary was not institutionally equipped to serve as guardian of the Constitution (HV 12–70). In Schmitt's opinion, the highly democratic, fragmented state created by the Weimar Constitution required an institutional center of gravity, and only the Federal President (*Reichspräsident*) could provide this stable pole (HV 132–159).

This chapter focuses on a particular aspect of Schmitt's argument. In the post World War II era, the establishment of new nation-states in the aftermath of decolonization, combined with the democratization of formerly communist and authoritarian systems, has raised the issue of institutional borrowing from one system to another.[2] Schmitt's comparative history of the German judiciary anticipated these efforts not merely in his insistence on the importance of context (e.g. Kahn-Freund 1974 and Sokolewicz 1995) but also in his use of conceptual frameworks to integrate the comparative history of institutions into his contextual analysis (e.g. Allison 1996).

Schmitt's effort to utilize what we, today, term developmental studies to address a pressing normative question is not interesting merely because it anticipated current scholarship. Criticizing Schmitt's approach will demonstrate how one can better integrate conceptually driven comparative histories into normative debates over institutions.[3] The next chapter extends to the courts the argument of the previous one that Schmitt failed to grasp the full political implications of the composite nature of the German state in the *Reich* period. A proper understanding of how the German state worked in the pre-Weimar period demonstrates the potential contribution of courts to democracies in times of crisis, even if one adheres to a positivist understanding of law.

In what follows, I lay the groundwork for this argument by considering Schmitt's comparative history of the German court system. Commentators have rightly criticized the two-dimensional quality of Schmitt's reading of some aspects of the German legal tradition, especially his overly narrow understanding of subsumption jurisprudence (esp. Kelsen 1930/31). But little attention has been accorded Schmitt's treatment of German legal politics, which anticipates contemporary social scientific analyses of judicial politics in Europe and North America stressing the policymaking role of courts in modern democracies (e.g. Shapiro and Stone 1994). Apart from Schmitt's normative concern, his argument is similar in that he stresses that certain features of the system, such as an extensive set of constitutional rights and easy access to courts, encourage attempts to utilize courts to obtain political and social objectives frustrated in the normal political process. In doing so, Schmitt edges toward the sort of dynamic conceptual model I concluded was missing in his comparative-historical approach in *Constitutional Theory* (*Verfassungslehre*) (V) ([1928] 1989). His failure to develop a model of how the politicization of the judiciary is possible, despite the institutional limitations he outlines, deprives his normative argument for a strong executive of considerable force and, more importantly, clears a theoretical space for a larger role for courts outlined in the final chapter.

An extended review of Schmitt's comparative history of the institutional limitations of German courts (I) lays the groundwork for a critical evaluation of his treatment of the issue of the politicization of the judiciary (II). Taking at face value his stated aim of seeking to bolster the state's ability to respond to the Republic's considerable governability problems, I suggest how Schmitt might have made more effective use of conceptual models to address institutional issues. As in previous chapters, my purpose in doing so is to highlight the limitations of Schmitt's approach and not to bolster his case for presidential government, which is almost unlimited in practical terms.

I.

A recurring theme of Schmitt's analysis of German constitutional politics is the distinctiveness of the German legal tradition. It was especially important, in his view, to remain cognizant of the profound influence Revolutionary France had on German legal development, particularly of the failure to link constitutions with private law reform. French and American constitution-making differed in that, although the United States, with some very important exceptions, such as slavery, already had a democratic society, the French had to establish one. Constitutions were to play an important role in effecting this change, at least in the sense of indicating what was to be done and in hindering reactionary changes.[4] The elimination of the feudal regime in a few days in August of 1789 obscures the fact that very little tangible was accomplished in this regard. In fact, significant private law reform was only carried out under Napoleon. In other words, the Revolution gave higher law status to the idea of civil equality guaranteed by law, and yet the laws necessary for ensuring this were only passed after the revolutionary decade ended (Grimm 1982, 23–33). The permanence of the Napoleonic code indicates the important public-law character of private law on the Continent (Casper 1989, 311–332, esp. 320–321). But the Napoleonic constitutions effectively eliminated the political rights of the people. It is perhaps a bit overdramatic, but one can say that the French received formal civil equality in exchange for their political liberty.[5]

Schmitt believed it was difficult to underestimate the importance of this pattern for German developments, for the French Revolution and its aftermath produced important changes in the object of judicial reform in Germany. Frederick the Great's judicial reforms aimed at bolstering the absolutist state by loosening the grip of the nobility on judicial offices and by promoting legal unity over local custom. In the late 18th and early 19th centuries, the goal was not merely to improve state control in this way. It was also to dampen calls for radical democratic change inspired by the French Revolution and the Napoleonic Wars. By instituting liberal reforms of the economy and the state apparatus, including the judiciary, which fell short of full or extensive rights of democratic participation, the reformers preserved important aspects of the absolutist state, further weakened the nobility, and derailed democratic reform efforts (Koselleck [1967] 1989).[6] Whereas the French Revolution aspired to effect democratic change through law, one of its great legacies on the continent in the 19th century came to be the hindering of democratic change through law. Prussia, for example, ironically became more like France in order to limit potential French influence. But, even when more substantial rights of political participation were achieved in Germany under Bismarck's Constitution, law still played this role as spoiler. The drafting of the German Civil Code illustrates this quite well.

By the time the Code took effect in 1900, the character of German politics had changed fundamentally. The most notable change was the rise of mass parties and the decline of the National Liberal party, which, in the initial decade of the *Reich*, claimed to speak for the "nation." The legal bureaucrats and professionals who drafted the Code on behalf of the *Reich* government structured political participation so that competing groups, other than the Social Democrats, had a say in the drafting and revision of the Code, though in a way that moderated potential opposition. This lent legitimacy to the final product, which was completed without major revisions, even though various groups had fundamental objections to it. In this way, the drafters of the Code successfully executed a rearguard action for a formerly solid liberal consensus which was already rapidly disintegrating (John 1989).

Leaving aside Schmitt's claim that liberalism and democracy are necessarily antithetical,[7] he was right that as a factual matter, the cause of liberalism in the 19th century on the Continent advanced apart from that of democracy. In other words, an ever more liberal social order was established without corresponding democratic change. This was clear in France to varying degrees under the Restoration, the July Monarchy, and the First and Second Empires, for example, but especially in Germany during the *Reich* period. Schmitt faulted liberals for not pushing their cause to a decisive conclusion, and yet he recognized that liberals had achieved many of their most important aims by the late 19th century. In this reading, clearly influenced by Weber, the bourgeoisie achieved great prosperity in a generally liberal economic and social system, settling for only limited, though ever growing, political influence.[8]

At this point, the peculiarly German notion of *Rechtsstaat* becomes relevant. This term is not directly translatable. Its closest English equivalent is the "rule of law," and yet even this is an inadequate rendering, because the German term does not include a necessary connection between civil and political liberties.[9] Schmitt argues that this protean concept is perhaps best explained in regard to the German view of the state (HP; V 125–220, esp. 125–126; and HV 22–36). Until the mid-19th century in Germany, the state was defined substantively in terms of purpose, and yet there were no judicial means for reviewing whether and/or how the state fulfilled its tasks. Administration was an internal affair, not subject to review by regular courts. Gradually, administration became more subject to judicial control, though by special administrative courts at the *Land* level. The state was defined less in regard to certain tasks and purposes, but its activity was increasingly subject to judicial control. The concern became how it defined and executed its will, not the content of these actions (V, 125–220, esp. 125–134; Scheuner 1968, 461–503). This idea of the state culminated in that of "*Kompetenz-Kompetenz*" in the *Reich* period. This term also has no English equivalent, but it can be rendered literally as the authority to determine the legitimate scope of authority. Only the state had this self-defining capacity. In other words, the state could define the extent of its authority, whereas that of other associations was limited by the state. It is important to stress the peculiarly circular character of this idea. If the state followed proper procedures, which it itself established, then it could do whatever it wished. Nevertheless, this was seen as an important limit on state authority. Because the state could define itself only through law, it expanded the sphere of law as it extended the reach of its own authority, perfecting the *Rechtsstaat* idea (Emerson [1928] 1979, esp. 47–91).

Schmitt was quite critical of the "murky legal conditions of the old German *Reich*" (1985 (PT), 10), particularly its legal theory. He thought the dominant school of thought, legal positivism, could achieve great theoretical precision and symmetry because it abstracted away from the unresolved tensions and ambiguities of the system. In fact, the state in the *Reich* period was not a unity which defined itself, as suggested by the concept, *Kompetenz-Kompetenz;* rather, it was a composite constructed, quite literally, from a series of compromises between formerly sovereign states with separate identities and differing systems (Schmitt 1958 (VRA), 29–33). Put differently, the Constitution was less a social contract among the people than one between independent groups (HV 60–62). This contractual character of the Constitution explains why many provisions involved quite specific concessions to individual *Länder*. The *Reich* government, for example, was given control of the postal service, but the important *Länder* of Bavaria and Württemberg retained authority over the postal services in their jurisdictions (Schuster 1983, 83–85). Under these conditions, central state action was quite cumbersome. Any legislative initiative affecting the *Reich* required attaining agreement among powerful actors and groups at different levels of the system. The execution of these dictates also required cooperation of the individual *Länder* governments, because administrative and judicial organs were located primarily at the *Länder* level (Deuerlein 1972, 135–154).

This splintered political identity had several important implications for the court system in Germany. Most generally, unlike France, which had a unified, centralized court system by this time, the German court system remained quite fragmented. Germany followed the basic civil law pattern of establishing separate courts for different sorts of cases, but this took place mostly at the individual *Land* level. Most *Länder* had highly developed legal systems,[10] which, after unification, continued to handle the vast majority of cases. In fact, there was only one court established at the national level during the *Reich* period, the Federal High Court, the high court for civil and criminal cases.[11] Finally, there was no court established at the *Reich* level comparable to the *Tribunal des Conflits* (Conflicts Court) in France, which could settle conflicts over the jurisdiction of the respective courts (Deak and Rheinstein 1936, 846–876).

Another important institutional peculiarity of German courts in the *Reich* period was that, with a few minor exceptions, the jurisdiction of German courts was enumerative in the strictest possible sense. In other words, access to the courts was explicitly and narrowly defined by statute. The jurisdiction of courts, generally, in civil law countries is enumerative, but Germany carried this to the greatest possible extreme. In this important respect, Germany differed from France, where statutes often established a general right of access for a much more broadly defined class of cases. The most striking example, of course, is the jurisdiction of the Council of State (*Conseil d'Etat*), which is truly general in a wide range of administrative cases (Deak and Rheinstein 1936, 846–863, esp. 858–862).[12]

German court jurisdiction was so strictly enumerative, because agreement on a general proposition was difficult to attain among the various *Länder* composing the *Reich*. The difficulty in forging policy at the national level was complicated by the emergence of mass political parties, which became increasingly influential through the budgetary power of the Federal Parliament (*Reichstag*),[13] a development with no parallel in France at the time (Mayeur and Reberioux 1987, 214–220). Most major legislative initiatives reflected these difficulties. The German Civil Code, for example, was passed partly because many issues were left open, to be decided locally or through special legislation dealing only with a particular issue (John 1989, 160–198).

The establishment of central governmental organs, particularly the Federal Chamber (*Bundesrat*), moderated the centrifugal forces created by the federal system, but, in a certain sense, at the expense of courts. Composed of *Länder* governments and dominated by Prussia,[14] the most powerful German *Land* by far, the Federal Chamber provided the unwieldy system with a center of gravity.[15] Article 76 of Bismarck's *Reich* Constitution assigned the Federal Chamber the task of resolving disputes of a "nonprivate law nature" among *Länder* and constitutional disputes within *Länder* when no other authority has been established for this purpose. Because most important disputes arising from the federal system were resolved politically in the Federal Chamber (Scheuner 1976, 36–39), a potentially significant role for courts in policing the system, as some courts have in the United States for example,[16] was practically precluded.

The development of German legal institutions, therefore, followed that of France in certain important respects, but the idiosyncrasies of German federalism placed courts in an even more subordinate position vis a vis the political branches than was true of their French counterparts. The collapse of the *Reich* system, according to Walter Simons, the president of the Federal High Court between 1922–1929, provided great opportunities for a fundamental restructuring of the court system and a recasting of the traditional understanding of the role of courts in constitutional government (1924). Schmitt insisted that though in some senses courts attained new prominence during the Weimar period, there was no fundamental change in their position in the system.

The principal drafter of the Weimar Constitution, Hugo Preuß, preferred that the judiciary generally exercise the power of judicial review, as in the United States. Preuß thought that without any specific provisions regarding judicial review, the practice of judicial review would develop much as it had in America. For this reason, he opposed provisions assigning a special court the power of judicial review in certain specified cases; as well as prohibitions against judicial review altogether (HV 23).[17] In the end, the drafting committee did not decide the question one way or the other. Except for a few provisions concerning impeachment and certain quite limited federalist questions, the Weimar Constitution had little to say regarding judicial review (Friedrich 1928, 188–200).

Judicial review of the substantive constitutionality of statutes did develop without an explicit constitutional basis, much as Preuß predicted. The Federal High Court, for example, asserted this authority, either explicitly or implicitly, in three different cases and actually invalidated one *Reich* statute. Several courts besides the Federal High Court also asserted the power of judicial review. A special court, the State High Court (*Staatsgerichtshof*) was charged with resolving certain constitutional disputes, mainly federalist questions. Nonetheless, it considered two cases involving the constitutionality of a *Reich* statute. There were also several permanent high courts, each responsible for different sorts of cases. One of these, the Federal Tax Court (*Reichsfinanzgericht*), like the Federal High Court, could draw on only a tenuous textual basis for exercising the power of judicial review over the substantive constitutionality of *Reich* statutes, and yet it also declared a federal statute unconstitutional. In a word, the German system went from no courts with the power of judicial review over the substantive constitutionality of federal statutes to several courts claiming this authority simultaneously (Lenoir 1940, 361–383; Mattern 1928, 590–613).

Schmitt was troubled by such developments, partly because he considered the German judiciary ill-suited institutionally for exercising judicial review like that wielded by the U.S. Supreme Court. According to Schmitt, the German proponents of judicial review correctly pointed out that courts have a more prominent position in the common law countries, particularly in America before World War I, than courts on the Continent. The difficulty was not so much that the German advocates of judicial review overlooked important institutional differences between the courts in the two countries, though this did occur and was a problem. It was that these supporters of judicial review tended to exaggerate these differences, basing their arguments on perceptions of the U.S. Supreme Court which were so erroneous they almost constituted a "mythology" about it (HV 12). This mythology, in turn, obscured the important limits on the Supreme Court as an American political institution. For Schmitt, any adequate consideration of the proper place of judicial review in the Weimar constitutional system required clarity not only as to the appropriateness of the American analogy for the German context but also in regard to the U.S. Supreme Court as a political institution in the American context (HV 12–14).

A central organizing principle of Schmitt's critique of the German judiciary was his claim that states can be categorized "according to the area, in which they find the center of their activity," conceding, of course, that no state falls clearly into only one category (HV 75–77). According to this schema, the United States was a "jurisdiction state" (*Jurisdictionsstaat*) in that it was primarily concerned with defining and enforcing jurisdictional boundaries among rival centers of power (HV 13).[18] This designation fit the United States rather well in regard to the pre–World War I period, but especially in the early 19th century. Schmitt rightly pointed out that American judges have always had the authority to question the legal foundations of executive action, whereas ordinary courts on the Continent have never had jurisdiction over administrative acts. Schmitt also correctly emphasized that American courts often nullified and restricted the relatively infrequent, limited legislative initiatives of the time. In this period, legislative activity was quite limited, and the United States had very little formal bureaucracy, in contrast to Continental countries, so courts served as a shadow state of sorts, regulating and guiding economic development on the basis of common law categories (Horwitz 1977).

This is not to say that courts had free rein in the United States. There was considerable hostility toward the common law due to its association with

England.[19] This inspired calls for codification, which aimed to limit the authority of judges, who were seen as elitist and undemocratic. But the common law proved to have enormous staying power. According to Perry Miller, American lawyers staged one of the world's most successful public relations campaigns between the Revolution and the Civil War, replacing the clergy as America's elite (Miller 1965).[20]

Schmitt was right, however, to stress the importance of the common law tradition in the emergence of the U.S. Supreme Court as the most powerful court in the world at the time. That the U.S. Supreme Court claims the authority to review statutes on the basis of "general principles of law," not merely explicit constitutional provisions (HV 18), is not surprising considering that the common law is a set of concepts developed by judges through the process of application. The fact that the origin of the system is difficult to identify with great precision bolsters the view of judges as the instrument of reason by obscuring the centrality of human action in its establishment (Corwin [1928–29] 1995).

Just as important in the development of the American form of judicial review, Schmitt argues, is the position of the Supreme Court as the sole high court in the American system (HV 12–13). This gives the Supreme Court an authority not matched by any German high court during the Weimar period, because judgments of a German high court had to compete with those of other high courts. Poised at the pinnacle of a legal system based upon the idea of the supremacy not just of constitutional over ordinary law but that of higher law over constitutional law, it is not surprising that the Supreme Court over time took up the role of the authoritative interpreter of the American constitutional tradition generally.[21]

Schmitt was also right to stress that the political effectiveness of the Supreme Court depends on a societal consensus in support of its doctrine (HV 13 and 18). Besides the Supreme Court's failed attempts to settle fundamental conflicts, such as the slavery controversy,[22] this is clear, Schmitt pointed out, in the economic substantive due process cases, where the Court protected established economic and social interests by striking down social legislation, such as minimum wage and hour laws, long accepted in Germany. Though Schmitt did not explicitly predict the Supreme Court's about-face in response to considerable popular pressure during the 1930s, he would not have been surprised by it. The long-standing common law system of social ordering had been called into question by fundamental economic and social changes, and it was only a matter of time, Schmitt would have argued, before the Supreme Court would be forced to give way (McCloskey [1960] 1994).[23]

Relative to their American counterparts, courts in the Weimar system were disadvantaged on both counts. The German judiciary could not build upon a social consensus even as tenuous as that in the United States at the time. By placing the center of gravity in the Federal Chamber dominated by the conservative *Land* Prussia, the *Reich* constitutional system successfully contained rising social tensions, according to Schmitt. In addition to what was said about the *Reich* system in the first section, it is important to note that each *Land* had its own selection system for the *Länder* government delegations which constituted the Federal Chamber. Prussia had a tripartite voting system, for example, which was heavily weighted in favor of wealthy and generally conservative voters. This greatly limited the influence of groups, such as the emerging Social Democratic Party, first on the Prussian state government and secondly on the national government through the Federal Chamber (Berghahn 1994, 212 and Fairbairn 1997, 15).

The Weimar Constitution, in Schmitt's view, did not resolve the substantive disagreements between these opposing groups so much as set out the conditions for a temporary "cease fire" (HV 63). The conflict between competing groups was so intense that any judicial efforts to mediate their differences, even a well-intentioned effort to reestablish the delicate balance between them, would be perceived as one-sided and thus rejected. To illustrate the implications of this ideologically charged atmosphere for possible judicial resolution of disputes, Schmitt turned to the controversy concerning Chancellor Brüning's dissolution of the Federal Parliament in 1930 and subsequent reliance on presidential emergency decrees. The central issue was whether Brüning could have forged a workable parliamentary majority, making recourse to presidential emergency powers unnecessary. Schmitt noted that even the Social Democrats were divided on this basic factual question. In view of this, he argued, it is difficult to see how a court, such as the State High Court, could resolve such a question to the satisfaction of the Social Democrats, let alone other leading parties (HV 29–31).[24]

Schmitt identified an essential feature of Weimar politics and correctly pointed out its implications for the possible judicial resolution of explosive political disputes. It was bad enough that the party system was increasingly fragmented and included parties opposed to the Republic. But matters were made much worse by the fact that even those parties committed to supporting the Republic and essential to any workable governing coalition could not themselves agree on terms for participation in government coalitions. The fragmentation of the bourgeois block of parties, along with the bitter divisions among socialists, meant that parties supporting the Republic were hesitant to risk any actions that might alienate core supporters. This situation was exacerbated by the economic collapse late in the Republic, for the state did not have the money to fund tradeoffs necessary to hold together fragile governments.[25]

Even if there had been a societal consensus supporting judicial mediation of these fundamental disputes, Schmitt argued, the potential influence of the judiciary would have been hopelessly diluted by the fragmented character of the German court system. As noted, the especially splintered German court system was intimately connected to the peculiarities of German federalism. The situation did not improve during the Weimar period, despite the transfer of most legislative authority to the center under the Weimar Constitution. In some senses, in fact, the situation worsened.

After World War I, federalism had been discredited due to its association with the dynasties, particularly that of Prussia, which had dominated German affairs for half a century. Federalism could not be merely wished away, however. Practically all of the administrative organs of the state were at the *Land* level, and most *Länder* governments were controlled by either traditional authorities or by various radical groups. In the space of one year, for example, the *Land* Bavaria went from a radical leftist state, organized in worker and soldier councils, to a traditional rightist one, sympathetic to extreme right-wing groups like the incipient Nazi party. Maintaining the federal structure in some form was unavoidable (Deuerlein 1972, 171–193).

A substantial portion of legislative authority, however, had been transferred to the *Reich*. Lacking an administrative substructure, the *Reich* government more or less constructed a central bureaucracy as it legislated in different areas or continued to rely on *Länder* governments, creating enormous execution problems. The resulting patchwork character of the federal system was quite evident in regard to courts. Article 108 of the Weimar Constitution called for the establishment of a State High Court (Schuster 1983, 118), and Articles 19, 59, and 170 indicated its range of possible jurisdiction (103, 109, 129–130, respectively). Article 172 even provided for its provisional formation until the necessary statutes were passed (130). This ensured there would be such a court, but not that it could do anything. In fact, on the basis of the legislative-reservation clauses of the relevant constitutional provisions, the government could have rendered the State High Court an effective nullity by dividing its possible jurisdiction among existing courts or establishing new courts.

Legislation was passed in 1921 providing for the formation of the State High Court and specifying its jurisdiction and procedure (Federal Parliament 1921). Though this enabling legislation gave it the power of final judgment in an important range of cases, this legislation did not resolve the problem of fragmentation of institutional competence. In fact, it exacerbated the problem in certain respects. According to the statute, the State

High Court was to be comprised of judges from different courts depending on the type of case. In constitutional cases arising under Article 19, the Court was to be formed principally of judges from leading administrative courts, particularly from the anticipated federal high administrative law court (Schuster 1983, 103). Until this federal high court for administrative cases was established by law, the statute provided that in relevant cases, the State High Court would be comprised of the president of the Federal High Court, several judges of the latter chosen by him or her, and several judges from state administrative courts.

Walter Simons, president of the Federal High Court from 1922 to 1929, when he resigned because of a dispute with the Federal President over the jurisdiction of the court, was a vocal advocate of widening the authority of the Court to rival that of the U.S. Supreme Court. Simons thought the German court should be a coordinate branch of government with independent constitutional status, like the Supreme Court. Moreover, he thought that the Federal High Court should be the final arbiter of constitutional disputes as well as authoritative interpreter of the Weimar Constitution.[26] The court, under Simons' stewardship, took tangible steps in this direction, asserting in varying degrees of explicitness the power of judicial review of the material constitutionality of *Reich* legislation, much in the way the Supreme Court did in *Marbury v. Madison*, that is, without an explicit textual basis in the Constitution or appropriate enabling legislation. Thus, though the State High Court arguably might have been best suited to take on a role similar to the Supreme Court or even the French Council of State, it was manned by justices from other courts with their own agendas.

The result was lack of unity in the court system. In addition to the retention of the Federal High Court and the establishment of the State High Court, Article 107 of the Weimar Constitution called for the establishment of administrative courts at both the *Reich* and *Länder* levels (Schuster 1983, 118). Most *Länder* already had administrative courts; some even had a high court for administrative cases, as well as a court to resolve conflicts between the administrative court and the other high courts. Efforts were focused, therefore, on establishing administrative courts on the *Reich* level. The tendency was for the *Reich* government to establish administrative courts, often including a high court for that particular area, when it passed a major piece of legislation. But the *Reich* never established a high court for administration to resolve conflicts between administrative courts at the different levels, nor did it set up a court to resolve conflicts between these various high courts, ordinary and administrative, at the federal level (Deak and Rheinstein 1936).

There were legislative efforts to unify the system. The most important proposal would have given the State High Court the authority to review the substantive constitutionality of *Reich* statutes and regulations in certain specified, narrowly defined instances. The State High Court could do so, if called upon by the Parliament, the Federal Chamber, or the *Reich* government. It could also settle doubts about the constitutionality of laws and regulations raised by a particular high court as well as resolve conflicts between competing high courts. In all cases, the State High Court would confine itself to the question of constitutionality, defining the law for future cases; it could not actually decide the case at hand, as could the U.S. Supreme Court (Lenoir 1940, 369).

The failure of these reform efforts encouraged a free-for-all of sorts among various high courts claiming authority for final judgment in regard to different cases. It is not necessary to recount in detail all of the leading decisions of these competing tribunals. A brief example should make clear the extent of the problem. Financial questions are explosive in any system, but particularly in a federal system, which divides governmental tasks among different levels. This was particularly so in the Weimar period. During the *Reich* period, most administrative and judicial organs were concentrated at the *Länder* level, where primary authority of direct taxation also rested. This led to considerable federal indebtedness, because the *Reich* government had few direct means of paying for its substantial and ever growing military programs. With the transfer of much legislative authority to the center under the Weimar Constitution, the situation was reversed. The individual *Länder* had substantial obligations, for which they could not raise the necessary funds through direct taxes (Deuerlein 1972, 171–193).

It is difficult to underestimate the enormous problems this produced for the Weimar state. Several provisions of the Weimar Constitution established legal mechanisms to resolve these explosive financial disputes between the *Reich* and *Länder* governments. Article 8, for example, charged the *Reich* government with considering "the preservation of the viability of the *Länder* governments" when it absorbed revenue generating mechanisms which formerly belonged to the *Länder* governments (Schuster 1983, 100–101), and Article 11 indicated in general terms for what purposes the *Reich* government could restrict the revenue generating mechanisms of the *Land* governments (101). Most important for the role of courts in the constitutional system was Article 13, which established the supremacy of *Reich* laws and stipulated that disputes over whether *Länder* provisions were reconcilable with *Reich* ones could be resolved by "one of the high courts of the *Reich*," if specified officials at either level called upon it to do so (101).

The problem was that this provision only indicated "a" high court, not "which" high court could resolve these disputes. Numerous statutes were passed during the Weimar period pursuant to this article. Two in particular illustrate the considerable jurisdictional confusion. These statutes, passed within a little over a week of one another in 1920, gave the Federal High Court and the Federal Tax Court (*Reichfinanzgericht*) jurisdiction over different sorts of cases under Article 13. Each high court, however, was responsible for determining the extent of its own jurisdiction, since there was no tribunal of conflicts to authoritatively settle competing claims. The Federal High Court claimed that the Federal Tax Court's jurisdiction was limited to tax law questions, but that it, the Federal High Court, could exercise concurrent jurisdiction in this area. The Federal High Court never carried out its threat, but there would have been no judicial means of preventing it from doing so, because no other judicial body could legitimately invalidate its claims (Lenoir 1940, 370–375).

In addition to the confusion resulting from the overlap of institutional competence, there was also considerable uncertainty in regard to the sources of law, particularly in constitutional cases. Schmitt was especially concerned with the extensive catalogue of rights and duties contained in the Second Principal Part of the Weimar Constitution, which he labeled an "almost a bottomless pit of doubts" and "differences of opinion" about the Constitution (HV 49). This catalogue included some traditional civil and political liberties but numerous social and economic rights as well. The problem, Schmitt argued, was that the precise legal status of these myriad rights provisions was unclear. The text of the Weimar Constitution did not indicate clearly whether many of these provisions were directly enforceable by courts without enabling legislation or whether they had merely a programmatic status, indicating the general future direction of legislative activity in regard to rights. This catalogue was especially peculiar, in Schmitt's view, not only because the legal status of various provisions was unclear but also because what little guidance the Weimar Constitution offered ran counter to any sensible understanding of constitutional rights (HV 47–48). For example, certain essential constitutional guarantees, such as "freedom of the person" protected by Article 114 (Schuster 1983, 119) seemed subject to definition through ordinary legislation, making possible their effective gutting by the legislature, whereas other guarantees, such as the "well-earned rights of civil servants" guaranteed by Article 129 (121), did not appear subject to legislative restriction at all. It is absurd, Schmitt claimed, to permit Parliament to legislate without restriction in regard to essential constitutional rights, and yet not allow it to lower the salaries of civil servants in order to respond to a pressing fiscal crisis. But the presence of simple legislative reservation clauses in the former, but not the latter, suggested this, according to Schmitt (VRA, 180–231).[27]

Under certain conditions, Schmitt argued, it would be possible to hammer out workable compromises in regard to these rights, but the tumultuous political climate during the Weimar period militated against resolving these ambiguities through evolving political practice (HV 71–91). The troubled domestic and international position of the Republic often rendered it difficult to form coalitions necessary to address certain pressing problems of order and public welfare, let alone determine the fundamental orientation of the system.[28] What was true of the legislature applied even more to courts, because of their more limited normative claim to authority (HV 60). It was also not clear, according to Schmitt, on what legal basis courts could address questions of constitutional rights. The State High Court was the principal organ for addressing constitutional disputes, but it was not a permanent court, nor did it handle claims of individual rights. It was called into session by governmental organs to resolve disputes regarding their authority, and this only on the basis of enabling legislation. The State High Court itself widened the right of access by defining parliamentary minorities as representing *Land* parliaments, providing an opening for opposition political parties to press their claims, which, in turn, might involve certain of these provisions. But it never recognized individuals as parties before the court (HV 48–54).

The Federal High Court, interestingly, may have been a more effective vehicle for judicial resolution of these ambiguities. The State High Court could authoritatively settle points of law for all future cases. As Schmitt pointed out, it could only consider disputed questions referred to it by narrowly defined groups of governmental officials, and, moreover, these disputes primarily involved federalist questions (HV 48–60, esp. 54–60). The Federal High Court, like the U.S. Supreme Court, had no explicit authorization to address constitutional questions. Nonetheless, it was the high court for civil and criminal cases which might impinge on disputed rights provisions. The Federal High Court could authoritatively settle points of law for lower courts in the immediate case and then remand these to the appropriate court for final disposition. But, unlike the Supreme Court, which is constrained by the "Cases and Controversies Clause," the Federal High Court could address any point of law on its own initiative, not merely those necessary for deciding the case at hand. This gave the Federal High Court an important potential institutional advantage over the Supreme Court in enhancing its own authority, because it did not need to wait for an appropriate case to settle an important point of law.

The Federal High Court was still hesitant to review the material constitutionality of *Reich* laws, even under the leadership of Walter Simons, who, as president of the court, was a vocal advocate of widening its authority. As noted, it explicitly ruled only one *Reich* statute unconstitutional, and this involved a law of little consequence. Moreover, as Schmitt pointed out, the Federal High Court refused to evaluate the constitutionality of statutes and regulations according to their conformity to general principles of law, as the Supreme Court does on occasion (HV 12–22, esp. 16–19).

It is significant, Schmitt argued, that the clearest elaboration of the Federal High Court's position on its authority of judicial review was a case in which it did not strike down the statute in question: specifically, the famous decision of November 4th, 1925, concerning the constitutionality of a *Reich* law for the revaluation of debts (HV 16–19). According to the Federal High Court, judges were strictly bound to the law, which was understood to mean both constitutional and ordinary law. In cases of clear conflict between the two, judges must refuse to enforce the statute, since constitutional provisions have a higher legal status. However, if a statute is passed according to the procedures necessary for a constitutional amendment, there is no longer a conflict, and it has the force of law. A constitutional amendment was not necessary in this case, reasoned the Federal High Court, because there was no conflict between any constitutional provision and the statute in question (111 *RGZ* 320; Friedrich 1928, 196–97).[29]

Schmitt did not object to this limited understanding of judicial review, since, in his view, it did not violate the traditional understanding of the judicial function based on the notion of the "subsumption" of a set of facts under a particular norm. In cases of an obvious conflict between a constitutional provision and a statute (HV 50 and 52–53),[30] the courts served a useful function by not enforcing the statute. By serving as guardians of "part" of the Constitution, courts could contribute to ensuring that the Constitution was "respected" (HV 21).

The problem, in Schmitt's view, was that the decisive challenges to the Republic involved the use of existing institutions to further political aims inimical to the basic principles of the Republic, such as the establishment of a communist or a fascist dictatorship through constitutional amendments. German courts were unable to respond to such legal challenges to the Republic, because doing so would require judges to interpret, rather than merely apply the law, and this would violate the Continental stricture against judge-made law. Moreover, due to the relative institutional weakness of courts generally, it was unlikely that even a court legitimately empowered to interpret the law in this way, such as the U.S. Supreme Court, could decisively resolve this type of dispute. German courts, however, were especially disadvantaged in this regard, since the fragmented character of the German court system diluted the potential impact of such a judgment, even if a German court were bold enough to render it. Though courts could serve as guardians of part of the Constitution, Schmitt concluded, one must look elsewhere for a guardian of the Constitution generally (HV 18–22).

II.

When the issue is defined as whether courts can effectively defend the system from efforts to transform it from the inside, Schmitt's argument is quite powerful. American courts have proven incapable of preventing unconstitutional use of established institutions and legal mechanism in times of crisis. American courts also cannot invalidate a properly enacted Constitutional amendment, though, through interpretation, they might alter the scope and substance of some of its provisions, especially if they conflict with other constitutional norms. Leaving aside, for now, Schmitt's overly narrow reading of the traditional German understanding of adjudication, one must concede that his incisive analysis of the comparative institutional disadvantage of German courts, stemming from the structure of the judiciary, demonstrates that it was particularly unrealistic to expect eleventh-hour heroics from German judges.

This begs the question, of course: Why measure courts, or any institution for that matter, against such high standards? Perhaps one should give up the quixotic quest for a single guardian of the Constitution. It might be better to focus, as Hermann Heller insists, on the system as a whole fulfilling this role.[31] The next chapter works internally to Schmitt's argument to offer an understanding of the role of the judiciary that better serves constitutional democracy in this sense. But, first, it is necessary to consider a major deficiency in Schmitt's understanding of the changing nature of legal politics in the Weimar period.

European courts have traditionally been quite deferential to political authorities. This traditional passivity changed markedly once many states established special constitutional courts in the postwar era. Now that constitutional courts play a prominent role in the politics of many European democracies (Shapiro and Stone 1994, 397–561; also Tate and Vallinder 1995), there is considerable scholarly interest in the political implications of the institutional design and jurisdictional rules of these courts (e.g. Kommers 1976; Landfried 1984; and Stone 1992). With the acceptance of courts as policy makers comes the recognition that constitutional principle is defined not by the political branches or courts acting alone, but rather through a dynamically interactive process involving both political branches and courts (Stone 1994).

Schmitt was a precursor of this scholarly interest in the political role of courts. In *Guardian of the Constitution*, he argued that features of the Weimar Constitution, such as its extensive catalogue of basic rights, along with changing understandings of the role of courts in government and the expansion of the specialized system of courts, encouraged the use of courts for political purposes (HV 60–70). Before the so-called Road to Karlsruhe was built, Schmitt spoke in a now familiar scholarly vernacular, arguing that individuals, groups, and even governmental organs may use court challenges as a means of obtaining through the judiciary what they failed to gain via the political process. Schmitt pointed out, for example, that even the *Reich* government itself was not above seeking to use the State High Court to circumvent its own policies (HV 59).

In *Guardian of the Constitution*, therefore, Schmitt continued the trend toward institutional analysis begun in earnest in *Constitutional Theory*. A consistent criticism of Schmitt has been his tendency to compare ideal standards with actual conditions, in order to discredit moderate normative or institutional alternatives. While this tendency is evident throughout Schmitt's Weimar era works, his use of this tactic became more sophisticated over time. In his treatment of the role of courts in Weimar democracy in *Guardian of the Constitution*, Schmitt displayed extraordinary insightfulness regarding the institutional basis of constitutional politics. The problem is that Schmitt extrapolated from trends in scholarship about the role of courts in democratic government (HV 67–70) to issue a warning about the possibly negative consequences of a "politicization of the judiciary" (HV 22).[32]

These speculations would not be troubling, if they represented one part of a larger argument. Schmitt needs to show the reader how one gets from there to here. The expansion of the Catalogue of Rights, along with uncertainty about the legal status of these rights, can be seen as an incentive to individuals and groups to use court challenges to circumvent the political process. Seeing the Constitution as a contract, to which they are parties, individuals and groups may challenge state action, claiming they are entitled to goods and services or perhaps a share in political authority. Such groups might also challenge positive state action, claiming it violates their well-earned rights or constitutional liberties. In this way, intense pluralistic competition is not eliminated or ameliorated so much as displaced into the court system (HV 62–70 and 102–103).

Schmitt pointed out, however, that the State High Court did not take the bait. For example, it granted political parties standing to sue, but only in regard to narrowly defined issues concerning the conduct of elections. Moreover, access to the Court was only granted to those parties whose support in prior elections suggested they would gain representation in Parliament in the disputed contest (HV 84–85). In this way, the State High Court effectively resisted the effort to transform it into an "instrument of state pluralism" (HV 69).

The steadfastness of the State High Court begs the question of why one should be so concerned. Parties to many cases before the Federal High Court, Schmitt pointed out, were clearly party coalitions from different levels and branches of government (HV 64–66). Pluralist forces were banging at the gates, clammering to get in and foul up this arena as well. Though the tower guards wavered from time to time, they never succumbed to the temptation to grant entry to the temple. So why all the fuss?

That more is needed for Schmitt to make his case is illustrated well by revisiting Max Weber's ideal-typical method. We have seen that though ideal types are one-sided exaggerations of actual conditions, they are useful heuristic devices in that they enable one to develop and test hypotheses about empirical reality (Weber 1949, 63–112). J.W.F. Allison rightly points out that in the case of institutional borrowing, one can develop ideal-typical understandings of the conditions under which one can expect particular institutional arrangements to work or not. One can then examine empirical cases to determine whether or to what extent the postulated conditions seem to account for the development, success, or failure of particular institutional forms (Allison 1996, 27–33).

The potential usefulness of this approach is illustrated by the controversy over rights provisions in the constitutions of the new democracies in Central and Eastern Europe. A recurring point of controversy is the question: Should the newly democratic states recognize only traditional political and civil liberties, such as guarantees against arbitrary arrest and detention, or should they also recognize economic and social rights like those to free health care or adequate housing? This debate revolves not merely around philosophical questions of the appropriate role of law in regulating the relation between the state and individuals.[33] It also involves arguments about the likely practical impact of different legal protections. Some argue, for example, that recognition of economic and social rights may not be illegitimate per se. However, attempts to enforce such rights might have negative practical consequences, such as placing demands on governments that they are unable to fulfil, which, in turn, might call into question the very legitimacy of the constitutional system. This is a particularly important concern in newly democratic countries, the argument goes. Because such countries lack a firmly established democratic tradition, they have very little margin for error in the early stages of democratic consolidation. For the sake of the long-term effectiveness of democratic government, it is better for states not to recognize economic and social rights, leaving provision of such services to the political process over time (e.g. Sunstein 1992, 18–21 and 1993, 35–38).

Guarding against the deleterious consequences of this sort of judicialization of politics is an important goal. But merely the presence or absence of particular types of constitutional provisions is not alone sufficient grounds for its development. The particular institutional configuration, either singly or in combination with other factors, such as prevailing political constellations or aspects of legal culture, might produce unexpected forms of constitutional politics (e.g. Seitzer 1999). The model-building focus of Weber's ideal-typical method (Kalberg 1994, 12) is an especially useful means of combating a tendency toward what Wojciech Sokolewicz terms "constitutional nominalism," or the confusion of terminology with actual conditions (Sokolewicz 1995, 269). This is because the background assumptions of a typical normative argument should lend themselves readily to construction of a model, which then can be tested. By postulating the relationship of factors that can be expected to bring about such a judicialization of politics, theorists would render their claims falsifiable through controlled comparison with other systems, both past and present (Burke 1992, 28–33).

Allison rightly senses the potential usefulness of Weber's ideal-typical approach in debates over institutional borrowing. But Weber's understanding of the comparative method has wider applications. Any proposed changes in legal practices or institutional structures and procedures are based upon assumptions about the nature of these practices, structures, and procedures as well as about the expected impact of proposed changes. Rendering these assumptions explicit in a formal model would introduce an experimental element into normative debate about institutions. As thought experiments postulating expected relationships among possible causal factors, ideal-typical models enable one to develop and test hypotheses about possible causal factors in specific contexts (Kalberg 1994, 50–78 and 92–142).

Schmitt does not explicitly formulate such a model, let alone test it in an empirically rigorous way. Nonetheless, the very effort to construct a testable model provides a sort of threshold requirement for normative arguments about institutions and facilitates the critical review of their claims. In this spirit, I will distill a model from Schmitt's comparative analysis of the institutional limitations of courts by identifying the basic limitations of courts and formulating them conceptually. There are the institutional limitations of courts generally, such as post hoc decisionmaking and dependence on prevailing political and social power constellations for the effectiveness of their judgments. There are also conditions pertaining to German courts in particular, such as fragmented structure, jurisdictional overlap and uncertainty, and a narrow understanding of legal sources. From Schmitt's argument, one could postulate that courts could serve effectively as guardians of the Constitution in Schmitt's sense if the following conditions are met: courts have the power to act preemptively, have their own enforcement powers, and have a centralized hierarchical structure; also, courts are not limited to enforcing narrowly defined constitutional provisions; finally, courts are expected by dominant political and social groups to intervene in politics to preserve the constitutional framework.

Quite obviously, the Weimar judiciary did not fulfill these conditions, so Schmitt was quite right to stress that they could not serve as guardians of the Constitution in his sense. But the point of a carefully designed and executed comparative-historical study is to examine critically one's presuppositions. Schmitt developed a conceptually rich comparative-historical argument about the institutional limitations of courts, but he did not ask the further question of whether the comparative history of the institutional means of ensuring the basic integrity of the constitutional system called into question his implicit model of the role of courts in the Weimar constitutional system. In other words, for Schmitt to make his case he has not merely to set out conditions under which foreign models might operate successfully. It is also necessary for him to show how the politicization of the judiciary is possible, given the manifest institutional obstacles he outlines. Contrast Weimar with the Federal Republic in this regard.

A number of legal and institutional changes in the post–World War II era facilitate what contemporary social scientists term the "judicialization of politics." In addition to establishing a Constitutional Court explicitly empowered to adjudicate claims of individual rights, the German Basic Law also provides for easy access to the Constitutional Court. When joined with the continued cumbersomeness of the legislative process at the federal level and the relative fragmentation of the party system, it is not surprising that the Federal Constitutional Court is a key player in German politics. Those unable to achieve their political and social aims through the political process are encouraged to seek a favorable Constitutional Court judgment (Kommers 1976 and Landfried 1984).

Under the inchoate system of public law in the Weimar Republic, it was not clear whether or to what extent the extensive rights provisions established judicially enforceable legal claims. And, if so, it was uncertain how or to what extent these rights could be enforced institutionally. This lack of clarity regarding the sources of law and legal redress certainly could encourage efforts to utilize the courts for political purposes. The losing party in a political struggle, or one that anticipated losing, might have little to lose and much to gain in making recourse to the courts. Perhaps the still undefined system of constitutional protections and legal redress could be turned to their favor. As Schmitt pointed out, the State High Court especially and, to a much lesser degree, the Federal High Court were not so eager to lend a helping hand. But when one faces certain defeat, why not throw the dice again, particularly since the courts have little power to do direct harm without the cooperation of political authorities.

This suggests that despite the myriad changes stemming from the Weimar Constitution and ordinary law, Schmitt's own critique of the institutional posture and capacity of German courts compel him to make two additional arguments if his warning against a politicalization of the judiciary were not to ring hollow. The first had to do with the pluralist capture of the court system in practical terms. Schmitt noted that many of the cases before the State High Court were propelled by party coalitions controlling particular levels or branches of government. In many of these cases, there was an important federalism question involved. Moreover, the typical dispute was over the distribution of funds or of the costs of legally mandated governmental services. In this sense, these cases conformed to the model he outlined earlier where it was appropriate for the State High Court to become involved and when the civil law model had some applicability, because the dispute had an important contractual element (HV 64–66).

Extrapolating beyond these cases was more difficult. The State High Court had refused to consider a number of cases which are not easily reducible to a federalist question. The Court had also refused to serve as a subsidiary means of dispute resolution, stepping into the breach in the absence of another suitable forum. This suggests that the system, as it was then constituted, offered little incentive to utilize courts for political purposes. Schmitt needed to offer a model of judicial politics, rooted in the concrete institutional structure of the Weimar Republic, which could demonstrate how the court system as constituted could realistically become a pluralist battleground. Schmitt could argue, for example, that given their subordinate political position, courts are generally the less-preferred option of those seeking to utilize the system for their own ends. Under certain conditions, however, courts could become a much more attractive political option. The normal political process must not offer potential means for advancement of political aims. Groups must also have access to courts, with access meaning not merely that parties are granted standing before courts. It is also essential that potential claimants have the necessary resources to press their case,[34] even though they might not ultimately receive the relief they seek

(McCann 1994, esp. 57–58). As these conditions are filled over time, the unsuitability of courts for pluralist rent-seeking is reduced, and one can expect greater reliance on courts for this purpose.

With this model, Schmitt might have turned to the question of the politicization of the judiciary during the final years of the Republic. He might have conceded that the sort of manipulation of the judiciary he feared had not been such a problem until then. However, one might expect it to become more of a problem in the coming years. At the time *Guardian of the Constitution* was written, for example, the Republic had entered upon its final crisis period, when parliamentary government was replaced by rule through presidential decree. Schmitt might have argued that the sort of pluralist end-runs through the court system he feared were not as tangible a possibility before, because groups could still seek to control the normal political process to their advantage, making courts, with their restricted control over resources and limited power to provide remedies, a much less attractive option. With the effective end of parliamentary government, pluralist groups had little choice but to appeal to courts. Moreover, with the increased reliance on presidential decrees, there might have been greater occasion for court challenges, since presidential decrees violated statutory and constitutional rights to an ever greater degree in the final phase of the Republic. The legitimacy of court review of the legality of ordinances, while not unquestioned in all cases, particularly those involving emergency decrees, certainly was on more solid ground than judicial improvisations in terms of the review of the substantive constitutionality of national laws (Mattern 1928, 562–613, esp. 570–590). Given the acute hardships visited upon different groups, one might expect courts to make use of their decree powers to moderate these conditions.

One can take issue with this argument in a number of ways. The biggest problem for Schmitt was the final claim. The fact that the allegedly passive German judges were willing to circumvent the will of Parliament through expansive readings of general clauses was partly explicable on the basis of Schmitt's argument. As civil servants, Schmitt might have pointed out, German judges were inclined to defer to the state, not society as represented in Parliament. But Schmitt's reading of the restrictive outlook and methods of the German courts cut against the key component of this proposed model. Courts generally, but German courts in particular, were unlikely to counter executive action intended to preserve the system as a whole during times of crisis. So it was unlikely they would be moved by conventional human sympathies to circumvent executive decrees in the final phase of the Republic. To give his warnings against a possible politicization of the judiciary a claim to practical import, he needed to offer some explanation as to why courts might be inclined to forgo their traditional deference to the state, particularly in a time of crisis.

It is difficult to see how Schmitt could have made such an argument on the basis of his comparative history of courts. By recasting his comparative inquiry, he might still have argued that increased reliance on courts was a real possibility, despite the unlikelihood of immediate tangible benefit. Schmitt discussed with considerable acumen some of the key constitutional conflicts in American history for purposes of illustrating the institutional limitations of courts generally. His concern with the extent to which courts were able to counter challenges to the existing political and social order was overly narrow. It tended to obscure the events leading up to and following the dramatic confrontations and to discount possible motivations that did not involve tangible political benefits. Both of these factors were potentially very important in explaining any increased willingness to pursue court challenges and in identifying the consequences of recourse to courts over time. Litigants may not have been concerned to achieve tangible benefits from a court challenge. The attention generated by court cases, even certain losers, might have been the goal, because it encouraged more successful political action, just as unenforceable court judgments might have served symbolic political purposes (e.g. McCann 1994, esp. 57–58). This concern with symbolic politics and potential political mobilization was particularly important in the era of mass democracy, Schmitt might have argued. And the development of well-organized and funded political organizations facilitated the pursuit of such challenges. So increased recourse to courts could have been expected, even if German judges retained a steely reserve.

By adopting a more nuanced model of legal politics, Schmitt could have provided his argument with a more substantial claim to tangible relevance, even though he failed to show that the anticipated politicization of the judiciary would significantly reduce the state's capacity for governability in the short-term. Adapting a more finely textured model of legal politics, however, cuts against Schmitt's argument in another important sense. By broadening the time horizon, such a model shows that even an institutionally disadvantaged judiciary, such as that in Weimar, can make a far more substantial contribution to constitutional democracy than Schmitt conceded. Outlining such a role for the judiciary is the task of the final chapter.

NOTES

1. The President of the Federal High Court, Walter Simons, was a leading proponent of more active court involvement in German constitutional politics.

Hans Kelsen's expectations were not as high for the world's first constitutional court, founded in Austria in the interwar period. Nonetheless, he is a principle target of Schmitt's critique. Simons' position is discussed below, whereas Kelsen's exchange with Schmitt is considered in the next chapter. On the debate over judicial review generally, see Wendeberg (1984) and Caldwell (1997, 145–170).

2. An early extended treatment of the importance of institutional borrowing in political development was Thorstein Veblen's examination of Imperial Germany ([1915] 1954). Reinhard Bendix offers an excellent comparative study relating development issues to newly independent nations in the 1960s ([1964] 1977).

3. Schmitt's concern with foreign institutional models calls to mind the comparative studies of some American progressives (e.g. Wilson 1973). However, Schmitt's use of conceptually driven problem-oriented histories to examine the development and operation of institutions and systems points forward to more contemporary developmental studies. For an analysis of the differences between traditional institutionalism and political development studies, see Skowronek and Orren (1995).

4. On the programmatic character of the French *Declaration of the Rights of Man and Citizen*, see Wright (1994, 199–233).

5. In fact, under Napoleon, the French were subject to authority more absolute than that of Louis XIV (Godochet 1989, 45–76, esp. 57–58).

6. This discussion assumes Prussia as the modal case in terms of legal and political development, obscuring important regional and local differences. Prussia, for example, followed the Napoleonic model of social reform without granting rights of political participation. The South German *Länder* granted limited rights of political participation, and yet they did not go as far as Prussia in eliminating the vestiges of feudalism (Huber 1957, 1: 314–386). There were also major differences in terms of achieving uniformity of law, a major goal of reformers throughout Germany (Grimm 1986, 61–76), and many *Länder* differed significantly from Prussia in terms of types of legal remedies and courts established to enforce them (e.g. Henne 1995). Finally, regional differences persisted in the *Reich* era. In fact, the *Reich* itself was a composite state, constituted of myriad compromises, including those with *Länder* governments, preserving regional differences. On the importance of regional variation in understanding the politics of the *Reich*, see Retallack (1996, 221–256) and Herrigel (1996). Nonetheless, the basic Prussian pattern of civil law changes, without institution of full democratic reform, came to redefine Germany in the *Reich* period, even though there is substantial disagreement over the political and social implications of this combination. The works on this topic defy citation. Good overviews of the debate over the importance of the *Reich* for German political development are offered by Eley (1992), Retallack (1992), and Evans (1997, 12–22). Therefore, though taking Prussian developments as the modal case distorts overall developments somewhat, it is not unjustified in terms of the general features of the *Reich* system, which are of such importance to Schmitt's argument.

7. This claim emerges in works throughout the Weimar period, but it is especially associated with the polemical work, *The Crisis of Parliamentary Democracy* (CPD) (1988).

8. For a particularly clear elaboration of this familiar lament of Schmitt's, see *Hugo Preuß: Sein Staatsbegriff und seine Stellung in der deutschen Staatslehre* (HP) (1930, esp. 12–16). For Weber's influential argument regarding Bismarck and the German bourgeoisie, see Weber ([1918] 1978).

9. Maus (1986, 11–82) rejects the view that the *Rechtsstaat* concept only relatively recently included a necessary connection between *Recht* and *Gesetz*. It was only in the course of the 19th century that the view developed that law need not have a democratic foundation. The classic treatment of the political, social, and philosophical roots of this notion is Krieger (1957). Hesse (1962, 71–95) provides a good discussion of the more directly legal aspects of the concept.

10. Bismarck's *Reich* Constitution did not contain a Declaration or Bill of Rights, for example, but most *Länder* constitutions, even the Prussian Constitution of 1850, contained individual rights guarantees. Moreover, most *Länder* had passed the enabling legislation necessary to ensure that these provisions were enforceable in courts. Thus, civil rights, long ensured through private law, gained explicit public law status, but on the individual *Länder* level. In this limited sense, the *Reich* resembled the United States before the addition of the Bill of Rights to the Constitution (Luebbe-Wolff, 1990, 353–372).

11. The Federal High Court's jurisdiction was mostly appellate. It could review *Länder* laws to ensure their compatibility with those of the *Reich*, which were supreme in the limited area of federal legislative competence. It could also examine whether *Reich* laws were passed according to proper procedures, but it could not review their substantive constitutionality. On the history and institutional features of the Federal High Court prior to Weimar, see Müller (1997). The personnel and institutional features of the Federal High Court in the Weimar period are covered extensively in Lobe (1929).

12. As Schmitt points out, there were important exceptions to this general right of access (HV 50– 51).On the important place of the *Conseil d'Etat* in the French state and on the development of its adjudicatory procedures, respectively, see Allison (1996, 138–152 and 209–216).

13. On the importance of the transformation of the nature of political competition for reform efforts through Parliament during the *Reich* period, see Blackbourn and Eley (1984, 260–285).

14. Prussian dominance was ensured, because it had an effective veto over constitutional changes. Moreover, the Prussian king, the German Kaiser, not only appointed the Chancellor who presided over the *Bundesrat*, he also commanded the army in times of war or internal disorder. For an excellent summary of the complex structure of the *Reich* constitutional system, see Craig (1978, 38–60).

15. Even Max Weber, who was highly critical of Prussian dominance during the *Reich* period and preferred an unitary system, argued that adoption of a federal structure was unavoidable in Germany and thus suggested reviving the Fed-

eral Chamber (*Bundesrat*) in some form, making it the center of gravity of a liberal-democratic Germany ([1918] 1988, 448–483).

16. There is often considerable squawking when a federal court decision strikes down a state court decision or state law. Generally, however, the ten-mile-freeway rule applies in regard to courts and the federal system to a greater degree than courts and the Congress. In other words, there is greater agreement on the need for judicial supervision of the federal-state relationship, even though those affected by a particular ruling might for a time think otherwise. As James Thayer points out, federal court review of the compatibility of state action with the federal Constitution is on much firmer ground than that of the actions of coordinate branches of the federal government, because the Supremacy Clause of the Constitution creates an hierarchical relationship between federal and state laws in some instances ([1908] 1972, 35–36). On the tumultuous beginnings of federal court supervision of state-federal relations, see McCloskey ([1960] 1994, 39–52). Choper (1980) provides an argument against close court supervision of the state-federal relationship that is not based on opposition to particular doctrines of the Supreme Court, such as prohibition of racially segregated education.

17. Mauersberg (1991) examines Preuß' role in the founding of the Weimar Constitution.

18. In *Legalität und Legitimität* ([1932] 1988), Schmitt narrows the definition of a jurisdiction state considerably: judges themselves determine legal norms independently of non-judicial, political authorities ([1932] 1988, 12). The discussion of jurisdiction states in the next two chapters is based on the more broadly defined concept presented in *Guardian of the Constitution*.

19. On the complex relationship to English common law early in the Republic, see Nelson (1975) and Cook (1981).

20. For an in-depth study of the role of law in the American Revolution and the political factors shaping the American embrace of natural law as an alternative to the common law, see Clark (1994, 31–45 and 352–391).

21. In important respects, Schmitt's position mirrors that of James Bradley Thayer, who argues that the emergence of the wide-ranging authority of judicial review exercised by the Supreme Court is a "natural," though by no means "necessary" development ([1908] 1972).

22. For an excellent history of legal and political efforts to settle the slavery question, see Fehrenbacher (1978, 1–208). On the way in which these events reflected larger debates over the character of the American Revolution and polity, see Jaffa (1982).

23. For an overview of the shift from common law to statutory principles of social ordering, see Sunstein (1990, 12–31). Orren (1991) considers the political and social implications of the persistence of the common law system, while Skowronek (1982) offers an excellent treatment of the political conflicts surrounding the emergence of the administrative state.

24. The standard view of Brüning is of a well-meaning, in many respects capable, man, who seriously miscalculated in believing he could resolve the fiscal crisis

brought on by the Great Depression through an extra-parliamentary strategy (e.g. Craig 1978, 534–543). More disturbing is Brüning's concession that he considered significant Nazi gains in the subsequent elections a distinct possibility, which makes his dissolution order "difficult to understand" (542, n. 19). On top of that, Brüning admitted in his memoirs to secretly longing for the restoration of the Kaiser, which suggests that he may not have desired a parliamentary solution, even if it were possible. As reported by Schmitt (1987, 83). For a critical assessment of Brüning's tenure at the helm, see Mommsen (1991, 119–140). Patch (1998) offers a more sympathetic recent reassessment of Brüning.

25. Peukert ([1987] 1991, 207–246) offers an excellent analysis of how poor material conditions converged with cultural dissatisfaction to seriously limit the options of supporters of the Republic. Maier's account of postwar political stabilization also stresses resource limitations. See especially his treatment of the reparations issue ([1975] 1988, 233–304). On the considerable problems of forging a workable coalition containing both the Social Democrats and the German People's Party, see Eyck (1963, II: 155–202) and Craig 1978, 498–533. For a revisionist view on the political options facing the Social Democrats, see Berman (1998).

26. For Simons' version of the dispute with *Reichspräsident* Hindenburg and the role he envisioned for the Federal High Court, see Simons (1929, 762–779).

27. In his attempt to sort out and classify the myriad rights provisions according to their relative constitutional weight, Schmitt anticipated certain key concepts of current German constitutional theory and practice, most notably that of "the guarantee of the essential content of a right" (*Wesensgehaltgarantie*) as well as that of "institutional guarantees." Cf. Stolleis (1972) and Lietzmann (1988, 107–118) on the vexed question of Schmitt's influence on contemporary German constitutional theory.

28. Even in the middle period of the Republic from 1925–1929, when order had been restored, the *Reichstag* was barely able to pass important pieces of legislation. On the governability problems of the Republic, see Maier ([1975] 1988, 483–515).

29. On the implications of the case for German legal culture, see Nörr (1996) and Caldwell (1997, 153–155).

30. Schmitt's position here mirrors that of James Bradley Thayer, who argued that the American Supreme Court should review the actions of coordinate branches of government, such as Congress, only "when those who have the right to make laws have not merely made a mistake, but have made a very clear one" ([1908] 1972, 16–22, esp. 17). Also, like Thayer, Schmitt warns against applying private law understandings of judging in constitutional cases, because constitutions are not comparable to private contracts in important respects (HV 67) (Thayer [1908] 1972, 1–7).

31. Hermann Heller's concept of the state as organization (1983, 259–269) seems in accord with the more institutionally broadbased understanding of constitutional politics defended here. I do not take up Heller's suggestion because it is overly vague on the important question of how the state would function institu-

tionally. On the concept's relevance for German legal theory, see Caldwell (1997, 131–133).

32. There are two important differences between Schmitt's analysis of German judicial politics and the above-noted contemporary social science treatments. Most contemporary social science treatments do not take a normative position on the question of courts in politics (e.g. Stone 1992, 1994, and 1999), as does Schmitt. However, there are some exceptions. For contemporary works stressing the possible negative consequences of this trend for democratic politics, see Landfried (1984, 157–178) and Seitzer (1999, 42–51). The second difference concerns the extent to which court judgments are thought to shape policymaking in the political branches. Contemporary social science treatments stress the significant influence of courts on policymaking, with legislative deliberations actually coming to reflect the legal discourse of courts (e.g. Stone 1999, 8–41). Schmitt, by contrast, argues that "a juridification of politics" in this sense will not occur. Rather, the judiciary will merely become another pluralist battleground, but without effectively resolving any of the contentious issues brought before courts (HV 22).

33. Schwartz (1992, 25–28) provides a cultural argument for inclusion of social and economic rights.

34. The 1998 British *Human Rights Act* (*HRA*), for example, incorporated the *European Convention for the Protection of Human Rights and Fundamental Freedoms (ECHR)* directly into domestic law. If litigants' claims are deemed as not having a reasonable chance of success, they might not receive aid to press their claims before the European Court of Human Rights in Strasbourg. Therefore, the degree of judicialization stemming from the *HRA* depends not exclusively on the merits of particular cases or the receptiveness of European institutions to legal challenges to domestic law. On potential glitches in the protection of European human rights law under the HRA, see Wadham and Mountfield (1999, 47–49). Epp (1998) considers the importance of financial and institutional support for the successful legal mobilization in a number of common law countries. Unfortunately, no comparable study has been carried out for the Weimar period.

Chapter 4

Rethinking the Role of Courts: Constitutional Democracy as Institutional Dialogue

One of the most striking features of Schmitt's late Weimar constitutional writings is the combination of an emphatic insistence on a strictly defined separation of powers with astute observations about the disjunctions between the theory and practice of Weimar constitutionalism (Sontheimer [1962] 1978, 80–81). Parliament, according to Schmitt, has the authority to pass general laws introducing permanent changes in politics and society. The President is only permitted to issue emergency decrees that are addressed to a specific concern and valid only for a limited period. Parliament's preeminent normative position is also reflected in its authority to nullify presidential decrees. Yet, when the dust settles, the President almost always ends up on top. The basic problem is that Parliament is often incapable of acting at all, let alone forcefully and with dispatch. And, even when Parliament is willing and able to rescind presidential decrees, the President can dissolve Parliament and institute the decrees anyway. After the subsequent elections, Parliament can respond again. But, by that time, presidential action might be a *fait accompli*, or the new Parliament may not be inclined to respond at all. So, in practice, presidential decree powers are almost unlimited, due to the difficulty in achieving the necessary majorities, particularly late in the Republic.[1]

Regardless of one's position on the question of presidential government, one thing is clear: Schmitt leaves courts almost entirely out of account in this clash of the Titans. German courts were simply not much use during the sort of state crisis the Weimar Republic faced, according to Schmitt, first, because the court system was quite fragmented, but also because German courts were especially docile politically. In a word, one should not count on German courts in a pinch. For they were either fighting among themselves about how to respond, or cowering in the corner, hoping to escape notice.

Schmitt exaggerated on both counts. The ordinary courts' expansive readings of general clauses suggest that the traditional sources of the law were not an insurmountable obstacle to a larger judicial role, and the fact that the German judiciary was quite neighborly when it came to helping the state crack down on leftist agitators suggests that the courts were not strictly apolitical (Peukert ([1987] 1991, 222–225 and Unger 1976, 216–220). Even the fragmented character of the system did not deprive the judiciary of opportunities to assume a larger role. The State High Court (*Staatsgerichtshof*), for example, ruled on the legality of the Papen government's use of presidential decree powers to substitute its authority for the Social Democratic-led caretaker government in Prussia. Displaying the sort of risk-aversion often evident among the institutionally more heavily armed American judiciary, the court split the difference between the two parties in a way that gave the government essentially what it demanded. That the State High Court did not completely cave in to the government's position, however, suggests that perhaps it, too, might one day have been bold enough to challenge the government in such cases, as does the U.S. Supreme Court on occasion.[2]

This chapter concludes my critique of Schmitt by extending the comparative analysis of courts presented in the previous one. Schmitt's understanding of state types provides a methodologically sophisticated conceptual framework for considering the political role of different institutions (I), and yet his failure to appreciate the complex linkages among the subsumption concept, the fragmented court system, and the composite state in the *Kaiserreich* unnecessarily precludes the German court system from a larger role in responding to the Weimar state crisis (II). The concept of constitutional democracy as institutional dialogue elaborated here shifts the focus of the debate over judicial review away from the doctrinal elements of judicial decision-making. The important consideration, rather, is whether judicial review enhances the system's capacity for self-correction (III).

I.

Schmitt's rejection of a larger judicial role in the Weimar Republic was tightly bound up with his understanding of state forms.[3] Schmitt claimed that one can categorize states according to the institutional center of their activity. The state in the medieval period, the early *Ständestaat*, was a "jurisdiction state" (*Jurisdiktionsstaat*), in that it was primarily concerned with defining and enforcing jurisdictional boundaries among rival centers of power, whereas the absolutist state was a "governmental state" (*Regierungsstaat*) because its legitimacy was based on its capacity to establish circumstances under which norms could be valid (HV 74–76).[4] This is not to say that other branches of government were not operative. "Each state," Schmitt emphasized, is a "mixture of state forms" (HV 76). The assemblies in the early *Ständestaat*, for example, were concerned mostly with maintaining and/or renegotiating the rights and privileges of the monarch and nobility. In this sense, they functioned more as courts which adjudicated disputes over private law rights than as modern legislative assemblies formulating laws applicable to society generally.[5] Schmitt emphasized that though these concepts do not alone accurately portray complex reality, they provide a useful shorthand way of categorizing and comparing state forms, as well as of tracking changes in state forms over time. Even "Bismarck's powerful government was always on the defensive in its relations with the Federal Parliament" (1930, 8 [HP]), he wrote. The relative power of the Federal Parliament increased in the *Wilhelmine* period, as parties supporting the government lost ground to their opponents, particularly the Social Democrats.[6] Therefore, the *Reich* system remained a hybrid state form throughout the period.[7] In fact, according to Ernst Rudolf Huber, the complex mixture of traditional Prussian authoritarianism with modern democratic institutions makes it difficult to categorize the *Kaiserreich* as a state type (Huber 1963, 3: 785–1074).[8]

Comparisons such as these can play an important role in legal and political theory. For normative argument to have a significant claim to practical efficacy, it is necessary to identify and respond to disjunctions between theory and practice. It is an important question as to what extent a proposed institutional solution has a legitimate normative basis in the text of a constitution or in the prevailing understandings of constitutional legitimacy. But one must also ask whether reigning practice accords with these normative sources. And, one must determine whether, or to what extent, the institutional relations envisioned by the constitutional text, or those actually taking place on the ground, fulfill the larger goals of the polity, whatever they may be and however they are defined.

That conceptual frameworks like Schmitt's can aid in this task is illustrated by the issue of state form in the United States. Schmitt's designation of the United States as a jurisdiction state is an apt description of the American state in the first half of the 19th century. Though the Supreme Court had not yet taken up the central role in constitutional politics that it occupies today, the federal court system played an important political role during this period by providing a degree of policy leadership in the decentralized polity.[9] More important for purposes of evaluating Schmitt's conceptual framework is the fact that the dominant institution on the national level, the U.S. Congress, devoted much of its activity to the resolution of constitutional questions, such as whether it was permissible for the federal government to undertake internal improvements like road construction.[10] The United States in this period could be classified as a jurisdiction state insofar as the center of state activity was the resolution of conflicts over the normative legitimacy of particular governmental actions, even though, at the explicit level, the legislative branch was the primary institutional mechanism for resolving these disputes.

American political development in the 19th century also seems to confirm Schmitt's claim that during times of crisis, the true center of state activity emerges (HV 76). The original understanding of the federal government was that the President would be the executor of laws passed by Congress. With the outbreak of the Civil War, President Lincoln was compelled to take dramatic actions to save the Union, interventions which often violated the Constitution, particularly the Congress's constitutionally granted emergency powers.[11] Lincoln's willingness to use executive power independently of Congress seems to anticipate the sort of presidential leadership characteristic of the current American system, perhaps marking a shift from a jurisdiction to a governmental state form. If the outbreak of the Civil War itself cannot be seen as the failure of the jurisdiction state, Schmitt might argue, then, clearly, the failure of Congress to respond effectively to the crisis and the Supreme Court's inability to bring the President to heel in the midst of war does indicate that the traditional state form was no longer functioning. Only the President could respond effectively to the crisis, so, at least during the war, the United States was a governmental state.

The presidency attained greater prominence in the Civil War. But it is difficult to see Lincoln's dramatic actions in defense of the Union as a change in state form. The president's role as commander in chief of the armed forces gave Lincoln a degree of independence from Congress he would not have enjoyed in peacetime, as he himself was aware.[12] However, it is important to keep in mind that Lincoln's independence as chief executive did not signal so much a fundamental change in the nature of the American state as the fact that Congress was busy elsewhere. In this period, for example, Congress transformed the relationship of the people and the federal government through a number of programs, such as the Homestead Law, the Morill Land Grant College Law, the Railroad Act, and the National Bank. Moreover, one must not overestimate presidential discretion, even in the conduct of the war and the character of the postwar reconstruction, for, in many respects, Congress sought to go further than Lincoln in these areas.[13]

Congress remained in the driver's seat even during the Civil War, and, after the war, Congress reasserted its authority over all areas of policy. Congressional ascendancy continued for much of the 19th century. It was only with massive changes sparked by industrialization, the two World Wars, and the Great Depression that the office of the presidency attained its current prominence. The actions of President Lincoln during the Civil War, as with those of other relatively independent presidents like Andrew Jackson and Theodore Roosevelt, can be better characterized as opportunities for leadership seized by remarkable individuals than the emergence of the true center of state activity under times of stress or crisis.[14] Continuing with our driving analogy, one can say that, whereas in wartime, the president was permitted to take the wheel, in peacetime, the president was no longer even allowed to ride in the front seat.[15]

Congressional activity during the Civil War, however, might indicate the beginnings of a change in state form. Many of the bold legislative initiatives noted above, along with the slow movement away from the patronage system and toward the regulatory state at century's end, suggest a new understanding of the nature of law and government. The age of statutes had not yet dawned. For the better part of half a century, the Supreme Court would continue to defend common law categories by reading statutes quite narrowly. Nonetheless, there was increasing support for the idea of social experimentation through law, with the legislative branch as the primary institutional vehicle of these efforts. In this sense, one can see the emergence of what we today term the administrative state as a shift toward a lawgiving state.[16]

At the same time, it is necessary to qualify the notion of Congressional dominance of the system in this period. In the early 19th century, the office of the president was still rooted in the culture of deference of the early Republic, which meant that the office was not the object of partisan struggle. The reigning practice was to grant the position to the eldest, most prominent member of the elite, with Jefferson third in line after Washington and Adams. Under this patrician understanding of government, the president was an elder statesman, who ensured the overall security and integrity of the United States, while Congress, as the political focal point of the system, actually got its hands dirty with the business of governing. There was none too little chomping at the bit under this system. Jefferson, for example, had an agenda and wanted to lead. He was able to defer outwardly to Congress, because Congress was at his beck and call. Having an overwhelming partisan majority in Congress, he merely let his lieutenants know, behind the scenes, what he wanted, and they passed it (Skowronek 1993, 62–85).

Schmitt's typology of state forms provides a useful starting point for analyzing the theory and practice of politics. Certain features of different states suggest their inclusion in a particular category. One can test these categorizations against actual conditions over time. That after careful scrutiny, the initial classifications appear inappropriate is not necessarily a problem, for the purpose of the categories is to advance understanding of contexts that are complex and ever changing. If the subsequent investigation calls into question the explanatory power of the concepts, it is necessary to either discard or revise them (Allison 1996, 27–33).

Schmitt's record in this regard is ambiguous. In many respects, he utilizes his conceptual scheme effectively to chart complex changes in the nature of the German state. But at key points, he falls down on the job in that he does not call into question his application of these concepts and, more importantly, the usefulness of the framework itself. This is especially clear in regard to his claim that in emergencies the true center of state activity becomes apparent.

At such times, as Schmitt himself insists, the executive usually has an institutional advantage. This is because the executive can typically act with greater dispatch and effectiveness than branches of government which must reach decisions collectively or which cannot themselves enforce decisions. Given the institutional advantage of the executive, it is not surprising that, in an emergency, other branches of government would either defer to the executive or would seek to incorporate executive-like mechanisms into their modes of operation. Typically, Schmitt notes, jurisdiction states will adopt forms of summary justice, while a lawgiving state will pass enabling legislation establishing extraordinary governmental powers (HV 76).

Like the classification of state forms, Schmitt's claim regarding emergency situations and the center of state activity is also a useful heuristic device for analyzing actual situations with a view to determining to what extent they conform to the results that one would expect under the circumstances. One can ask, for example, whether jurisdiction states, in fact, respond to emergencies through some form of adjudication, whether carried out by ordinary courts or by extraordinary tribunals. The answer to this question might enable one to better understand state action in a particular context. That actual states do not conform to these one-sided concepts is not especially important. The types merely help one chart deviations from the postulated norm, which, in turn, might suggest avenues for further research.

Take, for example, Schmitt's early work, *Dictatorship* ([1921] 1989) (D), which is noteworthy for Schmitt's careful analysis of precise lines of authority in a number of different instances of the exercise of political power in times of emergency. Some of the incidents and developments examined are not surprising. Oliver Cromwell's protectorate, for example, as well as revolutionary and post-revolutionary France, both fall in the "usual suspects" category. This is also true of Wallenstein's execution of his commission during the Thirty Years War. Traditional histories tend to place such events in the context of long-term developments, such as 17th century England or Reformation Germany. Such narratives focus on the key players, decisive battles, high profile executions, and historic settlements.[17] Schmitt's account contains some high political drama as well. But he also inquires after the more mundane details of the exercise of political authority. This historical detail is useful for its own sake, if only to supplement traditional political and constitutional histories. However, Schmitt's purpose is not to tell it "as it really was," in the famous words of Ranke.[18] It is to determine the precise scope and limits of the authority of various actors in different contexts. Using the distinction between commissarial and sovereign dictatorship as a point of comparison, Schmitt classifies writings, incidents, and developments according to their degree of adherence or deviation from these concepts.[19]

In *Guardian of the Constitution*, Schmitt also uses conceptual frameworks to illuminate issues of contemporary concern, though institutional questions are more central to his analysis than in *Dictatorship*. On the other hand, *Guardian* does not achieve the level of conceptual clarity of the earlier work. In the former, specifically, Schmitt fails to clearly distinguish, at the conceptual level, between the institutional responses one would expect from different types of states. In institutional terms, all states are, at some level, governmental states, since they tend to utilize executive-like institutional mechanisms to respond to emergency situations (HV 76). A well-intentioned historian could put Schmitt's framework to good use despite this lack of conceptual sharpness, for she could revise or discard the categories as it became clear during subsequent research that other concepts might prove better for organizing and executing inquiry. Schmitt does not make this additional step. Schmitt reviews a range of institutional responses to emergency situations over time in different national and subnational contexts (HV 1–11); his claim regarding typical institutional responses to emergencies is clearly informed by this impressive comparative survey. Nonetheless, it was incumbent on Schmitt to continue his analysis by asking the central question of *Guardian of the Constitution*: Specifically, were there disjunctions between theory and practice that were relevant for addressing the constitutional crisis of the Weimar Republic? In other words, it is important to ask, as did Schmitt, what sort of institutional response different systems took to emergency situations and, to what extent, if at all, did these responses form discernible patterns. But far more important in terms of responding to the Weimar state crisis, are the further questions as to what extent these responses were successful and, if so, why. In terms of the constitutional text, a system might have utilized a particular institutional mechanism for responding to an emergency, and yet, in practice, some other institution, combination of institutions, or not immediately apparent practices might have been responsible for the success or failure of the system. Careful analysis of these disjunctions might have suggested how to best respond to the Weimar state crisis. The issue of the role of courts in German constitutional politics illustrates the consequences this methodological deficiency has for his overall argument.

II.

While Schmitt's conceptual approach in *Guardian* could prove useful in identifying and responding to disjunctions in the theory and practice of constitutional democracy, one very such disjunction lies at the heart of *Guardian*. Schmitt rejected a larger judicial role in the Weimar constitutional system, partly because it would have violated what he considered to be the traditional German understanding of jurisprudence as the subsumption of a particular set of facts under an explicit legal rule. As Schmitt's own prior work suggests, however, such an understanding of adjudication does not square with legal practice, which requires considerable judicial discretion even in clear cases. In his 1912 dissertation, *Statute and Judgment* (*Gesetz und Urteil*) (GU), Schmitt argues that legal judgments involve an element of individual decision, a creative act, which is not justifiable in objective terms. What matters is not that a decision can be justified on objective grounds, but rather that it exists and that it provides reasons considered valid by an ideal legal community (GU).

By refusing to ground legal decision-making in either legal or nonlegal sources, Schmitt "pushed the Free Law movement's critique of legal reasoning to the limit," according to Peter Caldwell (1997, 52–53).[20] Then, less than twenty years later, Schmitt considered the Free Law Movement's critique of traditional German adjudication as one of the central constitutional questions of his day precisely because it stressed the unavoidably personal element in adjudication (HV 19). Before turning to Schmitt's critical posture toward the Free Law Movement, it is necessary to examine another rather surprising feature of his critique of the German judiciary in *Guardian*. More intriguing than the tensions with his previous work is the fact that the great theorist of the political would fail to read the subsumption model politically. Not only is there a "political" history of the subsumption jurisprudence which Schmitt overlooks. The subsumption model is also bound up with the workings of the German composite state in a way that is important for evaluating Schmitt's critique of the German judiciary.

An appropriate starting point is the issue of legal reform, which was at the center of German politics during the 19th century (Stolleis 1992, 2: 116–117). This focus on law reform was a corollary of Germany's relatively late establishment of full democratic government. At crucial junctures, liberal reformers were unable to achieve their political aims, so they trained their sights on legal change. Even in regard to legal issues, however, reformers were compelled to tailor their demands so as not to run afoul of the state (Blackbourn and Eley 1984, esp. pp. 190–205).

Early in the 19th century, monarchs and liberal reformers shared a dual interest in legal codification and in the establishment of a system of independent courts not under the direct control of the nobility or the monarch. Such legal reforms were favorable to both monarchs and the bourgeoisie, because they broke the stranglehold of the aristocracy over legal development. These reforms also rendered law more calculable at the same time that general legal rules were made applicable to new forms of economic and social activity. This obviously worked to the benefit of the bourgeoisie, who attained greater prominence in an expanding liberal social sphere not subject to the direct control of monarchs. It also worked to the advantage of the latter, as liberal reforms enhanced the overall power of the Prussian state.[21]

This mutually beneficial marriage of convenience had its limits. In addition to a system of independent courts, liberal reformers also sought the establishment of courts of general jurisdiction. In contrast to the French system, such courts would have been empowered to review the legal foundation of executive action as well as more mundane private law issues, as was already the case with courts in the United States and Great Britain (Ogorek 1986, 35–38). Monarchs bristled, however, at a strict adherence to formal legality, for it could stymie bureaucratic creativity in pursuit of state goals. Just as liberal reformers seemed poised to make substantial gains both in the legal and political field, German states began to place important restrictions on the jurisdiction of courts, including prohibitions on the review of administrative questions. By mid-century, many *Länder* also sought to punish individual judges for what they deemed inappropriate political activity.[22]

With one ear to the ground, liberals sensed the approaching reactionary stampede and played dead in hopes of not being trampled. Besides no longer pushing for courts of general jurisdiction (Ogorek 1986, 287–290 and

Stolleis 1988–1999, 240–243), they assumed a decidedly deferential posture in terms of legal interpretation. Insisting that adjudication was neutral and nonpolitical, they portrayed judicial decision-making as a logical operation, requiring the exercise of no significant judicial discretion. Because courts would merely apply the letter of the law in machine-like fashion, the state need not fear that judges would circumvent its will through crafty legal interpretation. Though large portions of state action would escape review, courts could operate at least without political interference in their narrowly circumscribed sphere (Ogorek 1986, 306–318).

The drive for political unification in the final third of the 19th century rekindled interest in law reform (John 1989). Liberals remained in the forefront of these reform efforts. But the character of German politics had already changed considerably. Bismarck's attempts to politically marginalize the Catholics and Social Democrats failed,[23] and the political dominance of liberals in the *Reichstag* ended with the ascendancy of the Social Democratic Party and the continued strength of the Catholic Centre Party. Moreover, right-wing groups began to organize and agitate at the national level, further splintering the increasingly isolated bourgeois political block.[24] In this more crowded political landscape, the *Reich* led by the conservative *Land* Prussia was pressed increasingly into the role of mediating between competing social interests.[25] The politics surrounding the drafting and promulgation of the Civil Code illustrates the impact this changed political environment had on the German state.

A recurring criticism of the Code was that it represented contestable value choices for a particular form of bourgeois social order. Though the political position of liberals was weakening, they were able to achieve passage of a civil code with their fingerprints all over it. By packing the drafting committee with legal positivists concerned with formal equality, liberal bureaucrats effectively neutralized opponents like Otto von Gierke, who charged that the emphasis on formal equality lent legitimacy to social inequality. Once the Code was drafted, considerable opposition remained, which hard-pressed proponents successfully headed off by arguing that the Code, while imperfect, constituted an advance over current law. Any deficiencies, proponents argued, could be remedied through special legislation. Not wanting to be seen as responsible for the failure of the Code, most opponents set their sights on revision and special legislation (John 1989, 105–159). The fragmented, cumbersome character of the legislative process meant that, when such responses were possible, as they sometimes were, they would always lag behind concrete developments.

The new Code proved more adaptable than its German predecessor, the General Law of Prussia, in part because it did not seek to anticipate all possible fact situations with narrowly formulated legal rules. The new Code opted instead for more generally cast provisions lending themselves to flexible interpretation. More importantly, it included quite broadly formulated provisions, general clauses, making reference to principles like "good faith and credit" (*Treu und Glauben*). The drafters of the Code were aware of the potential abuses of general clauses and sought to limit their inclusion. However, general clauses were also seen as a way of compensating for the incompleteness of the Code as well as a means of ensuring adaptability.[26] Doctrinal developments confirmed these intuitions. Through broad-based interpretation of these generally cast provisions and especially of the general clauses, judges applied the Code to a diverse and changing array of circumstances. Even a leading critic of the general clauses conceded that the Civil Code would have been quickly rendered obsolete without their inclusion (Hedemann 1933).

Applying Oliver Wendell Holmes's famous dictum to the German context, one could say that the life of German law was not logic, but rather the general clause. The subsumption concept could work on the level of practice, only because broadly worded provisions enabled judges to subsume widely disparate and changing sets of facts under established legal principles. Otherwise, the express provisions of the Civil Code and other major statutes might have been obsolete, if not at their very inception, then soon afterward (Nörr 1988, 29–40).

Such unplanned obsolescence would have presented significant problems for the German state, which was increasingly beset by ideological polarization in the popularly elected legislature. In this context, the subsumption model of adjudication served a dual political role. As a functional equivalent of a loyalty oath, it proved useful in the push for liberal reforms. By deemphasizing the role of discretion in adjudication, the subsumption concept helped provide cover for the drive for major institutional changes, which could potentially limit the range of independent state action. For while legal forms ultimately stem from the state, the fact that state officials must conduct business in conformity with these forms excludes responses directly and explicitly in violation of them. By obscuring the role of judicial discretion in legal change, the subsumption model also maintained the fiction of legislative guidance of legal change.

This reconsideration of judicial politics in the *Kaiserreich* calls into question the lessons Schmitt draws from the period. In Schmitt's reading, it was the rocklike traditional state, anchored by Prussia, which ensured political stability in the *Kaiserreich*. For Schmitt, institutions like local self-government and the courts only function effectively in a system with clear boundaries between state and society and law and politics, respectively. This alternate reading of the *Kaiserreich* suggests that the relationship was reversed. Institutions Schmitt considered at best peripheral and at worst a major problem did not operate effectively because of the relatively settled conditions established by the strong German state. On the contrary, these institutions served as essential support beams of the weak German state, which was already relegated to the role of mediator among rival social groups. Therefore, just as Schmitt's comparative history of the German state obscured the potential contribution of vibrant local self-government to political stability in the Weimar Republic, so did his unquestioned assumptions about traditional German jurisprudence wrongly preclude a more active role for courts in responding to the Weimar state crisis.

Kelsen is no doubt right that Schmitt refused to recognize the essential role of judicial discretion in subsumption jurisprudence, because doing so, in Schmitt's opinion, would have hindered the sort of executive action he believed necessary in the context of late Weimar (1930/31). However, if Schmitt's aim was to preserve the basic integrity of the system and to ensure minimum political stability, then the political history of the subsumption concept suggests that Schmitt might have been well served to rethink his exceptionally limited model of adjudication. A positivist understanding of adjudication like Kelsen's, when read institutionally, could have better served Schmitt's professed aim of ensuring the basic structural integrity of the system, while it advanced the liberal aim of restraining arbitrary state power.

III.

A disturbing corollary of the effacement of the state/society distinction, according to Schmitt, was the privatization of public law.[27] Individuals and groups, even governments, were increasingly inclined to view the Constitution as a civil law contract rather than a decision reached by the German people collectively, and one not subject to change in piecemeal fashion either through legislation or through judicial precedents (HV 54 and 62). Under this emerging understanding, both private and public law disputes were deemed resolvable through litigation before the ordinary and special courts of the Republic (HV 62–66).

The imperial character of civil law understandings of public law prompts Schmitt to consider the Free Law Movement's critique of traditional civil law adjudication as the primary constitutional question in the Weimar period (HV 19). In Schmitt's view, the Free Law understanding of adjudication, stressing the creative role of judges, encourages the politicization of the judiciary. It does so by lending credence to the view that there is always a chance that courts will render a favorable judgment, despite the fact that the sources of the law, narrowly understood, do not appear favorable and there is no enabling legislation empowering courts to resolve such disputes. Cases involving "punitive criminal sanctions," by contrast, lend themselves to resolution through subsumption of a particular set of facts under a preexisting legal norm. This is because the legal issue involves the violation of specific legal provisions by concrete individuals, not a clash of norms. In such cases, courts can discern an infringement of a constitutional norm and enforce a sanction without reaching judgments on the relative weight of opposing constitutional provisions (HV 43 and 67).

Schmitt's easy acceptance of criminal law analogies is surprising given his criticism of legal positivism for its failure to grapple with issues of actual enforcement of norms. For the application of legal sanctions to public officials is not at all straightforward. It is fairly simple for a legal system to identify and respond to misuse of official discretion by minor officials. A contempt citation or removal from office is often sufficient to ensure compliance with legal dictates. Legal enforcement is much more difficult at high levels of authority, particularly when the official or institution in question has considerable democratic legitimacy. At this level, it is better to speak of persuasion rather than compulsion. U.S. Supreme Court decisions, for example, are not binding as general political principles, though the coordinate branches of government might choose to treat them as such for political reasons. Officials and governmental bodies might choose not to comply, either in the immediate case or in the long-term, initiating constitutional conflicts that make for great political theater. Such disputes can involve major questions of principle, though often less lofty motivations are behind the insistence on suspect or contentious readings of the Constitution.[28] The possibility of short-term political gain is a strong motivation for politicians, for whom Keynes' dictum "in the long-run you're dead" applies with special urgency.

The role of the legal system in such conflicts is to raise the stakes of the exercise of political power. As Madison emphasized in *Federalist* 51, the dispersion of political power gives officials the motivation and means to question the actions of other governmental officials. When one calls attention to questionable state action, one puts pressure on others to justify their behavior in terms appropriate for their place within the overall system. The offending party or institution might offer an alternate interpretation of existing law, or they might claim their actions are necessary to attain some higher end. In any case, the justification must persuade other officials and the general public. Whereas even autocratic states require some voluntary cooperation of the public to ensure the long-term viability of the regime, the need for public support in a democracy is especially acute.

An essential element in the persuasiveness of such official explanations is the extent to which the form of argument offered is considered appropriate for the official's position and for the circumstances of the case. Typically, for example, it would be considered unacceptable for an administrator to ignore or violate the guidelines established by the enabling legislation for her agency, merely because she believed these guidelines were immoral or because, in her opinion, another scheme would better serve the general welfare. It is quite different for high elected officials. One might object to a particular understanding of morality motivating a specific piece of legislation, but the fact that legislatures consider the moral implications of proposed statutes is not per se a cause for concern.

At this point, Kelsen's formulation of Merkl's "multi-tiered" (*Stufenbau*) understanding of the legal system,[29] ridiculed by Schmitt,[30] becomes especially relevant because it distinguishes in a useful way among forms of justification appropriate for different levels of the system. For Kelsen, the best means of ensuring the justness and efficacy of laws in the long-term is the careful calibration of the way actions are justified with the institutional means through which actions are taken. The scope of an actor's discretion depends on where within the system he or she is positioned. A constitutional norm requires a different level of justification and will be treated in a different way institutionally than an ordinary statute or a local ordinance.[31] If particular actors exceed the boundaries of their allowable discretion, it is the responsibility of others to call them to account for their actions, compelling them to justify their actions with arguments appropriate for the circumstances. Kelsen does not deny that there is a personal element in law; legal norms do not enforce themselves. But by insisting that personal authority be embedded in institutions in this way, one better ensures that personal authority remains responsible. Moreover, while a multi-tiered system does not prevent erroneous or objectionable interpretations of the law, such a linkage of norms and institutions increases the likelihood that such actions will be corrected in the long-term.

An excellent example of the importance of linking forms of argument with institutions is the controversy surrounding Lincoln's suspension of habeas corpus during the Civil War. "The privilege of the writ of habeas corpus shall not be suspended," according to Article I, Section 9 of the U.S. Constitution, "unless when in cases of rebellion or invasion the public safety may require it." Sitting at the time as a circuit court judge, Chief Justice Taney was right to question Lincoln's unilateral suspension of habeas corpus, for the constitutional provision in question accords this authority to Congress, not the President.[32] But Congress was not in session. And, since the president is also charged with upholding the Constitution, Lincoln argued, it was necessary for him to violate this particular constitutional norm, albeit an especially important one, in order to preserve the entire constitutional system.[33] It is not necessary here to determine whether Lincoln's actions were justifiable despite their unconstitutionality in the narrow sense.[34] The important point is that a dynamic tension between institutions preserves the normative and institutional means for criticizing and restraining the exercise of these powers. The Supreme Court's response placed the onus of responsibility on Lincoln's shoulders, forcing him to account for his actions with arguments appropriate for his place within the system and for the particular circumstances in question (Fehrenbacher 1987, 120–122 and 134–140). Even though the questioning of official conduct did not compel Lincoln to forgo presidential emergency powers during wartime, it helped ensure that the system of valid laws was respected in the long-term by limiting the potential usefulness of Lincoln's actions as a precedent.[35]

It is clear that a proper evaluation of any understanding of the legal system requires considering legal politics in reference to a much longer time horizon. When viewed at discrete points, court interventions might appear inefficacious. But this is true of the political branches as well. Focusing on Lincoln's suspension of habeas corpus, for example, makes the Supreme Court and even the Congress seem impotent. A proper understanding of law and politics requires analysis of the relations among different components of the system, not just at such isolated moments, but across time as well. The fact that Lincoln arguably usurped some congressional authority during the Civil War should not block from view the full range of governmental activity at the time. We have seen that Congress was content to let Lincoln manage the war effort, while it was busy promoting territorial expansion, industrialization, and significant social change. In the post–Civil War era, the office of the President became less prominent, while the Congress for a time seemed to occupy the entire field. From the final quarter of the 19th century until shortly before World War II, however, the Supreme Court went to the barricades in defense of the common law system of social ordering against reform efforts of the political branches. Moreover, formerly inefficacious precedents from the Civil War era were a thorn in the sides of both Presidents Roosevelt and Truman in their attempts to exercise extraordinary powers during wartime. In fact, the Supreme Court was successful at derailing President Truman's attempt to direct economic activity on his own authority, and court precedents have even hindered the President's ability to control the executive branch (Corwin 1976; Fisher 1988, 231–274 and [1978] 1997, 49–86; McCloskey [1960] 1994).

One might question the applicability of the American example, given the important differences between Kelsen's understanding of party democracy and the American system of divided government.[36] Kelsen advocates concentrating political authority in the majority party in parliament, whereas, in the American system, it is dispersed throughout the system in varying degrees. Nonetheless, the point is still valid for addressing the question of legal efficacy generally. As Kelsen emphasizes in his critique of Schmitt's *Guardian of the Constitution* (1930/31), any complex system of authority will experience difficulty in ensuring the proper enforcement of legal norms, simply because so many different persons and organs are involved in the process of legal application, but also due to the inherent ambiguity of language. No dictate can be formulated clearly and unambiguously enough to guarantee the proper enforcement of norms in all cases. There will be considerable give-and-take over the scope and substance of legal norms even in a fully centralized system with undisputed lines of authority. Echoing Kelsen's criticism of Schmitt's narrow understanding of the subsumption concept, one can say that in regard to the ongoing institutional dialogue over the meaning and the applicability of legal norms, the differences between the American and Kelsenian systems are really a matter of degree not kind.

The key consideration in determining legal efficacy in such a system is not merely whether there is an institution willing and able to act at a particular point in response to a specific problem, though Schmitt is right that this consideration is important. One must also examine how different components of the system interact in regard to a range of problems over an extended period. Under such a dynamic understanding of legal politics, the institutional deficiencies of courts do not pose an insurmountable obstacle to the judiciary, as a whole, playing an important role in constitutional politics. This is because courts need not be able to preempt the actions of the political branches, or be able to enforce their own judgments, in order to contribute to the ongoing dialogue over the scope, substance, and applicability of legal norms. The comparatively more fragmented German court system, held up by Schmitt as an insurmountable obstacle to a more prominent judicial role, might actually have had an institutional advantage in regard to facilitating institutional dialogue. Realizing the potential benefits of the fragmented German court system requires recognizing that what is true of relations among levels and branches of government in constitutional systems generally also applies to relations among courts with diverse jurisdictional bases. Even an hierarchical court structure with relatively clear jurisdictional boundaries cannot ensure that there will not be differences of opinion over particular issues which are not easily resolved (Seitzer 1999a). As in the system generally, these doctrinal and jurisdictional disagreements can prompt productive exchanges among courts over the scope and substance of important principles.

The diffuse form of judicial review in the United States, for example, permits courts at all levels to review the constitutionality of governmental action. The system remains hierarchical insofar as there are courts which serve as final arbiters of legal disputes at both the state and federal levels. In regard to federal constitutional questions, the U.S. Supreme Court has the last word. Nevertheless, the nature of the judicial process in a complex system like the United States means that the Supreme Court's position atop the federal court system is not comparable to that of the *pater familas*. Because of the decentralized structure of the judicial system, an appropriate case must work its way up to the Supreme Court before a definitive judgment is reached, so there is usually some delay before the Supreme Court hears an appropriate case. In the interim, changes in court composition, the outlook of judges, or in politics and society generally might prompt the Supreme Court to view the issue differently.[37] Stephen Carter aptly terms this possibility the "forced reconsideration" of Supreme Court decisions. Departures from Supreme Court precedents, in other words, present the Supreme Court with an opportunity to revisit a previous decision (Carter 1996). Though Carter was discussing political responses to the Supreme Court, this concept also applies to relations within the judiciary. While the Supreme Court has the upper hand in any conflict, lower courts can still question important holdings, perhaps bringing about changes in doctrine. Since, in the vast majority of cases, Supreme Court precedents are unquestioned, anarchy is not let loose upon the legal system. Moreover, when the Supreme Court acquiesces in lower court doctrinal challenges, it does not relinquish its authority to set precedents. On the contrary, the Supreme Court retains its authority as final arbiter of legal disputes, but it leaves itself open to criticism and change. In this way, the court system preserves its hierarchical structure, while it enhances its capacity for self-diagnosis and self-correction (Seitzer 1997, 127–128).

Despite the position of the Supreme Court at the pinnacle of the federal judiciary, the court system overall exhibits an openness to criticism and change. In this sense, Schmitt overstates the differences between the German and the American systems. The German system is also decentralized, though in a decidedly different way. Rather than one high court in the federal court hierarchy, as in the U.S., there are several high courts at the national level, each with its own jurisdiction (Seitzer 1997, 129–30 and 1999a,

200–203). This lack of a clear hierarchy at the national level, along with ambiguities stemming from changes in the sources of the law, did produce considerable uncertainty in the Weimar period. But the fact that the German system does not speak with one voice is not in itself a problem; in fact, this might even be an advantage in Schmitt's terms.

Schmitt's concern is to ensure that there is an institution capable of defending the constitutional system in times of crisis. He is right that the courts are ill-suited for this role in the narrow sense. Regardless of whether they are categorized "positive" or "negative" liberties, all legal rights require positive government action to be effective (Holmes and Sunstein 1999). Still, some rights require more energetic governmental action like enabling legislation and executive regulations. The need for such action means that some rights may be valid and yet "underenforced" in that they are not fully realizable at that time (Sager 1978 and Sunstein 1993a, 152–153). However, the fact that courts alone cannot ensure that legal norms are fully enforced is not a decisive objection to a prominent role for courts in constitutional politics. Despite their need for a strong supporting cast, courts can still make a positive contribution to constitutional democracy. Courts can call to account officials like the *Reichspräsident*, who are better positioned institutionally to respond in the way Schmitt deems necessary. Like their American counterparts, German presidents may choose to ignore an adverse ruling, if they believe that the consequences of complying are too high. As Abraham Lincoln asked in response to criticism of his suspension of habeas corpus during the Civil War, "(a)re all the laws, but *one*, to go unexecuted, and the government itself to go to pieces, lest that one be violated?" (Fehrenbacher 1987, 121). Though underenforced or ignored in the short-term, court judgments help ensure officials take responsibility for their actions. As Schmitt concedes, such precedents help ensure that the Constitution is "respected" (HV 21).

Because the German judiciary cannot speak with one voice, as can the American courts on occasion, its judicial interventions have even less of an impact in the short-term. If there had been a widespread consensus in Weimar Germany supporting a particular court as the final arbiter of legal disputes, even of a constitutional nature, the German judiciary might have had a greater chance of success in going toe-to-toe with rival branches and levels of government. Since this was not the case, German courts can seek to resolve contentious legal disputes with wider political and social implications without causing mayhem, because particular courts would rarely be able to deliver a knockout blow. Regarding the exercise of presidential emergency powers in the midst of a genuine constitutional crisis, the inability of individual courts to bring political officials to heel would be especially pronounced.

This consideration prompts one to ask, as in the last chapter, why all the fuss about courts? In a fragmented system like Weimar Germany, courts can question state action without preventing necessary measures in the short term. But in the process of adjudicating challenges to governmental action, individual courts might present understandings of principle that resonate with the wider public. Here, again, the nonhierarchical system of high courts is an institutional advantage in that it permits a larger number of participants in the dialogue over principle. Of course, such post-hoc judicial constructs violate Schmitt's top-down, front-loaded understanding of constitutional principle. But if his primary concern is to preserve the basic constitutional framework and ensure governability, then he should not oppose such innovations merely because they stem from courts. As Schmitt himself points out, many features of the system, such as extensive presidential government in lieu of an effective parliament, do not accord with the original constitutional design. So why not permit courts to try their hand at resolving disputes, if there are not significant adverse consequences in the near term? If particular courts exceed the bounds of their legitimate discretion by taking positions that do not conform to the subsumption model, for example, then other officials or governmental bodies, such as courts and legislatures, can dispute the holding in the case and perhaps the court's reasoning as well. The affected officials might base their refusal to comply fully with a court judgment on these criticisms. Another possibility is complying with the holding of the decision in the case at hand, while refusing to take the reasoning of the decision as a political principle controlling future governmental policy, as Abraham Lincoln advocated in the aftermath of the notorious Dred Scott decision (Lincoln 1989, 1: 390–403). This latter alternative is particularly suitable for the German context with its more restrictive understanding of court precedents as sources of law (Foster [1993] 1996, 4 and 60). Finally, officials might also claim that though the court decision is perhaps correct in a narrow legal sense, larger considerations, such as preservation of the system generally, require an alternative course of action that is perhaps not strictly legal.

Schmitt might point out that such a "cowboy" understanding of constitutional politics is not appropriate for the German context. The German concern with strict legality might cause an official to comply with a court ruling, even though doing so might prevent her from taking action she deems necessary. But such regard for legality might derail state action without an adverse court judgment. In the lead-up to the appointment of Hitler as Chancellor, for example, President von Hindenburg became hesitant to continue governing by legally questionable emergency decrees (Craig 1978, 564–568). The decline in Nazi electoral support in the previous election made this decision, rightly, the cause of much gnashing of teeth. Hindenburg's actions illustrate the flaws of a highly personal understanding of constitutional politics like Schmitt's and, therefore, speak powerfully for a dialogic alternative, in which all branches and levels of government are important participants. Such an understanding better provides for the reversal or alteration of a fateful decision by a particular official or organ of government.

There is another reason to provide courts a larger voice in constitutional politics even in times of crisis. Not only does the dispersion of power in this way enhance the system's overall capacity for self-correction but, depending on the system's precise configuration and the prevailing circumstances, a decentralized system of authority can better provide for political stability by establishing more avenues for the expression of opposition, as illustrated by the constitutional crisis leading up to the Civil War.[38] At the founding and during the early years of the Republic, there were fundamental disagreements over slavery, but compromises were reached which effectively prevented the slavery issue from becoming a focal point of sectional tensions. This set of compromises began to unravel in the 1840s, because the acquisition of new territories threatened to disturb the delicate sectional balance. The Compromise of 1850 successfully reestablished this balance, stabilizing the system by providing both pro- and anti-slavery forces approximately equal shares in the spoils. The federal government never had much say in the regulation of slavery within the existing states. Before the Civil War, the federal government's responsibility for protecting the institution of slavery steadily increased, while its authority over the institution of slavery decreased (Fehrenbacher 1978, 27–48). But the federal government's authority over slavery in the territories was still widely recognized. At the time of the Compromise of 1850, the federal government still provided institutional means for the effective mediation of sectional disputes. But the Kansas-Nebraska Act and the Dred Scott decision denied the federal government any legitimate authority over the issue of slavery in the new territories. These legal changes, taken together, were producing fundamental structural changes in the American system. Most relevant at this point was the fact that the federal government no longer served even a mediating role in sectional disputes. During the first half of the 19th century, civil peace was maintained by limiting consideration of slavery at the federal level; but excluding consideration of slavery at the federal level in a period of rapid change only served to intensify sectional hostilities (Holmes 1988, 31–43).[39]

It is exceedingly difficult to generalize about the tendency toward political stability of different systems (Lijphart, Rogowski, and Weaver 1993, 302–344). However, narrowly focused analyses of particular contexts can reveal specific features of a system that under certain circumstances might provide unexpected advantages for political stability. In the *Reich* period, for example, local self-government and court interpretation of the Civil Code bolstered the weak German state by providing an alternate avenue for political competition and by facilitating legal adaptation, respectively. Schmitt's understanding of the nature of political stability did not take account of these features of the German composite state, and his use of comparative history to analyze the institutional strengths and weaknesses of the Weimar Republic did not prompt him to question his own assumptions. A more nuanced application of comparative history would have revealed the possible advantages of a more decentralized response to the Weimar state crisis. Rehabilitating local self-government could have broadened and deepened existing avenues of political participation, while permitting courts to legitimately address a wider range of public law disputes might have created an alternate means of expressing opposition to the increasingly divisive presidential government advocated by Schmitt. Encouraging both of these developments might have increased support for the regime precisely when it was most needed. In regard to the subject at hand, court judgments compelling the President to rescind or scale back controversial actions on several occasions might have produced greater confidence in the system overall and perhaps more tolerance for specific emergency decrees. This is admittedly speculative. But the enhanced support for the regime stemming from a more lively and effective institutional dialogue early in the final crisis of the Republic might have enabled President von Hindenburg to use illegal emergency decrees to cross to safety, so to speak, rather than appoint Hitler chancellor. Even presidents can wear out the welcome mat.

Perhaps a more decentralized solution to the Republic's difficulties would have failed, as well. Obviously, the sort of historical counterfactual necessary to address this question is beyond the scope of this book. Nonetheless, the preceding is sufficient to suggest that such decentralized solutions offered distinct potential advantages without precluding the sort of executive action Schmitt deemed essential in terms of short-term system maintenance. Despite Schmitt's methodological sophistication, his use of comparative history did not serve his own stated purposes especially well. While his comparative history of the German state was carefully tailored to reinforce his predetermined understanding of the nature of political stability, it unfairly discounted institutional alternatives that might have been better suited to preserving the structural integrity of the system, which was Schmitt's explicit aim in both works.

NOTES

1. Finn (1991, 139–178, esp. 161–163) examines how Article 25 concerning presidential dissolution of parliament undermined the legislative control of presidential emergency powers under Article 48.

2. On the political implications of the State High Courts decision, see Dyzenhaus (1997, 28–37). In regard to the U.S. Supreme Court, the classic examples are the postponement of certain habeas corpus cases until after the Civil War and the Steel Seizure Cases. On the former, see McCloskey ([1960] 1994, 70–74); consult Corwin (1976, 121–137) on the latter.

3. Cristi (1998, 179–193) also examines Schmitt's typology of state forms, though for a different purpose. The typology is examined here as a means of analyzing the institutional implications of existing state forms, whereas Cristi uses it to highlight the importance of the state/society distinction for Schmitt.

4. On the emergence of the *Ständestaat* in the mid-13th century and the origins of the absolutist state, see Barraclough ([1946] 1949, 322–339 and 376–405). On the general contrast between the *Ständestaat* and the absolutist state, see Unger (1976, 154–158 and 181–184).

5. See Carsten (1959) on politics in the *Ständestaat*. Regarding law in the *Ständestaat*, see Unger (1976, 158–166).

6. Not only did the *Reich* government have to contend with a growing formal opposition from the SPD, but its political allies were also increasingly disunified. Fairbairn (1997, 209–240) provides a good discussion of the SPD's electoral success and increasing political influence. On the disunity of the support for the *Reich* government in the Wilhelmine period, see Eley (1980, 293–315).

7. Craig (1978, 38–60) provides a good overview of the complex structure of the *Kaiserreich*. See also Blackbourn and Eley (1984, 251–285, esp. 253–254) on the implications of the constitutional settlement for politics in the *Kaiserreich*.

8. Over time, the balance within this composite state shifted from a clear advantage for the government to a precarious balance, in which the government retained perhaps a slight edge mainly because of the constitutional position of Prussia. On how the *Reich* government went from a superior position vis à vis the *Reichstag* to one of mediating among rival social groups, see Eley (1980, 349–361).

9. See Horwitz (1977) on how the courts promoted capitalist economic development through their interpretation of common law categories. Skowronek (1982, 26–35) shows how courts, along with political parties, compensated in part for the lack of a centralized state in this period.

10. For an excellent history of constitutional debates in the first and second halves of the 19th century, see Kammen (1987, 3–94 and 95–155, respectively).

11. Fisher (1997, 260–262) discusses the legal issues involved in Lincoln's actions. The practical impact of Lincoln's suspension of Habeas Corpus is examined by Neely (1991).

12. See, for example, Lincoln's "Annual Message to Congress, December 3, 1961," in which he justifies the establishment of special courts to administer summary justice as a temporary necessity in wartime (Lincoln 1989, 1: 286–287).

13. On the complexity of presidential-congressional relations in this period, see Skowronek (1993, 198–227).

14. The way in which various presidents make use of opportunities for leadership provided by their "political time" is the theme of Skowronek (1993).

15. According to Blum, Theodore Roosevelt was the first president to make full use of presidential powers during peacetime (1980, 23–60). On the modern presidency generally, see Neustadt (1990).

16. Sunstein (1990, 12–24, esp. 12–18) provides a good overview of the legal and political changes involved in the emergence of the administrative state. For a then contemporary understanding of the need for a fundamentally new understanding of American governmental institutions after the Industrial Revolution, see Beard and Beard (1930, esp. 2–19). Purcell (1973) offers an excellent treatment of the intellectual climate of early 20th century America, particularly of the perceived need for government of experts because of the expansion of the electorate. Finally, on the social dimension of changes in thought and governmental forms in the Progressive era, see Weinstein (1968).

17. For an overview of developments in English, French, and German historiography in the 19th and 20th centuries, see Evans (1997, 15–44). On the "Prussian School" of political historians that served as the backdrop to the "methodological debate" (*Methodenstreit*) among German historians around the turn of the last century, see Iggers ([1968] 1983, 90–123).

18. On Ranke's understanding of history and his contribution to the establishment of the modern discipline of history, see Gilbert (1990, 11–45).

19. Schmitt's dichotomy conforms to the "yardstick" variety of ideal types. On ideal types in general and "yardstick" ones in particular, see Kalberg (1994, 71–142 and 87–91, respectively).

20. The theorists of the Free Law Movement are one of Schmitt's principal targets in *Guardian of the Constitution*. The Free Law Movement was sharply critical of the traditional model of jurisprudence. In stressing the subsumption of particular facts situations under existing legal rules, the traditional understanding overlooks the centrality of judicial creativity to the act of subsumption itself. According to a prominent Free Lawyer, Eugen Ehrlich, existing legal rules often do not fit precisely the case in question, so it is necessary to stretch the underlying concepts until they are abstract enough to settle the dispute. In this sense, adjudication involves "juristic construction" prior to the application of rules (Ehrlich 1976, 212–213). The task of ascertaining the appropriate position of concrete principles and rules as well as "societal oppositions" and "considerations of interests" within the evolving system of laws is mistakenly seen as one of "subsumption"

through deductive logic rather than "creation" through abstract extension of concepts or the scientific reordering of the interrelationships between system and principles (222–225). The classic commentary on the Free Law Movement in Germany and Austria remains that by François Geny, who was himself a contributer to the movement (Geny [1954] 1963, 519–564). See also the extended treatment of Riebschläger (1968). For an overview of the principal themes and works of the movement, see Herget and Wallace (1987, 401–419).

21. On the long-term political and social changes producing the modern state in Prussia, see Rosenberg ([1958] 1966). Habermas ([1962] 1989) provides the classic treatment of the defining features and normative implications of the emergence of a bourgeois social order in Europe. On German liberals' ambiguous attitudes toward the state and reform in the 19th century, see Sheehan (1978).

22. For an extensive empirical study of *Länder* efforts to discipline judges, see Ormond (1994).

23. Huber (1969, 645–831) provides an in-depth analysis of the *Kulturkampf*. On the Anti-Socialist Laws, see Craig (1978, 140–180).

24. On the decline of liberal political fortunes, see Eley (1980, 19–94).

25. See Steinmetz (1996, 257–318) on the weakened position of the German state in the Wilhelmine period.

26. Boerner (1989) offers an account of the origins and legal implications of the general clauses.

27. Schmitt's concern with the privatization of public law was widely shared at the time (Thornhill 2000, 92–129).

28. Fisher's concept of "coordinate construction" captures the complex ways in which constitutional principle forms and changes through dynamic interactions among coordinate branches as well as between coordinate branches and other portions of the federal and state governments (1988). More recently, Whittington (1999) emphasizes the role of presidents, legislators, and even private citizens, in the development of constitutional principle and political practice. For such dialogic views of constitutional politics, the American system of divided government engenders constitutional conflicts, which are productive of constitutional meaning.

29. Silverman (1962, esp. vol. 2, 604–625) offers an excellent study of Kelsen's position in the legal controversies of the first half of this century. For an extended recent critique of Kelsen, see Dyzenhaus (1997, 102–160).

30. Schmitt considered Kelsen's legal positivism empty normativism. According to Schmitt, there is always a personal element in the application of laws. Some person or persons must have the authority, institutional resources, and the motivation to execute the norm. Similarly, merely designating one norm as superior to another, or simply stipulating that one type of norm is not as easily altered as another, does not mean that the inferior norm will always give way or that the superior norm will be executed in accordance with its status. Here, too, there are a large number of nonlegal factors involved in determining legal efficacy (PT 16–35, esp. 28–35 and HV 38, n. 2).

31. According to Kelsen, Schmitt incorrectly sees a "qualitative" difference between the activity of the "lawgiver" and that of courts, assigning only the former a "political," "decisionistic" element. Actually, however, there is only a "quantitative" difference between their respective activities. Obviously, lawgivers are superior to courts in that they establish guidelines for courts to settle conflicts of interest and power, and yet courts must also create law insofar as they must resolve doubts and questions concerning the clarity and meaning of norms and facts. In this sense, Kelsen argues, there is an element of decision in all adjudication, although Schmitt denies it in ordinary cases. Constitutional cases are different only in that one must inquire into the content of the law to determine whether its substance amends the constitution. If so, then a proposed legal norm must fulfill other procedural requirements, such as a qualified majority, in order to be valid (Kelsen 1930/31).

32. *Ex parte Merryman*, 17 Fed. Case No. 9,487 (1861).

33. "Message to Congress, July 4, 1861." Reprinted in Fisher (1995, 333).

34. Recent historical research suggests that Lincoln's actions were necessary under the circumstances and rather moderate in execution (e.g. Fehrenbacher 1987, 134–140 and esp. Neely 1991).

35. On the controversy over Lincoln's actions during the Civil War as a precedent for expansion of executive authority, see Fehrenbacher (1987, 128–142).

36. Kelsen's understanding of democracy is elaborated in *Vom Wesen und Wert der Demokratie* ([1929] 1981). See also Kelsen's social scientific approach to democratic theory in *Allgemeine Staatslehre* (1925). Good brief discussions of his concept of party democracy are offered in Manin (1997, 211–224) and Dreier (1999, 71–74).

37. On the U.S. federal court system generally, see Wasby (1978). For an excellent case study of the difficulties of bringing a case to the Supreme Court, see Glennon (1991).

38. On the 1850s as a constitutional crisis, see Bestor (1988, 219–245).

39. For an historical overview of political conflict in the United States, see Gunther and Mughan (1993, 278–280).

Works Cited

WORKS BY SCHMITT

Schmitt, Carl. [1912] 1969. *Gesetz und Urteil: Eine Untersuchung zum Problem der Rechtspraxis* (GU). Munich: C.H. Beck.

———. [1922] 1989. *Die Diktatur: Von den Anfängen des modernen Souveränitätsgedankens bis zum proletarischen Klassenkampf.* 5th ed. Berlin: Duncker & Humblot.

———. [1922] 1985. *Political Theology: Four Chapters on the Concept of Sovereignty.* Translated by George Schwab. Cambridge: The MIT Press.

———. [1923] 1985. *Crisis of Parliamentary Democracy.* Translated by Ellen Kennedy. Cambridge: MIT Press.

———. [1925] 1996. *Roman Catholicism and Political Form.* Translated and annotated by G. L. Ulmen. Westport, Conn. and London: Greenwood Press.

———. 1926. *Unabhängigkeit der Richter, Gleichheit vor dem Gesetz und Gewährleistung des Privateigentums nach der Weimarer Verfassung: Ein Rechtsgutachten zu den Gesetzentwürfen über die Vermögensauseinandersetzung mit den früher regierenden Fürstenhäusern.* Berlin and Leipzig: Walter de Gruyter.

———. [1928] 1989. *Verfassungslehre.* 7th ed. Berlin: Duncker & Humblot.

———. 1930. *Hugo Preuß: Sein Staatsbegriff und seine Stellung in der deutschen Staatslehre.* Tübingen: J.C.B. Mohr (Paul Siebeck).

———. [1931] 1985. *Hüter der Verfassung.* 3rd ed. Berlin: Duncker & Humblot.

———. [1932] 1987. *Der Begriff des Politischen: Text von 1932 mit einem Vorwort und drei Corallarien.* Berlin: Duncker & Humblot.

———. [1932] 1988. *Legalität und Legitimität.* 4th ed. Berlin: Duncker & Humblot.

———. [1932] 1996. *The Concept of the Political*. Translated and with an introduction by George Schwab. Foreword by Tracy B. Strong. Chicago: The University of Chicago Press.

———. [1940] 1989. Schlußrede vor dem Staatsgerichtshof in Leipzig in dem Prozeß Preußen contra Reich (1932). In *Positionen und Begriffe: im Kampf mit Weimar-Genf-Versailles*. Berlin: Duncker & Humblot.

———. 1943/44. *Die Lage der Europäischen Rechtswissenschaften*. Tübingen: Internationaler Universitätsverlag.

———. [1958] 1985. *Verfassungsrechtliche Aufsätze aus den Jahren 1924–1954: Materialien zu einer Constitutional Theory*. 3rd ed. Berlin: Duncker & Humblot.

———. 1987. "The Legal World Revolution." Translated by U. L. Ulmen. *Telos* 72 (Summer).

ALL OTHER WORKS

Abraham, David. [1981] 1986. *The Collapse of the Weimar Republic: Political Economy and Crisis*. 2nd ed. New York: Holmes & Meier.

Ackerman, Bruce. 1991. *We the People: Foundations*. Cambridge: Harvard University Press.

Adam, Armin. 1992. *Rekonstruktion des Politischen: Carl Schmitt und die Krise der Staatlichkeit, 1912–1935*. Weinheim: Acta humaniora.

Allison, J.W.F. 1996. *A Continental Distinction in the Common Law: A Historical and Comparative Perspective on English Public Law*. Oxford: Clarendon Press.

Anschütz, Gerhard. 1930. *Die Verfassung des deutschen Reichs vom 11 August 1919: Ein Kommentar für Wissenschaft und Praxis*. 13th ed. Berlin: Verlag von Georg Stilte.

Apelt, Willibalt. 1946. *Geschichte der Weimarer Verfassung*. Munich: Biederstein Verlag.

Arendt, Hannah. 1973. *On Revolution*. London: Penguin Books.

Baker, Keith, ed. 1987. The Declaration of the Rights of Man and of the Citizen. In *The Old Regime and the French Revolution*. Chicago: University of Chicago Press.

———. 1989. Sieyès. In *A Critical Dictionary of the French Revolution*, ed. François Furet and Mona Ozouf. Cambridge: The Belknap Press of Harvard University Press.

Barraclough, G. [1946] 1949. *The Origins of Modern Germany*. Oxford: Basil Blackwell.

Beard, Charles A., and William Beard. 1930. *The American Leviathan: The Republic in the Machine Age*. New York: Macmillan.

Bendersky, Joseph W. 1983. *Carl Schmitt: Theorist for the Reich*. Princeton: Princeton University Press.

Bendix, Reinhard. [1964] 1977. *Nation-Building and Citizenship: Studies of Our Changing Social Order*. New Enlarged Ed. Berkeley: University of California Press.

———. 1987. "Values and Concepts in Max Weber's Comparative Studies." *European Journal of Political Research* 15: 493–505.

Bentin, Lutz-Arwed. 1972. *Johannes Popitz und Carl Schmitt: Zur wirtschaftlichen Theorie des totalen Staates in Deutschland*. Munich: Verlag C. H. Beck.

Berghahn, Volker. R. 1994. *Imperial Germany, 1871–1914: Economy, Society, Culture and Politics*. Providence, R.I.: Berghahn Books.

Bergler, Manfred. 1987. "Die Kontroverse zu Max Webers Thesen über die Entstehung des modernen westlichen Kapitalismus." *Zeitschrift für Religions- und Geistesgeschichte* 39, 1: 24–36.

Berman, Harold J. 1983. *Law and Revolution: The Formation of the Western Legal Tradition*. Cambridge: Harvard University Press.

Berman, Sheri. 1998. *The Social Democratic Moment: Ideas and Politics in the Making of Interwar Europe*. Cambridge: Harvard University Press.

Berthold, Lutz. 1999. *Carl Schmitt und der Staatsnotstandsplan am Ende der Weimar Republik*. Berlin: Duncker & Humblot.

Bestor, Arthur. 1988. The American Civil War as a Constitutional Crisis. In *American Law and the Constitutional Order: Historical Perspectives*. Rev. Ed., ed. Lawrence M. Friedman and Harry N. Scheiber. Cambridge: Harvard University Press.

Bien, David. 1987. Offices, Corps, and a System of Credit: The Uses of Privilege under the Ancien Régime. In *The Political Culture of the Old Regime*. Vol. 1 of *The French Revolution and the Creation of Modern Political Culture*, ed. Keith Baker. Oxford: Pergamon Press.

———. 1994. Old Regime Origins of Democratic Liberty. In *The French Idea of Freedom: The Old Regime and the Declaration of Rights of 1789*, ed. Dale Van Kley. Stanford: Stanford University Press.

Blackbourn, David, and Geoff Eley. 1984. *The Peculiarities of German History: Bourgeois Society and Politics in Nineteenth-Century Germany*. Oxford: Oxford University Press.

Bloch, Marc. 1961. *Feudal Society: Social Classes and Political Organization*. Translated by L.A. Manyon. Chicago: The University of Chicago Press.

Blum, John Morton. 1980. *Progressive Presidents: Roosevelt, Wilson, Roosevelt, and Johnson*. New York: W.W. Norton & Company.

Böckenförde, Ernst-Wolfgang. 1976. "Die Historische Rechtsschule und das Problem der Geschichtlichkeit des Rechts." In *Staat, Gesellschaft, Freiheit: Studien zur Staatstheorie und zum Verfassungsrecht*. Frankfurt am Main: Suhrkamp Taschenbuch Verlag.

Boerner, Fritjof. 1989. *Die Bedeutung der General/Klauseln für die Umgestaltung der Rechtsordnung in der Nationalsozialistischen Zeit*. Frankfurt am Main: Peter Lang.

Borchardt, Knut. 1982. Zwangslagen und Handlungsspielräume in der großen Weltwirtschaftskrise der frühen dreißiger Jahre and Wirtschaftliche Ursachen des Scheiterns der Weimarer Republik. In *Wachstum, Krisen, und Handlungsspielräume der Wirtschaftspolitik: Studien der Wirtschaftsgeschichte des 19. und 20 Jahrhunderts*. Göttingen: Vandenhoeck & Ruprecht.

Bossenga, Gail. 1987. City and State: An Urban Perspective on the Origins of the French Revolution. In *The Political Culture of the Old Regime*. Vol. 1 of *The French Revolution and the Creation of Modern Political Culture*, ed. Keith Baker. Oxford: Pergamon Press.

Bourdieu, Pierre. [1972] 1977. *Outline of a Theory of Practice*. Translated by Richard Nice. Cambridge: Cambridge University Press.

———. [1988] 1991. *The Political Ontology of Martin Heidegger*. Cambridge: Polity Press.

Bowen, Ralph H. [1947] 1971. *German Theories of the Corporative State: With Special Reference to the Period 1870–1919*. New York: Russell & Russell.

Bracher, Karl Dietrich. [1969] 1970. *The German Dictatorship: The Origins, Structure, and Effects of National Socialism*. Translated by Jean Steinberg. With an introduction by Peter Gay. New York: Holt, Rinehart and Winston.

Brand, Donald R. 1988. *Corporatism and the Rule of Law: A Study of the National Recovery Administration*. Ithaca and London: Cornell University Press.

Braunthal, Gerard. 1996. *Parties and Politics in Modern Germany*. Boulder, Colo.: Westview Press.

Brecht, Arnold. 1945. *Federalism and Regionalism in Germany; The Division of Prussia*. New York and London: Oxford University Press.

Brecht, Arnold, and Theodor Kutzer. 1928. *Neuordnung der dezentralisation im Deutschen Reich*. Berlin-Friedenau: Deutscher Kommunal-Verlag.

Breuer, Stefan. 1984. "Nationalstaat und pouvoir constituant bei Sieyès und Carl Schmitt." *Archiv für Rechts- und Sozialphilosophie* 70: 495–517.

Briggs, Asa. 1996. Local, Regional, National: The Historical Dimensions of Public Authority. In *Kommunale Selbstverwaltung/Local Government: Geschichte und Gegenwart im deutschen-britishchen Vergleich*, ed. Adolf Birke and Magnus Brechtken. Munich: K. G. Saur.

Brubaker, Rogers. 1993. Social Theory as Habitus. In *Bourdieu: Critical Perspectives*, ed. Craig Calhoun, Edward L. Buma, and Moishe Pestone. Chicago: The University of Chicago Press.

Burger, Thomas. [1976] 1987. *Max Weber's Theory of Concept Formation: History, Laws and Ideal Types*. New Expanded Edition. Durham: Duke University Press.

Burke, Peter. 1992. *History & Social Theory*. Cambridge: Polity.

Butler, D. E. 1963. *The Electoral System in Britain Since 1918*. 2nd ed. Oxford: Clarendon Press.

Caldwell, Peter. 1995. "Legal Positivism and Weimar Democracy." *American Journal of Jurisprudence* 39, 1 (Spring).

———. 1997. *Popular Sovereignty and the Crisis of German Constitutional Law: The Theory and Practice of Weimar Constitutionalism*. Durham: Duke University Press.

Callinicos, Alex. 1995. *Theories and Narratives: Reflections on the Philosophy of History*. Cambridge: Polity Press.

Carsten, F. L. 1959. *Princes and Parliaments in Germany: From the Fifteenth to the Eighteenth Century*. Oxford: Clarendon Press.

Carter, Stephen. 1996. "The 'Morgan Power' and the Forced Reconsideration of Constititutional Decisions." *The University of Chicago Law Review* 53, 3: 819–63.

Casper, Gerhard. 1989. "Changing Concepts of Constitutionalism: 18th to 20th Century." *The Supreme Court Review* : 311–32.

———. 1990. "Guardians of the Constitution." *Southern California Law Review* 53: 773–785.

Choper, Jesse H. 1980. *Judicial Review and the National Political Process: A Functional Interpretation of the Role of the Supreme Court*. Chicago: University of Chicago Press.

Clark, J.C.D. 1994. *The Language of Liberty 1660–1832: Political Discourse and Social Dynamics in the Anglo-American World*. Cambridge: Cambridge University Press.

Cohen, Joshua and Joel Rogers. 1995. *Associations and Democracy*. Edited by Erik Olin Wright. London: Verso.

Coing, Helmut. 1982. Allgemeine Züge der Privatrechtlichen Gesetzgebung im 19 Jahrhundert. In *Das 19 Jahrhundert, Gesetzgebung zum allgemeinen Privatrecht*. Vol. 3 of *Handbuch der Quellen und Literatur der Neueren Europäischen Privatrechtsgeschichte*, ed. Helmut Coing. Munich: C. H. Beck'sche Verlagsbuchhandlung: 1–16.

Constant, Benjamin. 1988. The liberty of the ancients compared with that of the moderns. In *Benjamin Constant: Political Writings*. Translated and edited by Biancamaria Fontana. Cambridge: Cambridge University Press.

Conze, Werner. 1968. Die Krise des Parteienstaates in Deutschland, 1929/30. In *Von Weimar zu Hitler, 1930–1933*, ed. Gotthard Jasper. Cologne and Berlin: Kiepenheuer & Witsch.

Cook, Charles M. 1981. *The American Codification Movement: A Study in Antebellum Legal Reform*. Westport, Conn.: Greenwood Press.

Corwin, Edward. [1928–29] 1955. *The "Higher Law" Background of American Constitutional Law*. Reprint. Ithaca, New York: Cornell University Press, Cornell Paperbacks.

———. 1976. *Presidential Power and the Constitution: Essays by Edward S. Corwin*, ed. Richard Loss. Ithaca: Cornell University Press.

Craig, Gordon. 1978. *Germany, 1866–1945*. Oxford: Oxford University Press.

Crew, David. 1996. The Ambiguities of Modernity: Welfare and the German State from Wilhelm to Hitler. In *Society, Culture, and the State in Germany, 1870–1930*, ed. Geoff Eley. Ann Arbor: University of Michigan Press.

Cristi, Renato. 1984. "Hayek and Schmitt on the Rule of Law." *Canadian Journal of Political Science* 17.

———. 1998. *Carl Schmitt and Authoritarian Liberalism: Strong State, Free Economy.* Cardiff: University of Wales Press.

Dahl, Robert. 1961. *Who Governs?* New Haven: Yale University Press.

Dahrendorf, Ralf. 1968. *Society and Democracy in Germany.* Garden City, N.Y.: Doubleday & Company, Anchor Books.

Dawson, William Harbutt. 1916. *Municipal Life and Government in Germany.* 2nd ed. London: Longman's, Green and Co.

Deak, Francis and Max Rheinstein. 1936. "The Machinery of Law Administration in France and Germany." *University of Pennsylvania Law Review* 84: 846–876.

Deuerlein, Ernst. 1972. *Föderalismus: Die historischen und philosophischen Grundlagen des föderativen Prinzips.* Munich: Paul List Verlag.

Dewey, John. [1927] 1954. *The Public and Its Problems.* Reprint. Athens: Ohio University Press, Swallow Press.

Dieckmann, Hildemarie. 1960. *Johannes Popitz, Entwicklung und Wirksamkeit in der Zeit der Weimarer Republik.* Berlin-Dahlem: Colloquium Verlag.

Dorondo, D. R. 1992. *Bavaria and German Federalism: Reich to Republic, 1918–33, 1945–49.* New York: St. Martin's Press.

Doyle, William. 1987. The Parlements. In *The Political Culture of the Old Regime.* Vol. 1 of *The French Revolution and the Creation of Modern Political Culture,* ed. Keith Baker. Oxford: Pergamon Press.

Dreier, Horst. 1990. *Rechtslehre, Staatssoziologie und Demokratietheorie bei Hans Kelsen.* Baden-Baden: Nomos Verlag.

———. 1999. The Essence of Democracy—Hans Kelsen and Carl Schmitt Juxtaposed. In *Hans Kelsen and Carl Schmitt: A Juxtaposition,* ed. Dan Diner and Michael Stolleis. Gerlingen: Bleicher Verlag.

Duguit, Leon. 1919. *Law in the Modern State.* New York: B. W. Huebsch.

Dworkin, Ronald. 1985. *A Matter of Principle.* Cambridge: Harvard University Press.

Dyzenhaus, David. 1997. *Legality and Legitimacy: Carl Schmitt, Hans Kelsen and Hermann Heller in Weimar.* Oxford: Clarendon Press.

Ehrlich, Eugen. 1976. Die Juristische Konstruktion. In *Theorie und Technik der Begriffsjurisprudenz,* ed. Werner Krawietz. Darmstadt: Wissenschaftliche Buchgesellschaft.

Eley, Geoff. 1980. *Reshaping the German Right: Radical Nationalism and Political Change after Bismarck.* Ann Arbor: University of Michigan Press.

———. 1992. Bismarckian Germany. In *Modern Germany Reconsidered, 1870–1945,* ed. Gordon Martel. London and New York: Routledge.

Elster, Jon, Claus Offe, and Ulrich K. Preuß. 1998. *Institutional Design in Post-communist Societies: Rebuilding the Ship at Sea.* With Frank Boenker, Ulrike Goetting, and Friedbert W. Rueb. Cambridge: Cambridge University Press.

Emerson, Rupert. [1928] 1979. *State and Sovereignty in Modern Germany*. Reprint. Westport, Conn.: Hyperion Press.

Epp, Charles. 1998. *The Rights Revolution: Lawyers, Activists, and Supreme Courts in Comparative Perspective*. Chicago: The University of Chicago Press.

Ertman, Thomas. 1997. *Birth of the Leviathan: Building States and Regimes in Medieval and Early Modern Europe*. Cambridge: Cambridge University Press.

Evans, Richard. 1997. Whatever Became of the *Sonderweg?* In *Rereading German History, 1800–1996: From Unification to Reunification*. London and New York: Routledge.

———. 1997. *In Defense of History*. London: Granta Books.

Eyck, Erich. 1963. *From the Locarno Conference to Hitler's Seizure of Power*. Vol. 2 of *A History of the Weimar Republic*. Translated by Harlan P. Hanson and Robert G. L. Waite. New York: John Wiley & Sons.

Eyck, Frank. 1968. *The Frankfurt Parliament, 1848–1849*. London: Macmillan; New York: St. Martin's Press.

Fairbairn, Brett. 1997. *Democracy in the Undemocratic State: The German Reichstag Elections of 1898 and 1903*. Toronto: University of Toronto Press.

Fehrenbacher, Don. 1978. *The Dred Scott Case: Its Significance in American Law and Politics*. New York: Oxford University Press.

———. 1987. *Lincoln in Text and Context: Collected Essays*. Stanford: Stanford University Press.

Feldman, Gerald D. 1997. *The Great Disorder: Politics, Economics, and Society in the German Inflation, 1914–1924*. New York and Oxford: Oxford University Press.

Fijalkowski, Jürgen. 1958. *Die Wendung zu Führerstaat: Ideologische Komponenten in der politischen Philosophie Carl Schmitts*. Cologne: Westdeutscher Verlag.

Finn, John. 1991. *Constitutions in Crisis: Political Violence and the Rule of Law*. Oxford: Oxford University Press.

Fischoff, Ephraim. 1944. "The Protestant Ethic and the Spirit of Capitalism: History of a Controversy." *Social Research* 11 (February): 53–77.

Fisher, Louis. [1978] 1997. *Constitutional Conflicts between Congress and the President*. 4th Rev. Ed. Lawrence: University of Kansas Press.

———. 1988. *Constitutional Dialogues: Interpretation as Political Process*. Princeton: Princeton University Press.

———. 1995. *American Constitutional Law*. 2nd. ed. New York: McGraw-Hill.

Foster, Nigel. [1993] 1996. *German Legal System & Laws*. 2nd ed. Foreword by Lord Hoffmann. London: Blackstone Press.

Fraenkel, Ernst. 1964. *Deutschland und die westlichen Demokratien*. Stuttgart: Kohlhammer.

Friedrich, Carl. 1928. "The Issue of Judicial Review in Germany." *Political Science Quarterly* 42, 2: 188–200.

———. 1963. *The Philosophy of Law in Historical Perspective*. Chicago: The University of Chicago Press.

Frotscher, Werner. 1983. Organization der Reichsverwaltung und der Länderverwaltungen einschließlich Vorschläge zur Reichsreform. In *Das Reich als Republik und in der Zeit des Nationalsozialismus*. Vol. 4 of *Deutsche Verwaltungsgeschichte*, ed. Kurt Jeserich, Hans Pohl, and Georg-Christoph von Unruh. Stuutgart: Deutsche Verlags-Anstalt.

Furet, Francois. 1981. *Interpreting the French Revolution*. Translated by Elborg Forster. Cambridge: Cambridge University Press.

———. 1984. *In the Workshop of History*. Translated by Jonathan Mandelbaum. Chicago: The University of Chicago Press.

Geiter, Mary K., and W. A. Speck. 1997. Anticipating America: American mentality before the Revolution. In *Britain & America: Studies in Comparative History, 1760–1970*, ed. David Englander. New Haven: Yale University Press.

Geny, François. 1927. *Science et Technique en droit privé positif, Seconde Partie: Elaboration Scientifique du Droit Positif (L'irreductible "droit naturel")*. Paris: Societe anonyme du Recueil Sirey.

———. [1954] 1963. *Methode d'Interpretation et Sources en Droit Privé Positif: Critical Essay*. 2nd ed. Translated by Jaro Mayda. St. Paul, Minn., West Publishing Company.

Gerloff, W. 1928. "Schwebende Fragen des Finanzausgleichs." *Schriftenreihe des deutschen Städtetages* 5.

Giddens, Anthony. 1976. Introduction. In *Max Weber: The Protestant Ethic and the Spirit of Capitalism*. Translated by Talcott Parsons. New York: Charles Scribner's Sons.

Gilbert, Felix. 1990. *History: Politics or Culture? Reflections on Ranke and Burckhardt*. Princeton: Princeton University Press.

Glendon, Mary Ann. 1991. *Rights Talk: The Impoverishment of Political Discourse*. New York: The Free Press.

Glennon, Robert Jerome. 1991. "The Role of Law in the Civil Rights Movement: The Montgomery Bus Boycott, 1955–1957." *Law and History Review* 9, 1 (Spring 1991): 59–112.

Glum, Friedrich. 1929. *Der deutsche und der französische Reichswirtschaftsrat: Ein Beitrag zu dem Problem der Repräsentation der Wirtschaft im Staat*. Berlin und Leipzig: Walter de Gruyter & Co.

Godochet, Jacques. 1989. "L'histoire constitutionelle de la France de 1789 a nos jours." *Das Jahrbuch des öffentlichen Rechts der Gegenwart* 38: 45–76.

Gottfried, Paul Edward. 1990. *Carl Schmitt: Politics and Theory*. New York: Greenwood Press.

Grimm, Dieter. 1982. Die Verfassungsrechtlichen Grundlagen der Privatrechtsgesetzgebung. In *Das 19 Jahrhundert, Gesetzgebung zum allgemeinen Privatrecht*. Vol. 3 of *Handbuch der Quellen und Literatur der Neueren Europäischen Privatrechtsgeschichte*, ed. Helmut Coing. Munich: C.H. Beck'sche Verlagsbuchhandlung: 17–173.

———. 1986. "Historische Erfahrungen mit Rechtsvereinheitlichung—das frühe 19. Jahrhundert in Deutschland." *Rabels Zeitschrift für ausländisches und internationales Privatrecht* 50: 61–76.

———. 1988. *Deutsche Verfassungsgeschichte, 1776–1866: Vom Beginn des modernen Verfassungsstaats bis zur Auflösung des Deutschen Bundes*. Frankfurt am Main: Suhrkamp Verlag.

Grund, Henning. 1976. *"Preußenschlag" und Staatsgerichtshof im Jahre 1932*. Baden-Baden: Nomos Verlagsgesellschaft.

Gunlicks, Arthur B. 1986. *Local Government in the German Federal System*. Durham: Duke University Press.

Gunther, Richard and Anthony Mughan. 1993. Political Institutions and Cleavage Management. In *Do Institutions Matter? Government Capabilities in the United States and Abroad*, ed. R. Kent Weaver, and Bert A. Rockman. Washington, D.C.: The Brookings Institution.

Haan, Heiner. 1968. "Kaiser Ferdinand II. und das Problem des Reichsabolutismus." *Historische Zeitschrift* 207: 297–345.

Habermas, Jürgen. [1962] 1989. *Structural Transformation of the Public Sphere: An Inquiry into a Category of Bourgeois Society*. Trans. Thomas Burger with Frederick Lawrence. Cambridge: MIT Press.

———. 1987. Die Schrecken der Autonomie. Carl Schmitt auf englisch. In *Eine Art Schadenabwicklung*. Frankfurt: Suhrkamp.

Hahn, Erich J. 1995. *Rudolf von Gneist, 1816–1895: Ein politischer Jurist in der Bismarckzeit*. Frankfurt am Main: Vittorio Klostermann.

Hardin, Russell. 1993. Public Choice v. Democracy. In *The Idea of Democracy*, ed. David Copp, Jean Hampton, and John E. Roemer. Cambridge: Cambridge University Press.

Hart, H.L.A. 1961. *The Concept of Law*. Oxford: Clarendon Press.

Hartung, Fritz. 1972. Imperial Reform, 1485–1495: Its Course and Its Character. In *Pre-Reformation Germany*, ed. Gerald Strauss. London: Macmillan.

Hayek, Friedrich. 1973. *Rules and Order*. Vol. 1 of *Law, Legislation, and Liberty*. Chicago: The University of Chicago Press.

Hedemann, Justus Wilhelm. 1933. *Die Flucht in die General-Klauseln: Eine Gefahr für Recht und Staat*. Tübingen: J.C.B. Mohr (Paul Siebeck).

Heffter, Heinrich. 1950. *Die Deutsche Selbstverwaltung im 19. Jahrhundert: Geschichte der Ideen und Institutionen*. Stuttgart: K. F. Koehler.

Hegel, G.W.F. [1821] 1967. *Philosophy of Right*. Translated by T. M. Knox. Oxford: Oxford University Press.

———. [1837]. 1953. *Reason in History*. Translated with an introduction by Robert S. Hartman. Indianapolis, Ind.: Bobbs-Merrill Educational Publishing.

———. 1956. *Lectures on the Philosophy of History*. Translated by J. Sibtree. New York: Dover Edition.

Heimpel, Hermann. 1972. Characteristic of the Late Middle Ages in Germany. In *Pre-Reformation Germany*, ed. Gerald Strauss. London: Macmillan.

Hekman, Susan J. 1983. "Weber's Ideal Type: A Contemporary Reassessment. *Polity* 16, 1 (Fall): 119–37.

Heller, Hermann. 1983. *Staatlehre*. 6th Rev. Ed.. Edited by Gerhart Niemeyer. Tübingen: J.C.B. Mohr (Paul Siebeck).

Henne, Thomas. 1995. *Verwaltungsrechtsschutz: Das Beispiel des Herzogstums Braunschweig, 1832–1896*. Frankfurt am Main: Vittorio Klostermann.

Herget, James E. and Stephen Wallace. 1987. "The German Free Law Movement as the Source of American Legal Realism." *Virginia Law Review* 73: 399–455.

Herrigel, Gary. 1996. *Industrial Constructions: The Sources of German Industrial Power*. Cambridge: Cambridge University Press.

Herzfeld, Hans. 1957. *Demokratie und Selbstverwaltung in der Weimarer Epoche*. Berlin: Kohlhammer.

Hesse, Konrad. 1962. Der Rechtsstaat im Verfassungssystem des Grundgesetzes. In *Staatsverfassung und Kirchenordnung: Festgabe für Rudolf Smend zum 80 Gebertstag am 15 Januar 1962*, ed. Hesse, Siegfried Reicke, and Ulrich Scheuner. Tübingen: J.C.B. Mohr (Paul Siebeck).

———. 1991. *Grundzüge des Verfassungsrechts der Bundesrepublik Deutschland*. 18th ed. Heidelberg: C. F. Müller Juristischer Verlag.

Heun, Werner. 1989. "Der Staatsrechtliche Positivismus in der Weimarer Republik: Eine Konzeption im Widerstreit." *Der Staat* 28: 377–403.

Hirst, Paul, ed. [1989] 1993. *The Pluralist Theory of the State: Selected Writings of G.D.H. Cole, J. N. Figgis, and H. J. Laski*. London: Routledge.

Hobbes, Thomas. [1651] 1968. *Leviathan*. Edited and with an introduction by C. B. Macpherson. Harmondsworth, England: Penguin.

Hofmann, Hasso. [1964] 1992. *Legitimität gegen Legalität: Der Weg der politischen Philosophie Carl Schmitts*. Berlin: Duncker & Humblot.

Hofmann, Wolfgang. 1974. *Zwischen Rathaus und Reichskanzlei: Die Oberbürgermeister in der Kommunal- und Staatspolitik des Deutschen Reiches von 1890 bis 1933*. Stuttgart: Verlag W. Kohlhammer.

Holmes, Stephen. 1988. Gag rules or the politics of omission. In *Constitutionalism and Democracy*, ed. Jon Elster, and Rune Slagstad. Cambridge: Cambridge University Press.

———. 1993. *The Anatomy of Antiliberalism*. Cambridge: Harvard University Press.

———. 1995. *Passions and Constraint: On the Theory of Liberal Democracy*. Chicago: The University of Chicago Press.

——— and Cass Sunstein. 1999. *The Cost of Rights: Why Liberty Depends on Taxes*. New York: W. W. Norton & Company.

Holtfrerich, Carl-Ludwig. 1984. "Zu hohen Löhnen in der Weimarer Republik? Bemerkungen zur Borchardt-These." *Geschichte und Gesellschaft* 10: 122–41.

Hong, Young-Sun. 1998. *Welfare, Modernity, and the Weimar State, 1919–1933*. Princeton: Princeton University Press.

Horwitz, Morton J. 1977. *The Transformation of American Law, 1780–1860*. Cambridge: Harvard University Press.

Huber, Ernst Rudolf. 1957–84. *Deutsche Verfassungsgeschichte seit 1789.* 7 vols. Stuttgart: Verlag W. Kohlhammer.

Hudson, John. 1996. *The Formation of the English Common Law: Law and Society in England from the Norman Conquest to Magna Carta.* London and New York: Longman.

Hunt, Lynn. 1976. "Committees and Communes: Local Politics and National Revolution in 1789."*Comparative Studies in Society and History* 18: 321–46.

———. 1978. *Revolution and Urban Politics in Provincial France: Troyes and Reims, 1786–1790.* Stanford: Stanford University Press.

Iggers, Georg G. 1983. *The German Conception of History: The National Tradition of Historical Thought from Herder to the Present.* Rev. ed. Hanover, N.H.: Wesleyan University Press.

Imperial Parliament, Germany. 1921. "Gesetz über den Staatsgerichtshof vom 9. Juli 1921."*Reichsgesetzblatt* 74.

Jaffa, Harry V. 1982. *The Crisis of the House Divided: An Interpretation of the Issues in the Lincoln-Douglas Debates.* With a New Preface. Reprint. Chicago: The University of Chicago Press.

Jaffe, Louis L. 1937. "Law Making by Private Groups." *Harvard Law Review* 60, 2 (December): 201–253.

Jellinek, Georg. 1922. *Allgemeine Staatslehre.* 3rd ed. Berlin: Verlag von Julius Springer.

Jellinek, Walter. 1930. Insbesondere: Entstehung und Ausbau der Weimarer Reichsverfassung. In *Handbuch des deutschen Staatsrechts: Vol. 2,* ed. Gerhard Anschütz, and Richard Thoma. Tübingen: Verlag von J.C.B. Mohr (Paul Siebeck).

Joas, Hans. 1993. *Pragmatism and Social Theory.* Chicago: The University of Chicago Press.

John, Michael. 1989. *Politics and the Law in Late Nineteenth-Century Germany: The Origins of the Civil Code.* Oxford: Oxford University Press.

Johnston, David. 1986. *The Rhetoric of Leviathan: Thomas Hobbes and the Politics of Cultural Transformation.* Princeton: Princeton University Press.

Jones, Larry Eugene. [1988] 1998. *German Liberalism and the Dissolution of the Weimar Party System, 1918–1933.* Chapel Hill: University of North Carolina Press; Ann Arbor: University of Michigan Press.

Jones, P. M. 1995. *Reform and Revolution in France: The Politics of Transition, 1774–1791.* Cambridge: Cambridge University Press.

Kahn-Freund, Otto. 1974. "On Uses and Misuses of Comparative Law." *Modern Law Review* 37 (January): 1–27.

Kal, Bongkun. 1988. Carl Schmitts Einfluß auf das koreanische Verfassungsleben. In *Complexio Oppositorium. Über Carl Schmitt,* ed. Helmut Quaritsch. Berlin: Duncker & Humblot.

Kalberg, Stephen. 1994. *Max Weber's Comparative-Historical Sociology.* Cambridge: Polity Press.

Kammen, Michael. 1987. *A Machine That Would Go of Itself: The Constitution in American Culture*. New York: Alfred A. Knopf.

Karsten, Klaus. 1995. "Die Reichssteuerpolitik in der Weimarer Republik." In *Zeitschrift für Neuere Rechtsgeschichte* 17, 1.

Katzenstein, Peter. 1987. *The Semi-Sovereign State: Policy and Politics in West Germany*. Philadelphia: Temple University Press.

Kelsen, Hans. 1925. *Allgemeine Staatslehre*. Berlin: J. Springer.

———. [1929] 1981. *Vom Wesen und Wert der Demokratie*. 2nd. ed. Aalen: Scienta Verlag.

———. 1930. *Der Staat als Integration: Eine Prinzipielle Auseinandersetzung*. Wien: Verlag von Julius Springer.

———. 1930/31. "Wer soll Hüter der Verfassung sein?" *Die Justiz* 6.

———. [1960] 1989. *Pure Theory of Law*. 2nd ed. Translated by Max Knight. Gloucester, Mass.: Peter Smith.

———. 1968. Was ist die Reine Rechtslehre? In *Die Wiener Rechtstheoretische Schule: Schriften von Hans Kelsen, Adolf Merkl, Alfred Verdross*, ed. Hans Klecatsky, René Marcic, Herbert Schambeck. Wien: Europa Verlag.

Kervégan, Jean-François. 1992. *Hegel, Carl Schmitt: Le Politique Entre Spéculation et Positivité*. Paris: Presses Universitaires de France.

Kocka, Jürgen, ed. 1986. *Max Weber, der Historiker*. Göttingen: Vandenhoeck und Ruprecht.

Kocka, Jürgen and Detlev Peukert. 1986. "Max Weber et l'Histoire. Derniers Développements en République Fédérale d'Allemagne." *Revue de Synthèse* 4, 1–2 (January): 8–37.

Kolb, Eberhard, ed. 1972. *Vom Kaiserreich zur Weimarer Republik*. Cologne: Kiepenheuer & Witsch.

Kommers, Donald. 1976. *Judicial Politics in West Germany*. Beverly Hills, Calif.: Sage Publications.

Koselleck, Reinhart. 1985. *Futures Past: On the Semantics of Historical Time*. Translated by Keith Tribe. Cambridge: MIT Press.

———. [1967] 1989. *Preussen zwischen Reform und Revolution: Allgemeines Landrecht, Verwaltung und soziale Bewegung von 1791 bis 1848*. 3rd ed. Munich: Deutscher Taschenbuch Verlag.

Krieger, Leonard. 1957. *The German Idea of Freedom: History of a Political Tradition*. Boston: Beacon Press.

Krockow, Christian Graf von. 1958. *Die Entscheidung: Eine Untersuchung über Ernst Jünger, Carl Schmitt, Martin Heidegger*. Stuttgart: F. Enke.

Kruedener, Jürgen von. 1985. "Die Überforderung der Weimarer Republik als Sozialstaat." In *Geschichte und Gesellschaft* 11, 3: 358–76.

———. 1987. The Franckenstein Paradox in the Intergovernmental Fiscal Relations of Imperial Germany. In *Wealth and Taxation in Central Europe: The History and Sociology of Public Finance*, ed. Peter-Christian Witt. Leamington Spa, Germany: Berg.

———, ed. 1990. *Economic Crisis and Political Collapse: The Weimar Republic, 1924–1933.* New York: Berg.

Kühne, Jörg-Detlef. 1990. "Die französische Menschen- und Bürgerrechtserklärung im Rechtsvergleich mit den Vereinigten Staaten und Deutschland." *Jahrbuch des Öffentlichen Rechts der Gegenwart* 39: 1–53.

Lambert, Eduoard. 1921. *Le gouvernement des juges et la lutte contre la législation sociale aux États-Unis: L'expérience américaine du controle judiciare de la constitutionalité des lois.* Paris: Marcel Giard.

Landfried, Christine. 1984. *Bundesverfassungsgericht und Gesetzgeber.* 2nd ed. Baden-Baden: Nomos.

Lehman, Hartmut and Guenther Roth. 1993. *Weber's Protestant Ethic: Origins, Evidence, Contexts.* Cambridge: Cambridge University Press.

Lehnert, Detlef. 1992. "Hugo Preuß als moderner Klassiker einer kritischen Theorie der 'verfaßten' Politik. Vom Souveränitätsproblem zum demokratischen Pluralismus." *Politische Vierteljahresschrift* 33.

Lenoir, J. J. 1940. "Judicial Review in Germany under the Weimar Constitution." *Tulane Law Review* 14: 361–83.

Lepsius, M. Rainer. 1993. "Parteiensystem und Sozialstruktur: Zum Problem der Demokratisierung der deutschen Gesellschaft." In *Demokratie in Deutschland: Soziologisch-historische Konstellationsanalysen, Ausgewählte Aufsätze.* Göttingen: Vandenhoeck & Ruprecht.

Lepsius, Oliver. 1994. *Die gegensatzaufhebende Begriffsbildung: Methodenentwicklungen in der Weimar Republik und ihr Verhältnis zur Ideologisierung der Rechtswissenschaft unter dem Nationalsozialismus.* München: C. H. Beck.

Lieberman, Ben. 1998. *From Recovery to Catastrophe: Municipal Stabilization and Political Crisis in Weimar Germany.* New York and Oxford: Berghahn Books.

Lietzmann, Hans. 1988. Vater der Verfassungsväter?—Carl Schmitt und die Verfassungsgründung in der Bundesrepublik Deutschland. In *Carl Schmitt und die Liberalismuskritik,* ed. Klaus Hansen and Hans Lietzmann. Opladen: Leske & Budrich.

Lijphart, Arend, Ronald Rogowski, and R. Kent Weaver. 1993. Separation of Powers and Cleavage Management. In *Do Institutions Matter? Government Capabilities in the United States and Abroad,* ed. R. Kent Weaver and Bert A. Rockman. Washington, D.C.: The Brookings Institution.

Lincoln, Abraham. 1989. *Speeches and Writings.* 2 vols. With notes by Don E. Fehrenbacher. New York: Library of America.

Lindbekk, Tore. 1992. "The Weberian Ideal-Type: Development and Continuities. *Acta Sociologica* 35: 285–297.

Lobe, Adolf, ed. 1929. *Fünzig Jahre Reichsgericht.* Berlin: Walter de Gruyter.

Lowi, Theodore. [1969] 1979. *The End of Liberalism: The Second Republic of the United States.* 2nd ed. New York: W. W. Norton.

Luebbe-Wolff, Gertrude. 1990. Safeguards of Civil and Constitutional Rights—The Debate on the Role of the Reichsgericht. In *German and American Con-*

stitutional Thought: Contexts, Interaction, and Historical Realities. Edited by Hermann Wellenreuther. New York: St. Martin's Press.

Madison, James, Alexander Hamilton, and John Jay. 1961. *The Federalist Papers*. With an Introduction by Clinton Rossiter. New York: Mentor Books.

Maier, Charles. [1975] 1988. *Recasting Bourgeois Europe: Stabilization in France, Germany, and Italy in the Decade after World War I*. With a new preface. Princeton: Princeton University Press.

———. 1985. "Die Nicht-Determinierheit ökonomischer Modelle: Überlegungen zu Knut Borchardts These von der 'kranken Wirtschaft' der Weimarer Republik." *Geschichte und Gesellschaft* 11: 275–94.

Malberg, Raymond Carré de. 1984. *La Loi, expression de la volonté générale*. Paris: Economica.

Manin, Bernard. 1997. *The Principles of Representative Government*. Cambridge: Cambridge University Press.

Mattern, Johannes, 1928. *Constitutional Jurisprudence of the German National Republic*. Baltimore, Maryland: Johns Hopkins University Press.

Mauersberg, Jasper. 1991. *Ideen und Konzeption Hugo Preuß für die Verfassung der deutschen Republik 1919 und ihre Durchsetzung im Verfassungswerk von Weimar*. Frankfurt am Main: Lang.

Maus, Ingeborg. 1969. "Zur Zäsur von 1933 in der Theorie Carl Schmitts." *Kritische Justiz* 2: 113–24.

———. [1976] 1980. *Bürgerliche Rechtstheorie und Fascismus: Zur sozialen Funktion und aktuellen Wirkung der Theorie Carl Schmitts*. München: Wilhelm Fink Verlag.

———. 1986. *Rechtstheorie und politische Theorie im Industriekapitalismus*. Munich: Wilhelm Fink Verlag.

Mayeur, Jean-Marie and Madeleine Reberioux. 1987. *The Third Republic from its Origins to the Great War, 1871–1914*. Translated by J. R. Foster. Cambridge: Cambridge University Press, 1987.

McCann, Michael. 1994. *Rights at Work: Pay Equity Reform and the Politics of Legal Mobilization*. Chicago: The University of Chicago Press.

McCloskey, Robert G. [1960] 1994. *The American Supreme Court*. Revised by Sanford Levinson. Chicago: The University of Chicago Press.

McCormick, John. 1993. "Introduction to Schmitt's 'The Age of Neutralizations and Depoliticizations." *Telos* 96.

———. 1994. "Fear, Technology and the State: Carl Schmitt, Leo Strauss and the Revival of Hobbes in Weimar and National Socialist Germany." *Political Theory* 22 (November): 619–52.

———. 1997. *Carl Schmitt's Critique of Liberalism: Against Politics as Technology*. Cambridge: Cambridge University Press.

McLemore, Lelan. 1984. "Max Weber's Defense of Historical Inquiry." *History and Theory* 23, 3: 277–95.

McNeil, William C. 1986. *American Money and the Weimar Republic: Economics and Politics on the Eve of the Great Depression*. New York: Columbia University Press.

McPherson, James M. 1988. *Battle Cry of Freedom*. New York: Oxford University Press.

Mehring, Reinhard. 1989. *Pathetisches Denken. Carl Schmitts Denkweg am Leitfaden Hegels: Katholische Grundstellung und antimarxistische Hegelstrategie*. Berlin: Duncker & Humblot.

———. 1990. "Politische Ethik in Max Weber's 'Politik als Beruf' und Carl Schmitt's 'Der Begriff des Politischen.' " *Politische Vierteljahressschrift* 31, 4: 608–626.

———. 1991. "Carl Schmitts Lehre von der Auflösung des Liberalismus: Das Sinngefüge der 'Constitutional Theory' als historisches Urteil." *Zeitschrift für Politik* 38: 200–216.

———. 1995. "Carl Schmitt und die Verfassungslehre unserer Tage." *Archiv des öffentlichen Rechts* 120: 177–204.

Meier, Christian. 1988. Zu Carl Schmitt's Begriffsbildung. In *Complexio Oppositorium. Über Carl Schmitt*, ed. Helmut Quaritsch. Berlin: Duncker & Humblot.

———. 1988a. *Carl Schmitt, Leo Strauss und "Der Begriff des Politischen": Zu einem Dialog unter Abwesenden*. Stuttgart: J. B. Metzlersche Verlagsbuchhandlung.

Meinecke, Friedrich. 1950. *The German Catastrophe: Reflections and Recollections*. Boston: Beacon Press.

Merryman, John Henry. 1985. *The Civil Law Tradition: An Introduction to the Legal Systems of Western Europe and Latin America*. Stanford: Stanford University Press.

Meuter, Günther. 1994. *Der Katechon: Zu Carl Schmitts fundamentalistischer Kritik der Zeit*. Berlin: Duncker & Humblot.

Michelman, Frank. 1986. "Foreword: Traces of Self-Government. The Supreme Court 1985 Term." *Harvard Law Review* 100 (November): 4–77.

Miller, Perry. 1965. *The Life of the Mind in America: from the Revolution to the Civil War, Books One Through Three*. New York: Harcourt Brace Jovanovich, A Harvest/HBJ Book.

Mohl, Robert. 1860. *Staatsrecht, Völkerrecht und Politik*. 3 vols. Tübingen: Lauppe, 1860–1869.

Mommsen, Hans. 1991. Heinrich Brüning as Chancellor: The Failure of a Politically Isolated Strategy. In *From Weimar to Auschwitz*. Translated by Philip O'Connor. Princeton: Princeton University Press.

Mommsen, Wolfgang. [1959] 1984. *Max Weber and German Politics, 1890–1920*. Translated by Michael S. Steinberg. Chicago: The University of Chicago Press.

———. 1974. *The Age of Bureaucracy: Perspectives on the Political Sociology of Max Weber*. New York: Oxford University Press.

———. 1989. *The Political and Social Theory of Max Weber*. Chicago: The University of Chicago Press.

Moses, John A. 1982. *Trade Unionism in Germany, 1869–1918*. Vol. 1 of *Trade Unionism in Germany from Bismarck to Hitler, 1869–1933*. London: George Prior Publishers.

Muller, Jan. 1999. "Carl Schmitt's Method: Between Ideology, Demonology and Myth." *Journal of Political Ideologies* 4, 1: 61–85.

Muller, Jerry Z. 1991. "Carl Schmitt, Hans Freyer and the Radical Conservative Critique of Liberal Democracy in the Weimar Republic." *History of Political Thought* 12: 695.

Müller, Kai. 1997. *Der Hüter des Rechts: Die Stellung des Reichsgerichts im Deutschen Kaiserreich 1879–1918*. Baden-Baden: Nomos Verlagsgesellschaft.

Mußgnug, Reinhard. 1988. Carl Schmitts verfassungsrechtliches Werk und sein Fortwirken im Staatsrecht der Bundesrepublik Deutschland. In *Complexio Oppositorium. Über Carl Schmitt*, ed. Helmut Quaritsch. Berlin: Duncker & Humblot.

Nedelsky, Jennifer. 1990. *Private Property and the Limits of American Constitutionalism: The Madisonian Framework and Its Legacy*. Chicago: The University of Chicago Press.

Neely, Mark E. Jr. 1991. *The Fate of Liberty: Abraham Lincoln and Civil Liberties*. New York: Oxford University Press.

Nelson, Benjamin. 1973. Max Weber's *The Protestant Ethic:* Its Origins, Wanderings and Foreseeable Future. In *Beyond the Classics: Essays in the Scientific Study of Religion*, ed. C. Y. Glock, and P. E. Hammond. New York: Harper and Row.

Nelson, William E. 1975. *Americanization of the Common Law: The Impact of Legal Change on Massachusetts Society, 1760–1830*. Cambridge: Harvard University Press.

Neustadt, Richard E. 1990. *Presidential Power and the Modern Presidents: The Politics of Leadership from Roosevelt to Reagan*. New York: The Free Press.

Newcomer, Mabel. 1937. *Central and Local Finance in Germany and England*. New York: Columbia University Press.

Nipperdey, Hans Carl, ed. [1930] 1975. *Die Grundrechte und Grundpflichten der Reichsverfassung: Kommentar zum 2 Teil der Reichsverfassung*. 3 vols. Berlin: Hobbing.

Noack, Paul. 1993. *Carl Schmitt: Eine Biographie*. Berlin: Propyläen.

Nörr, Knut Wolfgang. 1988. *Zwischen den Mühlsteinen: Eine Privatrechtsgeschichte der Weimarer Republik*. Tübingen: J.C.B. Mohr (Paul Siebeck).

———. 1993. "Labour Law and Constitution. The Example of the Weimar Reichsverfassung of 1919." *Festschrift für Joachim Gernhuber zum 70. Geburtstag*, ed. Hermann Lange, Knut Nörr, Harm Peter Westermann. Tübingen: J.C.B. Mohr.

———. 1996. *Richter zwischen Gesetz und Wirklichkeit: Die Reaktion des Reichsgerichts auf die Krisen von Weltkrieg und Inflation, und die Entfaltung eines neues richterlichen Selbstverständnisses*. Heidelberg: C.F. Müller.

Ogorek, Regina. 1986. *Richterkönig oder Subsumtionsautomat? Zur Justiztheorie im 19. Jahrhundert*. Frankfurt am Main: Vittorio Klostermann.

Orlow, Dietrich. 1986. *Weimar Prussia, 1918–1925: The Unlikely Rock of Democracy*. Pittsburgh: University of Pittsburgh Press.

———. 1991. *Weimar Prussia, 1925–1933: The Illusion of Strength.* Pittsburgh: University of Pittsburgh Press.

Ormond, Thomas. 1994. *Richterwürde und Regierungstreue: Dienstrecht, politische Betätigung und Disziplinierung der Richter in Preußen, Baden und Hessen 1866–1918.* Frankfurt am Main: Vittorio Klostermann.

Orren, Karen. 1991. *Belated Feudalism: Labor, the Law, and Liberal Development in the United States.* Cambridge: Cambridge University Press.

Ostrogorski, Moisei. [1903] 1922. *Democracy and the Organization of Political Parties.* Translated by Frederick Clarke. With a preface by James Bryce. New York: Macmillan.

Ott, Walter. 1992. *Der Rechtspositivismus. Kritische Würdigung auf der Grundlage eines juristischen Pragmatismus.* 2d. ed. Berlin: Duncker & Humblot.

Padgett, Stephen and Tony Burkett, 1986. *Political Parties and Elections in West Germany: The Search for a New Stability.* London: Hurst & Co.

Patch, Jr., William L. 1998. *Heinrich Brüning and the Dissolution of the Weimar Republic.* Cambridge: Cambridge University Press.

Petzina, Dietmar. 1984. "Soziale und Wirtschaftliche Entwicklung." In *Das Reich als Republik und in der Zeit des Nationalsozialismus.* Vol. 4 of *Deutsche Verwaltungsgeschichte*, ed. Kurt Jeserich, Hans Pohl, and Georg-Christoph von Unruh. Stuutgart: Deutsche Verlags-Anstalt.

Petzina, Dietmar, and Werner Abelshauser. 1974. Zum Problem der relativen Stagnation der deutschen Wirtschaft in den zwanziger Jahren. In *Industrielles System und politische Entwicklung in der Weimarer Republik*, ed. Hans Mommsen, Dietmar Petzina, and Bernd Weisbrod. Düsseldorf: Droste Verlag.

Peukert, Detlev J. K. [1987] 1991. *The Weimar Republic: The Crisis of Classical Modernity.* Translated by Richard Deveson. London: Penguin.

Philip, Loïc. 1989. "La protection des droits fondamentaux en France." *Jahrbuch des Öffentlichen Rechts der Gegenwart* 38: 116.

Pilch, Martin. 1994. *System des transcendentalen Etatismus: Staat und Verfassung bei Carl Schmitt.* Wien & Leipzig: Karolinger.

Plessner, Helmut. 1974. *Die verspätete Nation: Über die politische Verführbarkeit bürgerlichen Geistes.* Stuttgart: Kohlhammer.

Pound, Roscoe. 1951. "The Development of American Law and Its Deviation from English Law." *The Law Quarterly Review* 67: 49–66.

Preuß, Hugo. 1964. *Staat, Recht und Freiheit: aus 40 Jahren deutscher Politik und Geschichte.* Hildesheim: Georg Olms Verlagsbuchhandlung.

Preuß, Ulrich K. 1993. "Constitutional Powermaking for the New Polity: Some Deliberations on the Relations between Constituant Power and the Constitution." *Cardoza Law Review* 14 (January): 639–60.

———. 1995. "Patterns of Constitutional Evolution and Change in Eastern Europe." In *Constitutional Policy and Change in Europe.* Edited by Joachim Jens Hesse and Nevil Johnson. Oxford: Oxford University Press.

Purcell, Edward. Jr. 1973. *The Crisis of Democratic Theory: Scientific Naturalism & the Problem of Value*. Lexington: The University of Kentucky Press.

Quaritsch, Helmut. 1988. Einleitung: Über den Umgang mit Person und Werk Carl Schmitts. In *Complexio Oppositorium. Über Carl Schmitt*, ed. Helmut Quaritsch. Berlin: Duncker & Humblot.

Rawls, John. 1993. *Political Liberalism*. New York: Columbia University Press.

Retallack, James. 1992. Wilhelmine Germany. In *Modern Germany Reconsidered, 1870–1945*, ed. Gordon Martel. London and New York: Routledge.

———. 1996. Liberals, Conservatives, and the Modernizing State: The *Kaiserreich* in Regional Perspective. In *Society, Culture, and the State in Germany, 1870–1930*, ed. Geoff Eley. Ann Arbor: The University of Michigan Press.

Revel, Jacques. 1987. Les corps et communautés. In *The Political Culture of the Old Regime*. Vol. 1 of *The French Revolution and the Creation of Modern Political Culture*, ed. Keith Baker. Oxford: Pergamon Press.

Riker, William H., and Jonathan Limco. 1987. The Relation between Structure and Stability in Federal Governments. In *The Development of American Federalism*, ed. William H. Riker. Boston: Kluwer Academic Publishers.

Roberts, Geoffrey K. 1997. *Party Politics in the New Germany*. London and Washington: Pinter.

Root, Hilton. 1987. *Peasants and King in Burgundy: Agrarian Foundations of French Absolutism*. Berkeley: University of California Press.

———. 1987. The Rural Community and the French Revolution. In *The Political Culture of the Old Regime*. Vol. 1 of *The French Revolution and the Creation of Modern Political Culture*, ed. Keith Baker. Oxford: Pergamon Press.

Rosenberg, Hans. [1958] 1966. *Bureaucracy, Aristocracy, Autocracy: The Prussian Experience, 1660–1815*. Boston: Beacon Press.

Rossiter, Clinton L. 1948. *Constitutional Dictatorship: Crisis Government in the Modern Democracies*. Princeton: Princeton University Press.

Roth, Guenther. 1963. *The Social Democrats in Imperial Germany: A Study in Working Class Isolation and National Integration*. Totowa, N.J.: Barnes & Noble.

Roth, Guenther, and Wolfgang Schluchter. 1979. *Max Weber's Vision of History: Ethics and Methods*. Berkeley: University of California Press.

Rückert, Joachim. 1984. *Idealismus, Jurisprudenz und Politik bei Friedrich Carl von Savigny*. Ebelsbach: Verlag Rolf Gremer.

Runciman, David. 1997. *Pluralism and the Personality of the State*. Cambridge: Cambridge University Press.

Rürup, Reinhard. 1972. Entstehung und Grundlagen der Weimarer Verfassung. In *Vom Kaiserreich zur Weimarer Republik*, ed. Eberhard Kolb. Cologne: Kiepenheuer & Witsch: 218–43.

Rüthers, Bernd. 1994. *Carl Schmitt im Dritten Reich. Wissenschaft als Zeitgeist-Verstärkung?* München: Verlag C. H. Beck.

———. 1999. "On the Brink of Dictatorship—Hans Kelsen and Carl Schmitt in Cologne 1933." In *Hans Kelsen and Carl Schmitt: A Juxtaposition*, ed. Dan Diner and Michael Stolleis. Gerlingen: Bleicher Verlag.

Sager, Laurence. 1978. "Fair Measure: The Legal Status of Underenforced Constitutional Norms."*Harvard Law Review* 91.

Sartori, Giovanni. [1994] 1997. *Comparative Constitutional Engineering: An Inquiry into Structures, Incentives, and Outcomes.* 2nd ed. London: Macmillan.

Savigny, Carl Friedrich. 1951. *Anleitung zu einem eigenen Studium der Jurisprudenz.* Stuttgart: K.F. Koehler Verlag.

———. 1968. *Vermischte Schriften.* 6 vols. Darmstadt: Wissenschaftliche Buchgesellschaft.

———. 1973. Vom Beruf unserer Zeit für Gesetzgebung und Rechtswissenschaft. In *Thibaut und Savigny*, ed. H. Hattenhauer. München: Vahlen.

———. 1975. *Of the Vocation of Our Age for Legislation and Jurisprudence.* London: Littlewood & Co.

Scheuerman, William. 1993. "The Rule of Law Under Siege: Carl Schmitt and the Death of the Weimar Republic." *History of Political Thought* 14: 265–80.

———. 1994. *Between the Norm and the Exception: The Frankfurt School and the Rule of Law.* Cambridge: The MIT Press.

———. 1995. "Is parliamentarism in crisis? A response to Carl Schmitt." *Theory and Society* 24: 135–158.

———. 1996. "Carl Schmitt's Critique of Liberal Constitutionalism." *The Review of Politics* 58: 299–322.

———. 1997. "The Unholy Alliance of Carl Schmitt and Friedrich A. Hayek." *Constellations* 4, 2 (October).

Scheuner, Ulrich. 1968. Die neuere Entwicklung des Rechtsstaats in Deutschland. In *Rechtsstaatlichkeit und Sozialstaatlichkeit: Aufsätze und Essays*, ed. Ernst Forsthoff. Darmstadt: Wissenschaftliche Buchgesellschaft.

———. 1976. Die Überlieferung der deutschen Staatsgerichtsbarkeit im 19 und 20 Jahrhundert. In *Bundesverfassungsgericht und Grundgesetz. Festgabe aus Anlass des 25jährigen Bestehens des Bundesverfassungsgerichts*, ed. Christian Stark. Tübingen: J.C.B. Mohr (Paul Siebeck).

Schieck, Hans. 1972. "Die Behandlung der Sozialierungsfrage in den Monaten nach dem Staatsumsturz." In *Vom Kaiserreich zur Weimarer Republik*, ed. Eberhard Kolb. Cologne: Kiepenheuer & Witsch: 138–164.

Schlink, Bernard. 1991. "Why Carl Schmitt?" In *Rechtshistorisches Journal* 10: 160–76.

Schönhoven, Klaus. 1972. *Bayerische Volkspartei 1924–1932.* Düsseldorf: Droste.

———. 1977. "Zwischen Anpassung und Ausschaltung. Die Bayerische Volkspartei in der Endphase der Weimarer Republik 1932/33." *Historische Zeitschrift* 224: 340–78.

Schulz, Gerhard. 1963–92. *Zwischen Demokratie und Diktatur: Verfassungspolitik und Reichsreform in der Weimarer Republik.* 3 vols. Berlin: Walter de Gruyter.

Schuster, Rudolf, ed. 1983. *Deutsche Verfassungen.* 15th ed. Munich: Wilhelm Goldmann.

Schwab, George. [1970] 1989. *The Challenge of the Exception: An Introduction to the Political Ideas of Carl Schmitt between 1921 & 1936.* 2nd Rev. Ed. Westport, Conn.: Greenwood Press.

Schwartz, Herman. 1992. "In Defense of Aiming High." *East European Constitutional Review* 1.

Seitzer, Jeffrey. 1993. "History, Political Practice, and Constitutional Change: A Comparative-Historical Approach to Constitutional Theory." Ph.D. diss., The University of Chicago.

———. 1997. "Courts as Democratic Institutions: Lower and Nonconstitutional Courts in the Constitutional Politics of Germany, Hungary, and the United States." *Journal of the Indiana Academy of the Social Sciences* 1: 126–35.

———. 1998. "Contextualizing the Positivist Separation Thesis: Abraham Lincoln on the Politics of Legal Systems." *Princeton Law Journal* (Fall): 34–41.

———. 1999. Experimental Constitutionalism: A Comparative Analysis of the Institutional Bases of Rights Enforcement in Post-Communist Hungary. In *Constitutional Dialogues in Comparative Perspective*, ed. Sally J. Kenney, William M. Reisinger, and John C. Reitz. With a foreword by Joseph P. Weiler. London: Macmillan.

———. 1999a. "Nonconstitutional Courts and Constitutional Change." *King's College Law Journal* (Fall): 198–221.

Sewell, William H. 1980. *Work & Revolution in France: The Language of Labor from the Old Regime to 1848*. Cambridge: Cambridge University Press.

Shapiro, Martin, and Alec Stone. 1994. "The New Constitutional Politics of Europe." *Comparative Political Studies* 26, 4.

Sharkansky, Ira. 1970. *Regionalism in American Politics*. Indianapolis, Ind. and New York: Bobbs-Merrill.

Sheehan, James J. 1978. *German Liberalism in the Nineteenth Century*. Chicago: The University of Chicago Press.

Shiyake, Masanori. 1988. Zur Lage der Carl Schmitt-Forschung in Japan. In *Complexio Oppositorium. Über Carl Schmitt*, ed. Helmut Quaritsch. Berlin: Duncker & Humblot.

Silverman, Paul. 1962. "Law and Economics in Interwar Vienna: Kelsen, Mises, and the Regeneration of Austrian Liberalism." Ph.D. diss., The University of Chicago.

Simons, Walter. 1924. "Das Reichsgericht in Gegenwart und Zukunft." *Deutsche Juristen-Zeitung* 29, 7–8 (April 1st): 241–46.

———. 1929. "Relation of the German Judiciary to the Executive and Legislative Branches."*American Bar Association Journal* 15: 762–779.

Skocpol, Theda. 1979. *States and Social Revolutions: A Comparative Analysis of France, Russia, & China*. Cambridge: Cambridge University Press.

———. 1994. *Social Revolutions in the Modern World*. Cambridge: Cambridge University Press.

Skocpol, Theda, Peter B. Evans, and Dietrich Rueschemeyer. 1985. *Bringing the State Back In*. Cambridge and New York: Cambridge University Press.

Skowronek, Stephen. 1982. *Building a New American State: The Expansion of National Administrative Capacities, 1877–1920*. Cambridge: Cambridge University Press.

———. 1993. *The Politics Presidents Make: Leadership from John Adams to George Bush*. Cambridge: Harvard University Press.

Skowronek, Stephen, and Karen Orren. 1995. Order and Time in Institutional Study: A Brief for the Historical Approach. In *Political Science in History: Research Programs and Political Traditions*, ed. James Farr, John S. Dryzek, and Stephen T. Leonard. Cambridge: Cambridge University Press.

Slagstad, Rune. 1988. Liberal constitutionalism and its critics: Carl Schmitt and Max Weber. In *Constitutionalism and Democracy*, ed. Jon Elster and Rune Slagstad. Cambridge: Cambridge University Press.

Soboul, Albert. 1988. *Understanding the French Revolution*. Translated by April Ane Knutson. New York: International Publishers.

Sokolewicz, Wojciech. 1995. The Relevance of Western Models for Constitution-Building in Poland. In *Constitutional Policy and Change in Europe*, ed. Joachim Jens Hesse and Nevil Johnson. Oxford: Oxford University Press.

Sontheimer, Kurt. [1962] 1978. *Antidemokratisches Denken in der Weimarer Republik: Die politischen Ideen des deutschen Nationalismus zwischen 1918 und 1933*. Munich: Deutscher Taschenbuch Verlag.

Sorel, George. 1950. *Reflections on Violence*. Translated by E. Hulme and J. Roth. London: Collier Books.

Spangenberg, Hans. 1912. *Vom Lehnstaat zu Ständestaat: Ein Beitrag zur Entstehung der landständischen Verfassung*. Munich: R. Oldenbourg Verlag.

Spitzer, Robert J. 1988. *The Presidential Veto: Touchstone of the American Presidency*. With a foreword by Louis Fisher. Albany: State University of New York Press.

Stein, Lorenz. [1850] 1964. *The History of the Social Movement in France*. 3 vols. Translated by Kaethe Mangelberg. Totowa, N.J.: Bedminister Press.

Steinberger, Helmut. 1987. *200 Jahre amerikanische Bundesverfassung: Zu Einflüssen des amerikanischen Verfassungsrechts auf die deutsche Verfassungsentwicklung*. Berlin: Walter de Gruyter.

Steinmetz, George. 1993. *Regulating the Social: The Welfare State and Local Politics in Imperial Germany*. Princeton: Princeton University Press.

———. 1996. The Myth of the Autonomous State: Industrialists, Junkers, and Social Policy in Imperial Germany. In *Society, Culture, and the State in Germany, 1870–1930*, ed. Geoff Eley. Ann Arbor: Michigan University Press.

Stolleis, Michael. 1972. Carl Schmitt. In *Staat und Recht: Die deutsche Staatslehre im 19. und 20. Jahrhundert*, ed. Martin J. Sattler. Munich: List Verlag.

———. 1988–99. *Geschichte des öffentlichen Rechts in Deutschland: Reichspublizistik und Policeywissenschaft, 1600–1800*. 3 vols. Munich: C. H. Beck.

Stone, Alec. 1992. *The Birth of Judicial Politics in France: The Constitutional Council in Comparative Perspective*. New York: Oxford University Press.

———. 1994. "Judging Socialist Reform: The Politics of Coordinate Construction in France and Germany." *Comparative Political Studies* 26.

———. 1999. Constitutional Dialogues: Protecting Rights in France, Germany, Italy and Spain. In *Constitutional Dialogues in Comparative Perspective*, ed.

Sally J. Kenney, William M. Reisinger, and John C. Reitz. With a foreword by Joseph P. Weiler. London: Macmillan.

Strauss, Leo. 1996. Notes on Carl Schmitt, *The Concept of the Political*. Translated by Harvey Lomax. In Carl Schmitt, *The Concept of the Political*. Translated and with an introduction by George Schwab. Foreword by Tracy B. Strong. Chicago: The University of Chicago Press.

Strayer, Joseph R. 1970. *On the Medieval Origins of the Modern State*. Princeton: Princeton University Press.

Stürmer, Michael. 1967. *Koalition und Opposition in der Weimarer Republik, 1924–1928*. Düsseldorf: Droste.

Sunstein, Cass. 1990. *After the Rights Revolution: Reconceiving the Regulatory State*. Cambridge: Harvard University Press.

———. 1992. "Rights, Aspirations and State Action." *East European Constitutional Review* 1.

———. 1993. "Against Positive Rights." *East European Constitutional Review* 2.

———. 1993a. *The Partial Constitution*. Cambridge: Harvard University Press.

Tate, C. N. and T. Vallinder, ed. 1995. *The Global Expansion of Judicial Power*. New York: New York University Press.

Tay, Alice Erh-Soon and Eugene Kamenka. 1983. Public Law—Private Law. In *Public and Private in Social Life*, ed. S. I. Benn and G. F. Gaus. New York: St. Martin's Press.

Taylor, Charles. 1975. *Hegel*. Cambridge: Cambridge University Press.

———. 1985. Social Theory as Practice. In *Philosophy and the Human Sciences*. Vol. 2 of *Philosophical Papers*. Cambridge: Cambridge University Press.

Thayer, James Bradley. [1908] 1972. The Origin and Scope of the American Doctrine of Constitutional Law. In *Legal Essays*. Reprint. South Hackensack, N.J.: Rothman Reprints.

Theiner, Peter. 1983. *Sozialer Liberalismus und deutsche Weltpolitik: Friedrich Naumann im Wilhelmischen Deutschland (1860–1919)*. Baden-Baden: Nomos Verlag.

Thoma, Richard. 1922. "Das richterliche Prüfungsrecht." *Archiv des öffentlichen Rechts der Gegenwart* 43: 267–86.

———. 1932. Das System der subjectiven öffentlichen Rechte und Pflichten. In *Handbuch des deutschen Staatsrechts: Vol. 2*, ed. Gerhard Anschütz and Richard Thoma. Tübingen: Verlag von J.C.B. Mohr (Paul Siebeck).

———. 1985. On the Ideology of Parliamentarism (1925). In *The Crisis of Parliamentary Democracy*, by Carl Schmitt. Translated with an introduction by Ellen Kennedy. Cambridge: The MIT Press.

Thornhill, Chris. 2000. *Political Theory in Modern Germany: An Introduction*. Cambridge: Polity.

Tilly, Charles. 1975. On the History of European State-Making. In *The Formation of National States in Western Europe*, ed. Charles Tilly. Princeton: Princeton University Press.

———. 1993. *European Revolutions, 1492–1992*. Oxford: Blackwell.

Tocqueville, Alexis. 1955. *The Old Regime and the French Revolution*. Translated by Stuart Gilbert. Garden City, N.Y.: Doubleday & Company.

———. 1969. *Democracy in America*. Translated by George Lawrence and edited by J. P. Mayer. New York: Harper & Row.

Tomlins, Christopher L. 1985. *The State and the Unions: Labor Relations, Law, and the Organized Labor Movement in America, 1880–1960*. Cambridge: Cambridge University Press.

Tracy, David. 1987. *Plurality and Ambiguity: Hermeneutics, Religion, Hope*. Chicago: The University of Chicago Press.

Tribe, Keith, ed. 1987. *Social Democracy and the Rule of Law: Otto Kirchheimer and Franz Neumann*. Translated by Leena Tanner and Keith Tribe. London: Allen & Unwin.

Ulmen, G. L. 1985. "The Sociology of the State: Carl Schmitt and Max Weber." *State, Culture, Society* 1: 3–57.

———. 1991. *Politische Mehrwert: Eine Studie über Max Weber und Carl Schmitt*. Weinheim: VCH Acta humaniora, 1991.

Unger, Roberto Mangabeira. 1976. *Law in Modern Society: Toward a Criticism of Social Theory*. New York: The Free Press.

Van Kley, Dale. 1987. The Jansenist Constitutional Legacy in the French Revolution. In *The Political Culture of the Old Regime*. Vol. 1 of *The French Revolution and the Creation of Modern Political Culture*, ed. Keith Baker. Oxford: Pergamon Press.

Veblen, Thorstein. [1915] 1966. *Imperial Germany and the Industrial Revolution*. New Brunswick, N.J.: Transaction Publishers.

Vogt, Martin. 1974. Die Stellung der Koalitionsparteien zur Finanzpolitik, 1928–1930. In *Industrielles System und politische Entwicklung in der Weimarer Republik*, ed. Hans Mommsen, Dietmar Petzina, and Bernd Weisbrod. Düsseldorf: Droste Verlag.

Voth, Jans-Joachim. 1993. "Wages, Investment, and the Fate of the Weimar Republic: A Long-term Perspective." *German History* 11, 3: 265–92.

Wadham, John, and Helen Mountfield. 1999. *Blackstone's Guide to the Human Rights Act 1998*. London: Blackstone.

Warrender, Howard. 1957. *The Political Philosophy of Hobbes: His Theory of Obligation*. Oxford: Clarendon Press.

Wasby, Stephen L. 1978. *The Supreme Court in the Federal Judicial System*. New York: Holt, Rinehart and Winston.

Watkins, Frederick. 1939. *The Failure of Constitutional Emergency Powers Under the German Republic*. Cambridge: Harvard University Press.

Weber, Max. [1906] 1977. *Critique of Stammler*. Translated by Guy Oakes. New York: The Free Press.

———. [1918] 1978. Parliament and Government in a Reconstructed Germany: A Contribution to the Political Critique of Officialdom and Party Politics. In *Economy and Society: An Outline of Interpretive Sociology*, 2 vols., ed.

Guenther Roth and Claus Wittich. Berkeley: University of California Press.

———. [1918] 1988. Deutschlands Künftige Staatsform. In *Gesammelte Politische Schriften*, ed. Johannes Winckelmann. 5th ed. Tübingen: J.C.B. Mohr (Paul Siebeck).

———. 1949. *The Methodology of the Social Sciences*. Translated and edited by Edward A. Shils and Henry A. Finch. New York: The Free Press.

———. [1958] 1976. *The Protestant Ethic and the Spirit of Capitalism*. Translated by Talcott Parsons. With an introduction by Anthony Giddens. New York: Charles Scribner's Sons.

Wehler, Hans-Ulrich. 1985. *The German Empire, 1871–1918*. Leamington Spa, England: Berg.

Weinstein, James. 1968. *The Corporate Ideal in the Liberal State, 1900–1918*. Boston: Beacon Press.

Wendenburg, Helga. 1984. *Die Debate um die Verfassungsgerichtsbarkeit und der Methodenstreit der Staatsrechtslehre in der Weimarer Republik*. Göttingen: Verlag Otto Schmwartz.

Westbrook, Robert A. 1991. *John Dewey and American Democracy*. Ithaca and London: Cornell University Press.

Whimster, Sam. 1987. Karl Lamprecht and Max Weber: Historical Sociology within the Confines of the Historian Controversy. In *Max Weber and his Contemporaries*, ed. Wolfgang J. Mommsen and Jürgen Osterhammel. London: Allen & Unwin.

White, Hayden. 1987. *The Content of the Form: Narrative Discourse and Historical Representation*. Baltimore: The Johns Hopkins University Press.

White, Morton. [1947] 1957. *Social Thought in America: The Revolt Against Formalism*. With a new preface and an epilogue. Reprint. Boston: Beacon Press.

Whitman, James Q. 1990. *The Legacy of Roman Law in the German Romantic Era*. Princeton: Princeton University Press.

Whittington, Keith E. 1999. *Constitutional Construction: Divided Powers and Constitutional Meaning*. Cambridge: Harvard University Press.

Wilson, Woodrow. 1973. *Congressional Government: A Study in American Politics*. With an introduction by Walter Lippmann. Gloucester, Mass.: Peter Smith.

Winckelmann, Johannes, ed. 1978. *Die protestantische Ethik II: Kritiken und Antikritiken*. Gütersloh: Gütersloher Verlaghaus Gerd Mohn.

Winckler, Heinrich, August, ed. 1985. "Kontroversen über die Wirtschaftspolitik in der Weimarer Republik." In *Geschichte und Gesellschaft* 11, 3.

Wirching, Andreas. 1996. Zwischen Leistungsexpansion und Finanzkrise: Kommunale Selbstverwaltung in der Weimarer Republik. In *Kommunale Selbstverwaltung/Local Government: Geschichte und Gegenwart im deutschen-britishchen Vergleich*, ed. Adolf Birke and Magnus Brechtken. Munich: K. G. Saur.

Wolin, Richard. 1992. "Carl Schmitt: The Conservative Revolutionary Habitus and the Aesthetics of Horror." *Political Theory* 20: 424–47.

Wood, Gordon S. [1969] 1972. *The Creation of the American Republic, 1776–1787*. Reprint. New York: W. W. Norton & Company.

Woodward, C. Vann. [1951] 1956. *Reunion and Reaction: The Compromise of 1877 and the End of Reconstruction*. Garden City, N.Y.: Doubleday Anchor Books.

Wright, J. K. 1994. "National Sovereignty and the General Will: The Political Program of the Declaration of Rights." In *The French Idea of Freedom: The Old Regime and the Declaration of the Rights of 1789*, ed. Dale Van Kley. Stanford: Stanford University Press.

Index

Ackerman, Bruce, Schmitt and dualist democracy, 37 n.29, 38 n.39

Adams, John. *See* United States

Adenauer, Konrad. *See* Local Self-Government

Allison, J.W.F., Weberian ideal types and institutional borrowing, xx n.9, 92–93

American Civil War: in congressional policy leadership (Homestead Act, Morill Land Grant Act, Railroad Act, and National Bank), 106–107; constitutional crisis of 1850s (Compromise of 1850, Kansas-Nebraska Act, and Dred Scott), 122. *See also* Lincoln, Abraham

American Supreme Court, 89; the Cases and Controversies Clause, 88; civil rights in late 19th century, 65; common law and Supreme Court authority, 82; common law categories in age of statutes, 107; constitutional amendments, 90; and the Federal High Court, 74; and "general principles of law," 82; *Marbury v. Madison*, 85; "mythology" of the Supreme Court in Weimar, 81; and the New Deal, 82; and the political branches, 104; and presidential emergency powers, 117–118; policy leadership in 19th century, 81, 105–106. *See also* Constitutional Politics; Courts; Lincoln, Abraham

Anschütz, Gerhard: commentary on Weimar Constitution, 25; on limits of constitutional law, 14

Berman, Sheri, on the political base of the Social Democratic Party, 69 n.9

Bien, David, corporate bodies and French self-government, 32

Bismarck, Otto von, government of, 105. *See also* Constitutions; Parliament; Political Parties

Blackbourn, David, and Geoff Eley, bourgeois revolution, 36 n.15

Borchardt, Knut. *See* Economy

Bourdieu, Pierre, *habitus*, 7, 35 n.7
Brecht, Arnold. *See* Federalism
Breuer, Stefan, on Sieyès and Schmitt, 38 n.35
Brüning, Heinrich, role in collapse of Weimar Republic, 69 n.9, 100–101 n.24. *See also* Schmitt, Carl
Bureaucracy, civil servant rights and governability problems, 13, 14; construction of the federal bureaucracy, 84; policymaking and administrative-supervisory role in Reich, 50; and political leadership, 50; and 19th-century reform, 10, 60. *See also* Rights

Caldwell, Peter, on Schmitt and the Free Law Movement, 110
Carter, Stephen, "forced reconsideration" of constitutional norms, 119
Catholic Centre Party (Centrum). *See* Political Parties
Civil Code. *See* Law; Legal Reform
Common Law. *See* American Supreme Court; Law; Tomlins, Christopher
Conceptual Frameworks, comparative history and contextual analysis, 75; and empirically grounded constitutional theory, 26; and normative argument, 105; and Schmitt's typology of state forms, 108–110; and state form in the United States, 105–108; and the Weimar state crisis, 42–44. *See also* Mehring, Reinhard; Schmitt, Carl; State; United States
Constant, Benjamin, and ideal types, 27
Constitutional Politics, 80, 87, 88, 89, 99 n.11, 121–122; constitutional dualism in the 19th century, 60; institutional determinants of in postwar Germany, 94; in Prussian reform era and in the Wilhelmine period, 60–63; structural basis for Prussian dominance in Reich, 99 n.14; in the United States, 81, 115; in Weimar, 93–97. *See also* American Supreme Court; Courts; Federal Chamber; United States
Constitution-Making, 38 n.35; American and French Revolutions and, xv, 19–22; centralization/decentralization in, 29–34; as decision and core principles, 17; and the French Municipal Revolution, 32–33; and French national consciousness, 32–33; and national identity, 18–22, 27–28, 30–34. *See also* Preuß, Hugo; Schmitt, Carl
Constitutions, 77–78, 106–107, 122; 1831 Belgian, 10; 1850 Prussian, rights provisions under, 99 n.10; Bismarck's Imperial Constitution, 10–11; English, 18–19; French, 19–22; no rights provisions in, 99 n.10, normative, 17–18, 21–22; substantial rights of political participation under, 77; United States, 19; universal manhood suffrage under, 61; Weimar, 1–3, 8–9, 12, 46–47, 83. *See also* American Supreme Court; Constitutional Politics; Corporate Mediation; Federal Chamber; Local Self-Government; Rights
Corporate Mediation, in Old Regime France, 31–34, 55, 56–57, 73; under the Weimar Constitution, 46–47
Cortes, Donoso, 6
Counterrevolutionaries:
antidemocratic outlook, 6;
Schmitt's caginess about in *Political Theology*, 6. *See also* Schmitt, Carl
Courts, 88, 89, 97 n.1, 99 n.11; administrative courts in Weimar, 85; Austrian Constitutional Court and the Federal High Court, 74; courts and symbolic politics, 97; as democratic

institutions, xix n.5; enumerative jurisdiction of German courts, 79; federalism and the court system, 78–80, 83; fragmented judiciary and the political role of courts, 84, 103–104; French and German courts, 78–79; German courts as politically subordinate, 103–104; judicial politics in the United States, 119; and judicial review, 86–87; legislative efforts to unify court system, 86–87; as policymakers, 75, 90; political divisions and decentralized court system, 79, 83; political divisions and the political role of courts, 84; reactionary jurisdictional restrictions in 19th century Germany, 111; Schmitt and judicial politics studies, 91, 102 n.32. *See also* American Supreme Court; Democracy; Federalism; Legal Reform; Local Self-Government; State High Court

Cristi, Renato. *See* Liberalism; Schmitt, Carl

Cromwell, Oliver, 109

Decisionism, 37 n.29, 38 n.39; counterrevolutionaries and, 6; French Revolution as decisionist, 19–22; and the German state, 9; and the liberal constitutional tradition in Schmitt, 2, 22; Schmitt on historical continuity through, 16; in Schmitt's constitutionalism, 5; and understandings of law and politics, 41

Democracy, 115–116; comparative history and democratic theory, xvii-xviii; court-centered understandings of, xix n.6; court systems as democratic institutions, xvi, xix n.6; decentralization and constitutional compromises and, xv; direction of change in, xvii; fragmented judiciary and, xv–xvii; as ongoing experimentation, xvii, xix–xx n.7; procedural limitations and democracy, 27. *See also* Institutional Dialogue; Legal Positivism

Dictatorship, commissarial and sovereign 27, 109. *See also* Schmitt, Carl

Diremption. *See* Sorel, George

Duguit, Leon, public services and state legitimacy, 21

Economy, 43, 58, 68 n.4; Borchardt controversy, 69 n.9; coal crisis, 50; Great Depression and parliamentary government, 83–84; industrial autonomy, 50; industry and social compromise, 46; inflation, causes of, 68 n.5; inflation, government indebtedness and social services, 54; inflation and social compromise, 33; intra-government conflict over economy, 56; productive capacity, 1, 47; state intervention in, 55; temporary class compromises, 1–2, 46–47; unified, long-term leadership of, 50–51, 55; work conditions, 1, 46–47

Ehrlich, Eugen. *See* Free Law Movement

Elections: and liberal concept of representation, 51–52; the presidency and party mergers, 53; proportional representation and political paralysis, 51–53; Reich-Weimar comparison, 51–52; Sartori on stability of electoral system, 69 n.7; single-member districts and party leadership in the United States, 52–53; single-member districts in Reich period, 51–52

Emergency powers: German president, and parliament, 8; and Roo-

sevelt and Truman, 117. *See also* Lincoln, Abraham
Erzberger, Matthias, Finance Minister, on local self-government financial crisis, 54

Federal Chamber (*Bundesrat*), 83; and the composite state, 61, 80; and constitutional disputes in Reich, 79–80; Prussian control in Reich, 11, 99 n.14
Federal High Court (*Reichsgericht*): and American Supreme Court, 88; decision of Nov. 4, 1925, 89; and Federal Tax Court, 87; and judicial review, 80, 88; jurisdiction of, 99 n.11. *See also* American Supreme Court; Courts
Federal Tax Court (*Reichsfinanzgericht*), 87, 88, 89, 99 n.11; and judicial review, 80
Federalism, Arnold Brecht's reform plan, 69 n.8; consolidation of Prussia through presidential decree, xiv; court supervision in the United States, 100 n.16; divergent views on reform, 54; and financial balancing, 53–54, 66–67; judicial federalism, 100 n.16; *Länder* conferences in 1924 and 1928, 54; *Länder* opposition to reform, 54, 67; and local self-government, 58; political stability of, 70 n.24; Prussian dominance of Reich (federation) system, 50; reform of Weimar system, 66–68, 69 n.8; Schmitt's concept of, 42. *See also* Constitutional Politics; Local Self-Government; Political Stability; State; Weber, Max
Federalist Papers, The: and strong central government, 40 n.52; Number 51, 115
Finance, 57; foreign borrowing, 56; presidential decree on Länder supervision of local government borrowing, 56; taxing power, different governmental levels and social services, 53–54; taxing power, legal ambiguity of, 86; taxing power, shifted to Reich in Weimar, 62–63. *See also* Local Self-Government; Political Parties
Fisher, Louis, coordinate construction, xix n.6, 126 n.28
Frederick the Great. *See* Legal Reform
Free Law Movement, Ehrlich on concept stretching in law, 125 n.20. *See also* Schmitt
French *Conseil d'Etat* (Council of State), general jurisdiction of, 79. *See also* State High Court
French *Tribunal des Conflits* (Court of Conflicts), no German equivalent at Reich level, 79

German Idealism, on history, 15–16
Gneist, Rudolf. *See* Local Self-Government

Habermas, Jürgen, on *Constitutional Theory*, xviii n.2
Hegel, G., the idea in history and historical continuity 16. *See also* State
Heller, Hermann, state as organization, 90, 101 n.31
Hindenburg, Paul von (*Reichspräsident*), legality in late Weimar, 121–122
Historical School of Law: and historical continuity, 15–16; cultural incommensurability, 16
History, xvii, 16, 18, 48–49, 98 n.6, 109; comparative history in *Constitutional Theory* and *Guardian of the Constitution*, 2; the comparative history of courts, 75–90; historical models and legal theory, xviii; history and democratic experimentation, xviii; inductive approach and

French radicalism, 23–24; the intent of the framers, 15; Marxist historiography and class conflict, 5–6; narrative in *Crisis of Parliamentary Democracy*, 2, 41–42; periodization and narrative in 19th century historiography, 23; political history of the subsumption concept, 111–114; problem-oriented history, 2; Savigny's *Volksgeistlehre*, 15; Schmitt's understanding of, 37 n. 26; time horizons in legal theory and constitutional democracy, 11, 97, 117–118. *See also* Schmitt, Carl; Sorel, George; Weber, Max

Hobbes, 9; and constitutionalism, 4–5; on constitution-making, 4; reason as a restraint on sovereign authority, 5; and religious wars of 17th century, 5; Schmitt's emphasis of personalistic core of the *Leviathan*,4

Holmes, Oliver Wendell, 113

Huber, Ernst Rudolf, 105

Hunt, Lynn, the Municipal Revolution and French political culture, 33

Identity, in *Constitutional Theory*, 27–28, 30–34; continuity between Reich and Weimar, 17. *See also* Constitution-Making; Revolution; Schmitt, Carl

Imperial Cameral Court (*Reichskammergericht*), as a means of dispute resolution, 59

Imperial Central Bank, and pluralism, 55

Institutional Dialogue, 126 n.28; and constitutional principle, xix n.6; courts and, xvii, 118–124; courts and political responsibility, 120; and democracy, 115–116; democracy as, xvii; diffuse judicial review in hierarchical court systems and, 119; Kelsen on the inevitability of, 118; linking norms with institutions, 116; the Weimar court system and, 119–121. *See also* Democracy; Kelsen, Hans; Lincoln, Abraham

Jackson, Andrew. *See* the United States

Jefferson, Thomas. *See* the United States

Jellinek, Georg, *General Theory of the State*, 29–30; ideal types and Weber, 29–30; and Neo-Kantianism, 29

Kaiserreich, 113–114

Kalberg, Stephen, on Weber's ideal types, 38 n.42; Weber's ideal typical method as testable models, 93

Kapp Putsch. *See* Social Democratic Party

Kelsen, Hans, xiv, 18; comparability of American divided government and Kelsen's party democracy, 118; critique of Schmitt, 16, 114, 118; multi-tiered (*Stufenbau*) understanding of law, 59, on Schmitt's contrast between lawgiver and courts, 127 n.31; 116; Schmitt's critique of Kelsen, 126 n.30; on Schmitt's reading of subsumption jurisprudence, 114. *See also* Institutional Dialogue; Legal Positivism

Kompetenz-Kompetenz, 62

Koselleck, Reinhard, on Weber and ideal types, 25

Krieger, Leonard, German concept of freedom, 69 n.12

Landmann, Ludwig. *See* Local Self-Government

Law, 73, 84, 87, 88, 89, 99 n.11, 106–107, 122; administrative law on the Continent and the United States, 81; common law, 81–82; constitutional and ordinary, 11, 14, 82; constitutions as civil law contracts,

114; expansive readings of general clauses, 104; general clauses and the adaptability of the Civil Code, 113; judicial review in Weimar, 80–81; legal theory as a form of action in Schmitt, 17; politics of legal sources, 94–95; private and public law, 58, 95, 114–115; "underenforced" constitutional norms, 120. *See also* American Supreme Court; Courts; Finance; Legal Reform; Lincoln, Abraham; Local Self-Government; Schmitt, Carl; State High Court

Legal Positivism: adaptability of Civil Code and General Law of Prussia, 112–113; and democratic experimentation, xvii; law as a complete, closed conceptual system, 15; official discretion and the personal element in law, 116; relative importance of constitutional provisions, 14; Schmitt and the issue of legal enforcement, 115; and status quo, 11, 29; Western constitutional history and the Schmitt-Kelsen controversy, 18. *See also* Kelsen, Hans; Schmitt, Carl; State

Legal Reform: Civil Code, 10–11, 77, 112–113; Frederick the Great and, 76; French influence in Germany, 76–77; General Law of Prussia, 10, 112–113; Gierke, Otto von, on the liberal social implications of Civil Code, 112; goal of independent courts, 76; legal without political reform in 19th century France, 77; liberals and, 111–12; political unification and, 112; the Napoleonic Code as, 76; public law character of private law reform, 76. *See also* Law

Legislative-Reservation Clause *(Gesetzesvorbehalt)*, and State High Court jurisdiction, 84; and rights, 73; Schmitt on legal politics implications of, 87–88. *See also* Law

Liberalism, 18, 20, 38 n.35; American and early French constitutions and, 21–22; Cristi on Schmitt's "authoritarian liberalism," 7; German liberalism in the 19th century, 10–11; liberals, codification, and independent courts in the 19th century, 111–113; Schmitt's apparent rapprochement with, 8–9; subsumption jurisprudence and liberal reform, 113. *See also* Decisionism; Elections; Schmitt, Carl

Lincoln, Abraham, defense of suspension of habeas corpus, 120; on Dred Scott decision, 121; emergency powers and independence from Congress, 106–107; emergency powers in American Civil War as precedent 117–118; and institutional dialogue, 120; Taney's reaction to Lincoln's suspension of habeas corpus, 116–117; use of emergency powers, 106–107

Local Self-Government, 30; Adenauer, Konrad, Mayor of Cologne, 54; in American political tradition, 19–34, 65; borrowing by cities, 54; "cold socialization" in Germany, 62; competition among cities, 54; constitutionalism and prewar local government, 60–61; and courts, 113–114; crisis of, 54–56; English "municipal socialism," 61; and federalism reform, 69 n.9; financial supervision by Reich and *Länder*, 56, 66–67; in French Revolution ("Municipal Revolution"), 19, 31–34; Gneist, Rudolf von, local self-government and French-inspired radicalism, 60; Landmann, Ludwig, Mayor of Frankfurt am Main, 54; law of, 62–63; liberal critics of, 62;

and "non-political" issues, 63, 70; Mulert, Oskar, financial reform plan of Association of Cities, 67; and refeudalization of the state, 59–68; Schacht, Hjalmar, and financial crisis of, 56, 66; social change and politics of, 61–62, 64; social welfare, governmental finance, and, 53–54, 66; and state/society distinction, 63–65; Stein, Karl vom, and Prussian reforms, 60; "universality principle" of, 62, 70 n.22. *See also* Federalism; Political Stability; State

Madison, James, 70 n. 23; democratic implications of dispersion of power 115–116. *See also Federalist Papers, The*; United States

Marbury v. Madison. *See* American Supreme Court

Maus, Ingeborg, on connection between *Recht* and *Gesetz*, 99 n.9

McPherson, James, narrative and contingency in history, 41

Mehring, Reinhard: on Schmitt's critique of parliamentary government, 48; on Schmitt's "sociology of concepts," 9; on Schmitt's use of Weberian ideal types, 39 n.46

Methodenstreit (debate on method). *See* Weber, Max

Miller, Perry, hostility toward common law and antebellum codification movements, 82; lawyers as America's elite in the 19th century, 82

Models: dynamic forms, 75; experimental historical method in normative argument, xvii-xviii; Prussia as modal case, 98 n.6. *See also* History; Schmitt, Carl

Mommsen, Wolfgang, on Weber's ideal types, 38 n. 42

Mulert, Oskar. *See* Local Self-Government

National Economic Council (*Reichswirtschaftsrat*): and pluralism, 55, 73; the problem of personal power, 56–57. *See also* Schacht, Hjalmar

National Identity. *See* Constitution-Making; Courts; Preuß, Hugo; Schmitt, Carl

National Liberal Party. *See* Political Parties

Naumann, Friedrich: and purpose of Weimar Republic, 47; and rights provisions under Weimar Constitution, 13; and Weimar Constitution as class compromise, 12–13

Nedelsky, Jennifer, Madisonian constitutional structure protects property, 70 n.23

Neo-Kantianism, 30; in Schmitt's constitutional theory, 29. *See also* Kelsen, Hans; Weber, Max

Non-Political Organizations: government by experts 55, 56; and political leadership, 55–56. *See also* Schacht, Hjalmar

Ostogorski, Moisei, and Schmitt's critique of parliamentary government, 44

Parliament: conflicts between Bismarck's government and Parliament, 105; English model, 49; government by discussion, 44–48; inducements to compromise, 55; modern mass democracy, 45; pluralism and parliamentary instability, 50–51; Schmitt on overbearing majorities, 12; Schmitt's concept of "equal chance," xiv; States-General and the common good, 59; and unified leadership, 51, 53–55; in

Wilhelmine period, 105. *See also* Elections; Political Parties; Schmitt, Carl; Weber, Max
Patch, William. *See* Brüning, Heinrich
Pluralism, American and English, 43; and the composite state 57–58; as concept 42–43; and in Weimar 50–55. *See also* Parliament; State
Political Parties: Bavarian People's Party and the 1930 governmental crisis, 58; Catholic Centre Party and Bismarck's *Kulturkampf*, 112; National Liberal Party and concept of "nation," 77; splintered party system and parliamentary paralysis, 51, 53, 55; two party system, United Kingdom and the United States, 52; *Weltanschauungsparteien*, 11–12. *See also* Social Democratic Party
Political Stability: degree of centralization/decentralization as factor in, 34–35; German president and, 74; lack of consensus on values as factor in, 70 n.21; local government and the channeling of political dissatisfaction, 65–68; national identity as factor in 34; in Revolutionary France, 34; the state and, 57–68, 110–124; system capacity for experimentation enhances stability, xvii, xx n. 8. *See also* Elections; Federalism
Polycracy, 66–67; hybrid organizations abroad, 68 n.4; and local self-government, 58; non-political organizations and the economy, 55–56; Schmitt's concept defined, 43
Popitz, Johannes: and federalism reform, 67; polycracy concept and Schmitt, 43; proposed reform of tax system, 66–67
Preuß, Hugo: and drafting of Weimar Constitution, 12; on judicial review, 80; and purpose of Weimar system, 47; on retention of term "Reich" in Weimar Constitution, 17; on Social Democrats and social compromise, 12
Preuß, Ulrich, regarding Schmitt on American and French Revolutions, 9

Ranke, Leopold, and the modern discipline of history, 23, 109
Rechtsstaat, 99 n.9; development of, 77–78; distinction from Anglo-American rule of law, 77; and the German understanding of state, 77; as product of French and American Revolutions, 17–18. *See also* Law
Reparations, and German politics, 50
Revolution, 17, 36 n.15, 77–78; American and French Revolutions, 19–22; English Revolution, 18–19; French Revolution and concept of nation, 32; French Revolution and concept of radical break, 33–34; French Revolution and democratic change through law, 76; German Revolution, 1, 45–48; role of national identity in, 19–22. *See also* Constitution-Making
Rights, 12, 47; ambiguity of Catalogue of Rights of Weimar Constitution, 14; British Human Rights Act, 102 n.34; Catalogue of Rights and local government, 59, 62; of civil servants, 87; comparison between 19th century *Länder* rights provisions and U.S. Bill of Rights, 99 n.10; and German politics, 13; political divisions and disagreements over rights, 88; political effects of constitutional rights in central and eastern Europe, 92–93; Schmitt and rights in the Federal Republic, 101

n.27; Schmitt on legal status of Weimar provisions, 13, 87; state action and rights, 120; under Weimar Constitution, 73–74, 87, 88, 94–95. *See also* Constitutions, Schmitt, Carl

Riker, William, and J. Limco, federal systems and political stability, 70 n.24

Roosevelt, Franklin. *See* Emergency Powers

Roosevelt, Theodore. *See* United States

Roth, Guenther. *See* Social Democratic Party (SPD)

Savigny, Carl von, role of legal profession in politics, 11. *See also* History

Schacht, Hjalmar, Imperial Bank President, and municipal borrowing and problem of personal power, 56–57. *See also* Local Self-Government

Scheuermann, William: comparative history in Schmitt, 18; Schmitt's critique of parliamentary government, 48–49; Schmitt's use of narrative in *Crisis of Parliamentary Democracy*, 2

Schlink, Bernard, on Schmitt's continuing appeal, xviii n.2

Schmitt, Carl, xix n.2, 6, 29, 39 n.46, 43, 44, 66, 67, 73, 84, 100 n.21, 101 n.30, 117; the amending power of Parliament, 14–15; Brüning government, the SPD, and the 1930 governmental crisis, 83; comparative history and *Legality and Legitimacy*, xix n.5; comparative history and the independent state, xv; comparative history of parliamentary government, 48–50; comparative history of the judiciary, xvi; concept of identity, 17–22, 27, 29–34; constitutional dictatorship and reactionary politicians, xiv; *Constitutional Theory* and Bourdieu's concept of habitus, 7; continuity between Weimar and Nazi era writings, xiv; controversy over Schmitt's position on rights, xx n.8; criminal law analogies, 115; Cristi on state forms in Schmitt, 124 n.3; criticism of the typology of state forms, 108–110; critique of legal positivism, 78; the critique of liberalism in *Constitutional Theory*, 2–3, 7–10; critique of the Weimar Constitution's Catalogue of Rights, 87–88; "equal chance" for political leadership, xiv; on founding moments, 17; Free Law Movement and *Statute and Judgment (Gesetz und Urteil)*, 110; the Free Law Movement and the politicization of the judiciary, 114–115; on Free Law Movement as a constitutional problem, 110, 114; *Guardian of the Constitution* and *Dictatorship* compared, 108–110; *Guardian of the Constitution* and Weimar state crisis, xv; *Guardian of the Constitution* as problem-oriented history, xv; model building and legal politics in, 93–97; and one-sided conceptual formulas, xiii; organizational minimum, 13–14; organizing empirical materials in *Constitutional Theory*, 26; on the personal element in adjudication, 126 n.30; political and legal components of the *bürgerlicher Rechtsstaat*, 1, 18; and political development and judicial politics, 75, 98 n.3, 102 n.32; political divisions and parliamentary paralysis, 83; politics of the subsumption concept, 110; redefining the democratic ideal, 7; response to Richard Thoma, 47–48, 49; on Savigny and history, 37 n.26; Sorel and *Constitutional Theory*'s argumentative strategy, 3; on the State High Court in the 1930 governmental crisis, 83; on subsumption jurisprudence, 89–90; theory and practice and neo-Kantian state theory, 27; theory and practice and the Weimar constitutional crisis, 103, 109–110; and Weber on federalism, 36 n.12; and Weber on liberal politics in the 19th century. *See also* Decisionism; History; Parliament; Subsumption Jurisprudence

Separation of Powers, 70 n.23, 115–116; courts and the president, 120; president and parliament, 8, 103, 108; Schmitt on the German president, 74

Sieyès, Abbe de, 38 n.35; concept of radical break and liberal constitution-making, 18, 20–21

Simon, Walter, president of Federal High Court: comparison between American Supreme Court and Federal High Court, 85; on the court system and the German legal tradition, 80; on *Marbury v. Madison* and the Federal High Court, 85; on political role of Federal High Court 85, 89, 97 n.1

Social Democratic Party (SPD), 17, 69 n.9, 80; Anti-Socialist Laws, 61, 63; and Kapp putsch, 47; postwar conciliatory stance, 12; and Prussian caretaker government, xiv, 104; Roth, Guenther, on reformism, 64; and the state, 63–64; and traditional elites, 46–47; Weimar parliamentary coalitions, 55. *See also* Local Self-Government

Sonderweg (German peculiarity), 9, 36 n.15

Sorel, George: the Catholic Church and the French state, 3–4; history as a political tool, 9–10; method of diremption, 3; the myth of the general strike, 5–6. *See also* Schmitt, Carl

State, 17–18, 39 n.46, 77; as composite, 10, 57, 62–66, 105, 111, 124 n.8; concepts and crisis of 42–44, 48; emergencies and center of state activity, 108; governmental state, 105, 106, 108, 109; Hegel and the unified science of the state 29; hybrid state 105; independent state, 57, 68; jurisdiction state, 81, 104, 105, 106, 108; jurisdiction state in *Legality and Legitimacy* (*Legalität und Legitimität*), 9–10; and the pluralism, 58; quantitative total state, 63; Reich state and legal positivism, 16, 78; and Social Democratic Party (SPD), 61; *Ständestaat*, 58–60, 69 n.12, 104, 105; state/society distinction, 57, 63, 64, 113, 114; totalization of, 51, 63; types/forms of, 104–110. *See also* Conceptual Frameworks; Schmitt, Carl; Social Democratic Party; Sorel, George; United States

State High Court, 87; and the American Supreme Court, 86; and the Catalogue of Rights, 73; composition and legal politics, 85; and the French Council of State, 85; and judicial review, 80; jurisdiction, 84–85, 86; Papen government emergency decree, xiv, 104; and parliamentary minorities, 88, 91–92; and political issues, 91–92, 95. *See also* Schmitt, Carl; State

State Theory *(Staatslehre)*, Schmitt's *Constitutional Theory* as 19th century state theory, 29. *See also* Schmitt, Carl

Stein, Karl von. *See* Local Self-Government

Strauss, Leo, on Schmitt and Hobbes, 5; Schmitt on liberalism, 9

Subsumption Jurisprudence, 125 n. 20; in criminal cases, 115; and the fiction of legislative dominance, 113; Kelsen's critique of Schmitt, 118; personal element in adjudication, 110; political neutrality of, 111–112; and reactionary legal and judicial changes in 19th century Germany, 112; Schmitt on "obvious" constitutional violations, 89; Schmitt on traditional adjudication, 110. *See also* Liberalism; Schmitt, Carl

Taney, Roger B., Chief Justice, United States Supreme Court. *See* Lincoln, Abraham
Taylor, Charles, "self-description" of practices, 7
Thayer, James Bradley, and Schmitt's position on judicial review, 100 n.21, 101 n.30
Thirty Years War: and the *Ständestaat*, 59; Wallenstein, leading general under Ferdinand II, 109
Thoma, Richard: criticism of *Crisis of Parliamentary Democracy*, 47; as a democrat, xiv. *See also* Schmitt, Carl
Tocqueville, Alexis: central authority and local government, 31; centralization in France and the United States, 30; local self-government and state in France and United States, 32
Tomlins, Christopher, the common law as check on labor movement, 70 n.23
Truman, Harry. *See* Emergency Powers

Ulmen, G.L., on Schmitt's "sociology of the state," 39 n.46
United States, 30, 31, 32, 70 n.23, 82, 122; the administrative state, 107; Congress and constitutional questions, 106, 116–17; the Great Compromise of 1877, 65; Jackson, Jefferson, and Theodore Roosevelt and presidential leadership, 107–108; the patrician understanding of the presidency in the early Republic (Washington, Adams, and Jefferson), 106–108, 116–118. *See also* American Supreme Court; Elections; Lincoln, Abraham

Wallenstein, Count Albrecht von. *See* Thirty Years War
Washington, George. *See* United States
Weber, Max, 9, 29–30, 39 n.46, 48; comparative history and normative debate, 26–27; concepts in historical research, 24–25; *Economy and Society*, 38 n.42; on federalism in Germany, 99 n.15; and Hintze, Otto, 23; ideal types, 24, 26–27, 47, 92–93; and Lamprecht, Karl, 22–23; *Methodenstreit*, 22–25; on parliamentary leadership, 52; *Protestant Ethic and the Spirit of Capitalism*, 25, 27, 38 n.42; and purpose of parliamentary government, 47; scholarly debate over ideal types, 42; the social sciences and history, 25. *See also* History; Schmitt, Carl
Workers and Soldiers Councils (*Räte*): as innovative institution, 1; and social compromise in early Weimar Republic, 46

About the Author

JEFFREY SEITZER has been a visiting scholar at the Max-Planck Institute for European Legal History in Frankfurt am Main, Germany and at the Institute for Advanced Legal Studies of the University of London. The author of numerous articles on legal and political theory and comparative constitutionalism, he is currently translating Schmitt's *Legality and Legitimacy* and *Constitutional Theory*.

Recent Titles in Contributions in Political Science

President Reagan and the World
Eric J. Schmertz, Natalie Datlof, and Alexej Ugrinsky, editors

Ronald Reagan's America
Eric J. Schmertz, Natalie Datlof, and Alexej Ugrinsky, editors

Germany for the Germans? The Political Effects of International Migration
Wesley D. Chapin

Out of Russian Orbit: Hungary Gravitates to the West
Andrew Felkay

Ideas of Social Order in the Ancient World
Vilho Harle

Voting Rights and Redistricting in the United States
Mark E. Rush, editor

Democratization in Late Twentieth-Century Africa: Coping with Uncertainty
Jean-Germain Gros, editor

Eisenhower's Executive Office
Alfred Dick Sander

Partisanship and the Birth of America's Second Party, 1796–1800: "Stop the Wheels of Government"
Matthew Q. Dawson

The Early Security Confederations: From the Ancient Greeks to the United Colonies of New England
Frederick K. Lister

Selected Works of Juan Donoso Cortés
Juan Donoso Cortés
Translated, edited, and introduced by Jeffrey P. Johnson

The Later Security Confederations: The American, "New" Swiss, and German Unions
Frederick K. Lister